MAR 1 8 1992

Heir To Empire

HEIR TO

EMPIRE

United States
Economic Diplomacy,
1916-1923

CARL P. PARRINI

University of Pittsburgh Press

SBN 8229–3178–8
Library of Congress Catalog Card Number 69–12334
Copyright © 1969, University of Pittsburgh Press

To Sandy

Preface

One of the few scholars who proposed useful methodology in the study of economic diplomacy in the years 1916–1923 was Charles A. Beard, who developed an approach that stressed group consciousness of interest as the major determinant of the foreign policies of the United States from roughly 1900 forward. To test his hypothesis, Beard posited categories of interest groups. The relationships which he claimed existed between these groups and American politics have partly, though by no means completely, failed the test of specific research. Beard's attempt to establish relationships among categories of economic interests was nonetheless illuminating.

He assumed correctly that American political leaders based the foreign policies they developed on their desire to solve present social problems, and to prevent future ones. In Beard's view, American leaders agreed that the fundamental cause of social conflict was the battle among economic interest groups to obtain larger *shares* of national income. To resolve the conflict, Beard contended, they believed they had to find a way to increase the total *volume* of income available for distribution by the free market. Each group could then receive a larger *volume* without impinging on the *shares* obtained by other groups. This was possible if American leaders could develop foreign outlets for goods and services produced at home.

The strengths of this approach are obvious and it is con-

sistent with much of the documentary evidence. But it does
not account for the pragmatic reformist system of ideas with
which American leaders approached their problems, except
by suggesting implicitly that such ideas were simply ration-
alizations of what American leaders wished to do for largely
short-run economic ends. Beard failed to see that significant
numbers of American leaders wished to extend their conception of domestic stability to the international sphere.

He also missed that aspect of American policy which tried
to organize the world as a community. He could see American markets expanding enormously in the years 1900 to
1929, but could not see very much in the way of World
Community. More significantly, however, Beard concluded
that the economic and intellectual crisis in which the nation
found itself by 1929 proved conclusively that the pursuit of
economic opportunity abroad had not solved the problem
of interest-group conflict over the apportioning of income
shares at home. Indeed, he implied that such action abroad
made the crisis more serious, because it tended to blind the
nation to domestic poverty. Beard was digging in the documents for an open door at home—a trend toward domestic
social reform.

Woodrow Wilson appeared to Beard as a figure representative of such a tendency, if not a trend. He viewed Wilson as a President who tried consciously to blunt pressures
on the state to pursue foreign markets single-mindedly.
Wilson's Christian humanism and his frequently expressed
desire to find institutional means of avoiding war led Beard
to regard him as a blessed abberation. The concomitant
to interpreting Wilson as a statesman partly capable of view-
ing the world as a political if not an economic community
was to interpret the Harding Administration as a reactionary
reversion to what Beard and most other historians believed

to be the old purely interest-conscious diplomacy of William Howard Taft.

Beard's approach raises the question of whether or not the Harding Administration did in fact differ from Wilson's with respect to economic foreign policy. More specifically, it suggests these questions: (1) To what extent did the Harding Administration subordinate interest consciousness and act to implement world commercial policies on such problems as international investment, allocation of raw materials, reparations, war debts, and tariffs which would help make a community of the western nations? (2) To what extent was foreign economic policy in the years 1916 to 1923 a continuum?

An examination of the documents shows that Warren G. Harding, Herbert Hoover, Charles Evans Hughes, and Andrew J. Mellon were interested in pursuing an economic foreign policy which would facilitate world community. Equally significant was the finding that these men's decisions appeared to be based on assumptions and analyses which originated in the preceding administration.

It then became necessary to ask: What was the specific relationship between business and government in each administration? Which business groups supported the concept of community? Which opposed it? How were their respective sectarian interests related to the construction of a Western Community? How did those who supported community arrive at their positions? How did political leaders plan to convince the rest of the world of the need for community? How did those supporting the concept of community agree or disagree on tactics for achieving it?

This study tries to answer the above questions. It is based on the assumption implicit in the earlier works of Beard that while business interests do not dictate to the political leadership the policies they pursue, they do establish an economic reality within which the alternatives available to the politician are rather sharply circumscribed. But even Beard did not believe that such circumscription absolutely determined action; he looked for politicians with an eye for the wide-open door of poverty at home.

In addition to my indebtedness to Beard, I wish to acknowledge my gratitude to William Appleman Williams for his unfailing advice and encouragement. His many insightful criticisms and suggestions have proven invaluable. To Fred Harvey Harrington, who first suggested the overseas activities of the American banking community in the 1920's as worthy of pursuit, I am grateful for the initial stimulus from which this study developed.

For all errors which may remain, I alone am responsible.

Contents

Heir To Empire

CHAPTER I

🦅 Americans and Their Mission

By 1916 AMERICAN political and business leaders had reached the conclusion that in order to market the goods and services which the American economy was producing they had to change the rules governing world trade and investment. Their shorthand expression for that goal was called the Open Door. By this term they meant that United States entrepreneurs ought to have the right to use their capital and managerial talents everywhere on a basis equal to that enjoyed by the businessmen of other nations. To obtain this open door world American leaders had to fashion simultaneously policies which would: (1) resolve by compromise interest-group conflicts at home between bankers and manufacturers, importers and exporters, industry and agriculture; (2) build an international commercial system which would allow American business to topple and replace British business interests as the managing component of the world economy; (3) create new institutional means of performing the politically stabilizing task which Great Britain alone had performed before 1914.

The premise upon which business and political leaders agreed was expressed best by C. K. McIntosh, Vice-president of the Bank of California, when he argued in an address entitled "Foreign Investment as an Aid to Foreign Trade," delivered to the 1917 National Foreign Trade Council (NFTC) Convention, that "we will produce more than our average domestic markets will absorb and . . . we must then either curtail our production and cease to employ some of our people, or find another market for the surplus. That means foreign trade and we seek it, not primarily that our investment in certain industrial enterprises may return us increased dividends, but in order that the greatest possible number of the citizens of our country may be engaged in profitable employment. That means more real prosperity to each of us than increased dividends could afford." To accomplish this goal successfully American business groups would have to cease "scrambling amongst each other for the plums which fall," and instead, learn "by cooperative effort to plant more plum trees that we might share the larger yield." Intelligent reflection upon real interest would reveal that "in struggling along the path leading to the goal of individual success, we were not on the best road."[1]

McIntosh summarized the main corollaries to the basic premise. The American economy needed foreign markets to bring about full employment, which meant that American businessmen had to remold their traditional conceptions of how they as members of sectarian interests operated. They had to give up their scramble for larger shares of national income. Instead they had to work cooperatively, and convince others to join in a campaign to expand the total volume of income available for allocation among all the contending groups. This would have the virtue of deflecting the sectarian groups from internecine conflicts over their relative shares of income, since even if shares (as they were initially apportioned by the market place) remained the same, each group could receive a successively larger volume of income. Since they had little successful experience in the *system-*

1. National Foreign Trade Council, *Proceedings of the Fifth Annual Convention* (New York, 1917), 146. (Hereafter cited as NFTC Convention *Proceedings.*)

atic marketing of American production, as opposed to what amounted to rather haphazard dumping, American government and business leaders established various study groups to find out how other nations achieved foreign market development. That effort goes back, in a formal way, to 1909, when under the administration of William Howard Taft Congress voted a resolution to study means of expanding the foreign trade of the United States. There were two broad results of this effort: certain of the publications of the National Monetary Commission outlined the ways in which Britain and Germany structured their national banking and credit systems to facilitate the development of foreign markets; and the Department of Commerce and Labor began a series of studies, most of which were published subsequently during Woodrow Wilson's tenure of office, which outlined the ways in which governments, as well as banking, manufacturing and shipping, and importing and exporting interests in other nations worked together to develop foreign markets for the goods and services produced by their national economies. In 1916 the Wilson Administration continued the work with a two-volume study, under the direction of the Federal Trade Commission, entitled *Cooperation in the Export Trade*. That study amplified and confirmed conclusions reached under the Taft studies; the key to organized development of foreign markets rested in cooperation rather than competition among domestic economic interest groups.[2]

But in 1916 bankers, manufacturers, shippers, and importers and exporters had real and immediate conflicting interests. For instance, all the studies the government had

2. National Monetary Commission, *Publications of the National Monetary Commission* (Washington, 1909–1913); Bureau of Foreign and Domestic Commerce, *Special Agents Series* (Washington 1912–1919); Federal Trade Commission, *Cooperation in the Export Trade*, 2 vols. (Washington, 1916).

made from the Taft through Wilson Administrations seemed to show that to develop repetitive foreign markets it was necessary that American banks establish the widest possible network of branches abroad. Such branch banks were needed to help finance the whole operation as well as to collect credit information on foreign customers, and to make the exchange transaction between dollars and foreign currency. But the bankers were frequently reluctant to establish such branches abroad, because there was little immediate revenue in the business, because it threatened the profitable relations American banks had with analagous European institutions, and because they lacked the capital to finance such ventures. To resolve the conflict the National Foreign Trade Council (NFTC) and the American Bankers Association (ABA) established a joint committee in 1917 to study "American banking as [it] related to the foreign commerce of the United States."[3] But the banking-manufacturing rivalry, though continuously compromised, erupted periodically.

There were other lesser conflicts disrupting cooperation in the program upon which the interest groups shared a consensus. The frequently adjusted—but never definitively settled—tariff was one such issue. From the Payne-Aldrich Act of 1909 through the Underwood-Simmons Bill of 1913,

---

3. Quoted in an address by Lewis E. Pierson, chairman of the board, Irving National Bank of New York, NFTC Convention *Proceedings*, 1917, 138–39. At the 1915 NFTC convention George E. Kretz, manager of the Foreign Department of the National Park Bank of New York outlined the bankers' reluctance; on the other hand the government representative, Edward Ewing Pratt, chief of the Bureau of Foreign and Domestic Commerce (BFDC), pressed the bankers to form foreign branches, and urged them to find techniques, such as combination, to avoid the risks and so make the banking interest consistent with the general interest. The remarks of both Kretz and Pratt are printed in the 1915 NFTC Convention *Proceedings*, 115, 121.

concluding with the Fordney-McCumber Act of 1922, the tariffs were all in great part products of conflict of interest as well as consensus. On this subject the breakdown was complex. The majority of American industrial corporations and associated merchandising groups viewed a highly protective tariff as absolutely necessary to keep them in business. Their profit margins were low; their labor costs seemed threateningly high; since they were smaller-sized concerns, frequently one-plant operations, they did not possess banking connections which would allow them to compete with the large corporations for foreign markets. All they had—and even here their footing was precarious—were domestic markets. They demanded continued protection.[4]

On the other hand, the large corporations for the most part regarded the tariff as something which gave them a hinterland to be developed, but one in which they could (under most conditions) compete quite effectively with imports. Yet they were not about to give up even a small part of that controlled market unless they got the equivalent of their generosity from foreign commercial beneficiaries. They would bargain away some protective aspects of the high tariff in exchange for equal opportunity abroad—for an expanded "hinterland" in the world market.[5]

Spokesmen for the large banks had a still different tariff interest. They shared with the large corporations a desire to expand into new markets, but as bankers they expected to earn large profits which had to be repatriated. At least until the foreign branch and subsidiary movement got well under

4. See the comments of George M. Gillette before the 1916 NFTC Convention Group Session on "The United States Tariff System and Foreign Trade," NFTC Convention *Proceedings*, 1916, 122–24.

5. It is interesting to note that the dispute between the large and the small corporations centered superficially on the desirability of a tariff commission. But what was really at issue was the power of such a commission to lower tariff rates within certain limits.

way, profits had to be brought back to the United States partly in the form of imports. The bankers accepted the reasonable maxim that to buy from Americans foreigners had to sell, to some extent, in America. These big bankers largely made their tariff judgments on the basis that they as an interest, and America as an economy, could prosper only in the context of a prospering world. To them the American tariff was one of the key rules determining the extent to which world markets per se could be expanded, and a significant means of harmonizing the expansion of American penetration of world markets with the interest of other industrial powers.[6]

Even where it seemed that there were no apparent conflicts among interests—as in the proposal for generally agreed-upon low tariffs on industrial raw materials—the reality was quite different. For instance, American exporters of copper, silver, and raw cotton believed the prices they received were being depressed artificially because foreign governments allowed fabricators of raw materials to organize "buying pools," which resulted in an absence of competitive bidding and, consequently, very low prices. Naturally, domestic producers tried to limit competition at home in order to buoy up their domestic prices. But this had the effect of increasing raw material costs to American industry, as well as incidentally violating the antitrust laws.[7]

6. Indeed, the very fact that the war in Europe so stimulated the demand for nearly all that the American economy could produce meant that bankers did not have to worry immediately about how to import their profits; consequently, they could and did spend a great deal of their efforts on devising plans to expand world markets per se.

7. See Federal Trade Commission, *Cooperation in the Export Trade*, I. Edward H. Huxley, president of U.S. Rubber Export Co., New York, proposed that such interests be allowed to do something in the "nature of the German Cartel system," but disclaimed any desire to go that far in changing the antitrust policies of the United States. On this, see NFTC Convention *Proceedings*, 1917, 254–55.

Against this background it became the duty of national-interest-conscious politicians to administer existing laws, and to induce Congress to pass new laws which, while protecting the basic interests of *all* groups, would innovate in a direction encouraging the groups to cooperate in establishing an interrelated systematic pattern of banking, shipping, and finance abroad which would converge and result in the installation of American technology in the economies of foreign nations.

As early as 1915 David R. Francis, Democratic Governor of Missouri and Woodrow Wilson's ambassador to Russia in the ensuing year, told the NFTC Convention that "we are willing that the transportation companies of the United States . . . should give lower rates for export than they do for domestic consumption. God knows the railroads of this country have been punished enough during the past two or three years."[8] Francis was committing the administration to a virtual pledge that it would not enforce the Interstate Commerce Act (of 1887) against shippers offering differential freight rates to businesses engaged in the development of American foreign trade. This pledge freed the railroads from the "incubus of fear" that the antitrust laws would be used against their participation in the campaign to expand the nation's foreign markets, and so incidentally increase the volume of income received by the shippers when the campaign succeeded.

The administration legalized its pledge when it enacted the Clayton Antitrust Act in 1916 and so removed "all inhibitions against combinations in foreign commerce." But the Clayton Act when passed resulted in positive action to bring about American economic expansion as a system. Before the 1916 NFTC Convention Maurice A. Oudin, man-

8. NFTC Convention *Proceedings*, 1915, 169–70.

ager of the Foreign Department of the General Electric Company, described the American International Corporation, permitted under the Clayton Act, as "by far the most conspicuous organization in the United States partaking of the nature of a cooperative enterprise . . . in which are associated banking, transportation, commercial and manufacturing interests. . . ." Its purpose was to be the financing and promoting of public and private undertakings in foreign countries, and it would be "destined to create world markets for American products."[9]

But under the Clayton Act it was still illegal for two analogous manufacturing corporations to cooperate to develop a foreign market. In 1918 when Congress passed and President Wilson signed the Webb-Pomerene Act, the last of the great antitrust prohibitions affecting foreign commerce were removed. It then became possible for competing corporations to divide a foreign market for purposes of developing it under American auspices. Under the Webb Act General Electric, for instance, could bid for sales in Cuba, and Westinghouse could theoretically do the same in Peru.[10] The era of individualism among manufacturing corporations was over, and the era of cooperation had legally begun.

The Webb-Pomerene Act was not designed, however, simply to facilitate cooperation among analogous corporations. Once the law was passed the producers of primary

9. NFTC Convention *Proceedings*, 1916, 265–66.
10. Neither in congressional hearings nor in business association meetings does anyone say that analogous corporations ought to be allowed to divide foreign markets in this way. But since noncompeting interests could already cooperate under the existing Clayton Act, it is apparent that the Webb-Pomerene Act allowed such cooperation by competitive industrial corporations. On this matter see full remarks of Maurice A. Oudin, NFTC Convention *Proceedings*, 1916, 265–66. Oudin's remarks indicate that this is what the large corporations wanted and finally received from the Wilson Administration in 1918.

products, such as copper, silver, or cotton, could form export trade associations in which they could jointly offer their products to foreign buyers at relatively stable (and usually high) prices, and be partly protected against the vicissitudes of world market pricing as influenced by foreign buying pools.

In the area of finance for foreign trade the Federal Reserve Act of 1913 was the first great innovation. In 1916 it was amended to allow bankers engaged in foreign trade to combine to establish foreign branches. Competition among bankers in foreign trade was ended legally. The high risks involved in establishing foreign branches, about which bankers had complained, could now be spread among many units, thus reducing the risk of loss for any particular unit.

In 1918 most of the requirements to allow and encourage the cooperative effort of American business to produce, finance, ship, and market American goods abroad seemed to have been met—except for the decision about the nature of the tariff. There were three possibilities open: the tariff could be protective; it could be a bargaining instrument; or it could be a combination of both. The U.S. Tariff Commission studied all aspects of the problem from 1916 to 1922, spanning the Wilson and Harding Administrations. In general the Commission, and the top-level national politicians for whom it spoke, came down hard in favor of a compromise protective and bargaining tariff, which resulted in the Fordney-McCumber Act of 1922. Again a decision was taken which largely assured harmony among competing interests, but which would at the same time facilitate the consensus end of expanding markets abroad.

Government leaders and business spokesmen did have serious tactical differences even while they were in accord on the need to act in the long-run interests of the system. The political leaders frequently believed the corporations and bankers were endangering the desired end by demanding that the government pursue a policy that would fill the coffers of a special interest. The bankers, for example, were constantly nagging the state to guarantee risky capital investments which they undertook with the encouragement, or at the behest, of the state. Their argument was: since the nation believes the action is in the national interest, the state ought to bear the risk. In general political leaders through Wilson, Harding, and Hoover refused to subsidize such ventures on the entirely reasonable grounds that the profits would go to the corporations, not the taxpayers.

Concurrent with these efforts to create legal sanction for business cooperation, American leaders had to conduct diplomacy in such a manner as to create an international political economy conducive to expansion by peaceful means. They had to give the other industrial nations of the world a *real* interest in the growing American direction of the world economy. The techniques they used were similar to the means they had worked out to harmonize competing domestic interests. Just as they were refashioning the domestic economy into a national community, they tried to reform the outside world into an international community. As they made the national interest the interest of each component group at home, they had to make American interest the world's interest. If they could do that, they could give potentially competing nations a stake in stabilizing and securing a system which was in the first instance beneficial to the United States.

In a sense the Wilson Administration tried to lay the groundwork for the world community of interest which the United States constructed between 1916 and 1923 when it tried to prevent the outbreak of World War I as early as January 1913, before Wilson's inauguration. Colonel Edward M. House, with Wilson's consent, tried to mediate a settlement which would make Britain "less intolerant of Germany's aspirations for expansion" by encouraging Germany "to exploit South America in a legitimate way . . . by development of its resources and by sending her surplus population there. . . . Such a move would be good for South America and would have a beneficial result generally." To Count Johann von Bernstorff, German Ambassador to the United States, House "suggested that it would be a great thing if there was a sympathetic understanding between England, Germany, Japan and the United States. Together . . . they would be able to wield an influence for good throughout the world. They could insure peace and the proper development of the waste places besides maintaining an open door and equal opportunity to everyone everywhere."[11]

Although Wilson, House, and the Administration failed to avert the war, they continued to try to bring about a compromise which would associate all powers together in disarmament and in cooperatively developing the underdeveloped nations. But Germany would not agree to disarmament, and the British would not agree to economic cooperation unless Germany first disarmed. American leaders concluded that Germany, by insisting on its right to maintain huge armaments, had become the major stumbling block to the creation of a true community. In the sense that American leaders believed that Germany blocked the path of harmony for all, the United States did go to war against German militarism.[12] This action had an obvious corollary: since Germany would not surrender its overwhelming armaments

11. Charles E. Seymour, ed., *The Intimate Papers of Colonel House* (Boston and New York, 1926), I, 239–40, 256–65, 272–75.

12. Burton J. Hendrick, *The Life and Letters of Walter H. Page* (New York, 1925), III, 139–40, 143–52, 172–74. I think Page is typical in 1914 of what Wilson more reluctantly became in 1917.

in the interests of community, Germany had to be smashed and a coalition of nations had to be built to force disarmament on like-minded militaristic states in the future.

In the midst of the war against Germany Wilson understood that the Allies, assured of victory due to American entry, were fast becoming a greater threat to community than the virtually defeated Germans. In his "Fourteen Points" address to Congress on January 8, 1918, Wilson tried to meet the danger when in point three he called for "the removal, so far as possible, of all economic barriers and the establishment of an equality of trade conditions among all the nations consenting to the peace and associating themselves for its maintenance."[13] This was directed at America's co-belligerents, not its enemies. Defeated Germany would have little power to enact commercial discrimination against any other state. On the contrary, in point three Wilson was propagandizing for the inclusion of Germany in the community of interest he was hoping to construct, because as he wrote on October 28, 1918, "the experiences of the past . . . have taught us that the attempts by one nation to punish another by exclusive and discriminatory trade agreements have been a prolific breeder of that kind of antagonism which oftentimes results in war."[14] President Wilson, and a consensus of American leaders, believed that a nation whose leaders thought it was denied legitimate trade opportunities would resort automatically to massive armaments as a technique to acquire what was its right; consequently, disarmament by itself would merely remove the symbols of conflict, not their causes, which were economic. Disarmament had to be combined with the open door—"equal opportunity to everyone everywhere," in the words of Colonel House.

But America's European co-belligerents showed every

13. Ray Stannard Baker and William E. Dodd, eds., *The Public Papers of Woodrow Wilson, War and Peace I* (New York, 1927), 159.
14. *Ibid.*, 289.

sign that they had no intention of accepting any "open door" rules for the functioning of the world economy. On the contrary, before American entry into the war the Allies had laid down plans to organize world markets on a preferential basis, with the preferences going to them. When the United States entered the war they were willing to share these preferences with America, but not to give them up.[15] To meet the threat which the Allied plans posed to the broader community, American leaders realized that they had to continue to perfect their own tools to Americanize the world commercial system, and they had to use American economic power as pressure to frustrate various aspects of the victors' program as these items appeared in *and* out of diplomatic and commercial meetings over the years 1916–1923.

Wilson and his Republican successors shared the belief that disarmament and the open door were the twin keys to peace and community. They also agreed that the United States would have to coerce the other great powers to act in the interests of the common system. If the world were disarmed the weapon which the United States would have at its disposal was its expanding economic power. This in turn tended to reenforce the necessity for the United States to displace Britain as the managing segment of the world economy.

The technical means within which Wilson, and those who

15. U.S. Ambassador in France William G. Sharp to Secretary of State Robert Lansing, March 14, 1918, in State Department files, National Archives, Record Group 59, 600.001/207. The permanent committee of the Paris Economic Conference of 1916 asked that the "American Government nominate [a] delegate. . . . [That the] Committee concerns itself with studying economic questions arising out of the conduct of the war, as well as those relating to transition, following conclusion of hostilities, such as preferential trade agreements. . . ." Though it was clear the Allies wished the United States to share the "advantages" and thus the responsibility for such decisions, Lansing avoided the trap when he, in a note of March 14, 1918, instructed Sharp that "we have no representative on the Committee."

agreed with him, chose to exercise American leadership toward these two ends was the League of Nations. In their view such a league could force disarmament *and* write open door rules to govern the world economy. On this tactical question the American political elite split wide open. A wide spectrum of Democrats, Republicans, progressives, conservatives, interventionists, and noninterventionists broke with the Wilsonians on the League as a tactic toward the consensus ends. Men such as Herbert Hoover, Charles Evans Hughes, Philander C. Knox, Henry L. Stimson, William Howard Taft, and Elihu Root to a greater or lesser degree concluded that Wilson's Article 10 of the League of Nations Covenant was too inflexible to achieve real disarmament or generate the pressure to widen successively the application of the open door to ever larger areas of the world. Further, they believed that American participation in the League would deprive the United States of the freedom to use its economic power.

The differences between Wilson and his Republican successors may be summed up as tactical disputes within the context of a broad consensus about ends.

CHAPTER II

❧ State Capitalism Versus the Open Door

AT THE Paris Economic Conference of 1916, the nations of the Entente rejected the laissez faire theory current in the nineteenth century and adopted a commercial policy based on a return to mercantilist concepts popular during the sixteenth, seventeenth, and eighteenth centuries.[1] The new mercantilism had a serious anti-American aspect. The program adopted at Paris, if put into operation, would have divided the world market into politically organized regional markets and discriminated against American specialty exports within the Allied bloc.[2]

The Paris meeting was concerned with formulating an economic policy for the Entente powers during the war and through the period of reconstruction after the war, and with the development of a permanent commercial policy after

---

1. U.S. Senate, Committee on Judiciary, *Trade Agreements Abroad*, Senate Document No. 491, 64th Cong., 1st sess. (Washington, 1916), 38–39. (Hereafter cited as *Trade Agreements Abroad*.) See also National Foreign Trade Council, *European Economic Alliances, A Compilation of Information on International Commercial Policies after the European War and their Effect upon the Foreign Trade of the United States. Also An Analysis of European and United States Commercial Inter-Dependence and Treaty Relations* (New York, 1916), 21–22. (Hereafter cited as *European Economic Alliances*.)

2. *European Economic Alliances*, 11.

reconstruction.[3] The central feature of the Allied program was the substitution of a system of trade preferences for the unconditional, most-favored-nation commercial policy that had been the broad basis on which European trade had been conducted from 1870 to 1914.[4] The policy agreed upon at Paris relied on four major means of giving the Entente powers control of postwar world trade. In their domestic markets the Allied governments were to subsidize, give direction to, or regulate private enterprise. Second, they were to grant financial assistance for scientific and technical research facilitating the development of national industries and resources. Third, they were to enact customs duties, or export or import prohibitions, of a temporary or permanent character. Finally, the state was to participate directly in the financing and development of foreign markets.[5]

In order to compensate for lack of efficiency in certain areas of production, the Allies planned to establish differential shipping rates discriminating against the enemy powers and neutrals in competitive markets. The Allies hoped a discriminatory shipping policy would encourage Allied capitalists to develop raw material resources within their system of states and dependencies. Conversely, differential shipping rates would be a means of discouraging enemy and neutral capital from attempting to develop those same resources. All raw materials not available within the alliance were to be purchased from the outside through cooperative buying pools.[6]

A London meeting of the Chambers of Commerce of the

3. *Trade Agreements Abroad*, 46–49.

4. *Ibid.*, 36, 44; *European Economic Alliances*, 21.

5. H. W. V. Temperley, ed., *A History of the Peace Conference of Paris*, 6 vols. (London, 1921), V, Appendix I, 368–69 (extract from Paris resolutions on most-favored-nation clause); *Trade Agreements Abroad*, 44, 46–49.

6. *European Economic Alliances*, 11.

United Kingdom on February 26, 1916, framed most of the policy advocated by British delegates in Paris and adopted by the Allies. Told by its president, Sir Algernon Firth, that England would suffer the earlier fate of Holland if it became more trader than exporter, the delegates at the meeting adopted a resolution embodying Firth's recommendations.[7] Firth argued that even without further substantial investment, the output of English industry could be increased considerably if foreign competition were limited by changing the laws on patent rights, by controlling shipping entry to British ports, and by limiting free access to British markets. What was needed, he said, was the recognition that "production at home is infinitely preferable to the purchase of goods abroad, even at slightly reduced prices [for the foreign goods]." He claimed that if the principle of stimulating production at home with every available means had been recognized, then the raw materials of the Empire would have naturally gravitated to British industries. He advocated the free entry of loyal Empire peoples to British markets while denying it to the Germans.[8]

Firth's campaign for a closed-door postwar British commercial policy was a complete reversal of British policy as it had developed over the previous hundred years. From 1815 to about 1870, England was the primary manufacturing nation of Europe. After 1815, under steady pressure from industrial manufacturers, Great Britain moved toward a policy of free trade. The major issue was between the manufacturing and agricultural interests. English manufacturers, without substantial competition in the markets of the world,

7. A speech by Sir Algernon Firth delivered to the associations of Chambers of Commerce of the United Kingdom, March 29, 1916, *London Times* Trade Supplement, April 1916, in *Trade Agreements Abroad*, 37–40.

8. *Ibid.*

and with production exceeding domestic needs, pressed vigorously for broader markets. The debates, both within the
English business community and in Parliament, centered on
food costs. English agricultural interests lost continuously;
by 1870 almost all English protective duties had been removed. English agriculture was virtually destroyed and agricultural foodstuffs and raw materials for industry entered
free. From 1870 to 1914, English commercial policy was
basically one of free trade.

Beginning about 1870, however, France and Germany
began to expand their industrial manufacturing and established protective tariffs to maintain the new industries and
guarantee them the national markets. In spite of the growth
of protectionism from 1870 to 1914, England retained a free
trade policy, relying more and more on its financial power to
expand and hold markets. During the same period, Germany
complemented its policy of a domestic protective tariff with a
drive to expand its financial power abroad in order to extend
its foreign markets. France likewise protected its domestic
market and expanded its foreign investments, particularly in
Russia, as a means of foreign market development. As the
weakest economic power in this competition, France made
the first move toward tariff preference by implementing a
policy of tariff assimilation in its colonial areas.

On the whole, these tariff systems gave protection to native industries in national markets to the extent that they
could be supplied by those industries. The residue of national markets in Europe was governed by commercial
agreements based on the most-favored-nation principle. This
meant that the nations of Europe could export freely the
surplus of their specialities. The most-favored-nation principle allowed protective tariffs and nondiscrimination to coex-
ist in Europe. For example, France, Belgium, and the
Netherlands imported English cutlery without discrimina-

tion, while at the same time maintaining protective tariffs on their own cutlery industries. National industries were preserved even as the most efficient producer of cutlery supplied the general European market to the extent that national industries did not produce enough to supply them. These specialty exports, added to those portions of national markets unsupplied by national industries, made up the main body of inter-European trade. Despite protective devices, therefore, the quantity of inter-European trade was considerable, since the commercial agreements mitigated the harshness of growing protectionism.[9]

The outbreak of World War I led to severe controls over the trade of the belligerents. Capital issues were regulated, the state took control of foreign investment resources of nationals, the holdings of residents of enemy states were seized, and exports and imports were sharply controlled in the interests of winning the war. In the domestic economy, governments were active in the management of certain vital industries. State management of national economies was substituted for the indirect management of the market.

An examination of the statistics on the direction, volume, and composition of prewar American exports illustrates dramatically the enormous impact the change from most-favored-nation to trade preference as the fabric of European commercial policy would have on American foreign trade. In 1913, the last prewar normal year, over 77 percent of United States exports were to the belligerents and their colonies. Over 75 percent of American imports were from the same source. Of these quantities over one-half of United States exports were to Britain and the Empire and one-third of the imports were from Britain and the Empire.[10] Under the

9. This brief history of European commerical policy in the text is based on the summary in *European Economic Alliances*, 18–22.
10. *Ibid.*, 8–9.

prewar European commercial system, United States grain
and cotton exports entered Europe free (or at least without
unequal discriminations). This market was one of America's primary stakes in the most-favored-nation system.

Under a regime of Allied tariff preferences, however, a
greater proportion of Allied food supplies would come from
Russia, the British Empire, and such neutral sources as
Latin America (particularly Argentina).[11] A change in tariff systems, implemented mainly by Britain, but also by the
other Allies, meant that the Allies could control and develop
the neutral markets, particularly those of Latin America, in
which the United States had made significant inroads in the
early war years. The basis for such development would have
been an exchange of preferences between the Allies, as well
as tariff concessions to Latin America on raw materials and
foodstuffs in exchange for Latin American concessions on
Allied manufactures.[12] Any organized tariff and shipping
preferences of the kind outlined at Paris posed a serious
threat to United States exports, as well as to its import of
raw materials.[13]

In a letter of June 23, 1916, Secretary of State Robert
Lansing called President Wilson's attention to the broad
implications for American policy of the Paris proposals. If
applied, Lansing pointed out, the Paris measures might have
"very far reaching" effects on the "commerce and the trade
of the whole world after the war. . . ." He argued that the
United States had to view the Paris measures "from two
standpoints, that of their effect on the present and future
trade of the enemies of the Allies, and that of their effect on
the present and future trade of neutral countries." The effect

11. *Ibid.*, 11.
12. *Ibid.*, 11–12.
13. *Ibid.*, 8.

of the clear Allied attempt to destroy the postwar commerce of the Central Powers, Lansing maintained, would "make the negotiations of a satisfactory peace most difficult" and would have the effect of "prolonging the war." From the point of view of the effects on neutral trade, Lansing feared the proposed preferential system was operable because of the great resources for implementing the program represented in factors such as the large Allied colonial empires and their "great merchant marine." The "consequent restriction upon profitable trade . . . will cause a serious if not critical situation for the nations outside the union by creating unusual and artificial economic conditions." Lansing concluded his letter by urging upon Wilson a conference of neutrals to meet the threat, since "the best way to fight combination is by combination."[14]

Wilson's reply came in the form of a memorandum entitled "Bases of Peace." In point three of the memorandum Wilson proposed a "mutual guarantee against such economic warfare as would in effect constitute an effort to throttle the industrial life of a nation or shut it off from equal opportunities of trade with the rest of the world."[15]

In effect Wilson rejected Lansing's proposal of a neutral

14. Lansing to Wilson, June 23, 1916, in U.S. Department of State, *Papers Relating to the Foreign Relations of the United States, The Lansing Papers 1914–1920,* 2 vols. (Washington, 1939), I, 311–12. (Hereafter cited as *Lansing Papers.*)

15. Wilson to Lansing, February 7, 1917, Lansing to Wilson, February 7, 1917, *Lansing Papers,* I, 19–21. In a "Note" Wilson qualified his position to the effect that "this would of course, not apply to any laws of any individual state which were meant merely for the regulation and development of its own industries or for the mere safeguarding of its own resources from misuses or exhaustion, but only to such legislation and such governmental action as could be shown to be intended to operate outside territorial limits and intended to injure particular rivals or groups of rivals."

"bloc" to combat the Allied preferential system. In its stead
he advocated the open door of nondiscrimination as the economic basis of peace. As the Bases of Peace gradually became transformed into the Fourteen Points, the President
defined point three more sharply. The final result was Wilson's advocacy, in point three of the Fourteen Points, of the
open door as the means to resolve all kinds of commercial
warfare.[16] Thus the threat emanating from the Paris Conference was an added stimulus to the existing concern of the
Wilson Administration to remodel American foreign trade
policy.

The program of remodeling had begun with the passage
of the Federal Reserve Act of 1913. That legislation, it is
true, was designed primarily to allow American domestic
currency to expand and contract with the vicissitudes of
trade in the domestic American market. At the same time,
this expansion and contraction was intended to free part of
the nation's domestic bank reserves for the development of
foreign trade on a continuing basis. Two additional sections
of the Act were concerned specifically with foreign trade
development. One allowed American banks to discount commercial acceptances; that is, to grant short-term credit for
financing American import and export trade.[17] Previous to
the Federal Reserve Act, nearly all American export and
import trade credit was handled in sterling "bills," for which
the London banks charged fees. American foreign traders
were now permitted to eliminate a portion of these fees when
and if the New York banks established a bill discount market roughly comparable to the London market. The second

16. Series of memoranda from Lansing to Wilson, Wilson to Lansing,
ibid., 21–25.
17. Federal Trade Commission, *Cooperation in the Export Trade*, 2
vols. (Washington, 1916), I, 65; Harold L. Reed, *The Development of
Federal Reserve Policy* (Boston and New York, 1922), 110.

provision allowed American National Banks (banks with federal charters) to establish branches overseas.[18]

While attempting to frame a workable act, Congress had ordered the National Monetary Commission to make studies of foreign banking systems. Several of those reports indicated that America's two major competitors, England and Germany, used a highly integrated network of foreign branch banks. In 1906, Germany had 13 overseas banks with 70 branches. England possessed 32 empire banks with head offices located in London and 2,104 branches throughout the colonies. In addition, 18 other British foreign banks operated outside of the colonies with some 175 branches. Even Holland possessed 16 overseas banks with 68 branches.[19] Rightly or wrongly, American leaders concluded that a reciprocal causative relationship existed between the export of capital and the growth of branch banks. They contended that branches were in part expanded to assist the export of capital, even if initially they were established to facilitate simple merchandise trade. They believed further that by 1914 branch banks had turned almost exclusively to organizing the foreign investment of the industrial nation's capital in such a way as to sustain and increase its volume of foreign trade.[20] Almost without exception the pattern of international branch bank growth meant that developed nations established branch banks in underdeveloped countries.[21] Even when the commodities whose sale was financed were those of the underdeveloped country, the organizers of the flow of commerce were the bankers of the industrial

18. Federal Trade Commission, *Cooperation in Export Trade*, I, 64–65.

19. J. Riesser, *The German Great Banks and Their Concentration* (Washington, 1911), 459–60.

20. Clyde Phelps, *The Foreign Expansion of American Banks* (New York, 1927), 20.

21. Riesser, *German Great Banks*, 456.

country. In fact, to use their own capital profitably, and hence market their own goods and services, the British, French, or German bankers had to undertake the marketing of the commodities produced in underdeveloped countries, even if the production of those goods was not financed by the capital of the industrial country.[22]

More important than the branch banks in the development of the European system of foreign trade, however, was the interrelationship, on the one hand, between banking, shipping, and manufacturing and, on the other, the vertical and horizontal integration of such activities by the banks. In the view of American leaders, every such development project undertaken by either a German or English combination resulted in orders to the industry of the respective countries over a long period. These projects allowed for long-term planning by industry, which in turn meant cost-cutting, widening of markets, and attaining economies of scale. All such considerations provided for continuous rationalization.

In London or Berlin, moreover, the American leaders argued, the home banks were tied directly to manufacturing industries. Before 1910, for example, the Dresdener Bank was represented on the boards of more than 200 industrial corporations. The Deutsche Bank held positions on the boards of 116 German and foreign concerns.[23] Its charter provision was typical, declaring that the "object of this com-

22. This should be readily obvious if, for example, one imagines a British branch bank operating in Argentina prior to 1914. The main export commodities in such a case would be wheat and beef; if the wheat and beef were not exported, the British branch bank would have nothing to do even if—as was so often the case—it concentrated its direct activities in "banking" British-owned railroads in Argentina. If the wheat and beef had no export markets, the British-owned railroads in Argentina would have little business of a profitable nature to do; hence, they would have little or no need of banking services.

23. Federal Trade Commission, *Cooperation in Export Trade*, I, 62.

pany is the transaction of all sorts of banking business, particularly in the fostering and facilitating of commercial relations between Germany, the other European countries, and overseas markets."[24] Bank representatives on the boards of the industrial concerns always took special care to market the products of these industries.[25] In addition, the German banks made loans to local and municipal governments of other countries conditional on an agreement that the funds be spent on German material.[26]

In its final report in 1916 on the investigation of cooperation in the export trade of foreign countries, the Federal Trade Commission commented, on the basis of information supplied by American General Electric, that the relationship between German banking and German General Electric (A.E.G.) "assisted the A.E.G. in financing many foreign undertakings in which electrical equipment was required, such as power plants, street railways, electric light plants, etc." The system also "assisted in the organization of special banks and trust companies for electrical enterprises . . . abroad, whose function was the financing of foreign electrical enterprises."[27]

In contracts which carried no provisions requiring purchases of materials from industries in the country of the bank managing the loan, other less obvious (but nonetheless effective) means of tying the loan to national technology were employed. For example, when the Argentine railways were built by British capital, the loan contract stipulated that the engineers in charge of construction be British nationals. Since they alone were familiar with British equip-

24. Riesser, *German Great Banks*, 421.
25. Federal Trade Commission, *Cooperation in Export Trade*, I, 62–63.
26. Riesser, *German Great Banks*, 384–86.
27. Federal Trade Commission, *Cooperation in Export Trade*, I, 276.

ment, these engineers used British engineering designs, built to track width for British gauge engines and cars, and followed their own construction methods. Almost all future supplies for those railroads thus had to be purchased from British firms, the only manufacturers using engineering specifications for locomotives, steel rails, and rolling stock serviceable as replacements. In this way British manufacturers of railway equipment had a permanent noncompetitive market for railroad equipment.[28]

The importance of establishing national technology in a newly developing area, particularly in railroad investments, was demonstrated by the British attempt to keep an American railroad builder from getting a contract to build a line in Uruguay in 1916. Even though British costs of production were higher, Britain underbid the American firm on the project, their avowed purpose being to keep American technology out of South American railroads.[29] From the British point of view, securing the noncompetitive replacement business was more important than making a profit on the actual construction of the original railroad.

In addition to railroads, public utility investments were of great importance in building a noncompetitive replacement-parts business. As in railroad construction, the engineers on the project, as well as the managers of the gas, electric, or street railway stations, were almost always of the same nationality as the owners of the capital or the bankers floating the loan. Again as in the case of the railroads, they used equipment made in their native land. Out of national pride in the superiority of their own technology, and often in ignorance of the accomplishments or even the features of foreign technologies, they habitually chose designs with which they

28. *Ibid.*, 74.
29. *Ibid.*, 176.

were familiar from their own fund of national engineering.[30]

The final authority in the acceptance or rejection of bids for equipment on a given project in an underdeveloped country rested customarily with the directors of the bank financing the purchases in the exporting industrial country. These were "men of large and varied property interests, often including steel works and machine works which turn out the materials that the foreign enterprise uses. Indeed, the direction of their investments to foreign countries may have been guided by the nature of their property at home."[31] The European system of export trade development rested on multiownership by bankers and manufacturers of domestic industrial corporations.

The legal sanction to establish foreign branch banks was one important move in the program to expand systematically such cooperation in the American export trade. In 1916, the Federal Trade Commission made a study of European practice. Its consequent report was based on hearings in which depositions were taken from American businessmen in an attempt to secure a consensus of American business opinion. In this report the Commission argued that banking and shipping facilities, under American control, were the first requisites of a better, more carefully organized foreign trade program. The Commission saw a clear tendency on the part of American industry to develop interlocking directorates and other communities of interest which would closely parallel German and English patterns of cooperation in export trade operations. Given the proper facilities, managed by men with the tendency to cooperate in foreign trade, speedier and more efficient development of foreign markets would be assured.[32] The main recommendation of the Commission

30. *Ibid.*, 73–74.
31. *Ibid.*
32. *Ibid.*, 8–9.

was that a law be passed allowing American exporters to combine when operating in foreign markets, thus bypassing the provisions of the Sherman Antitrust Act, which prohibited such cooperation. These recommendations became law in the Webb-Pomerene Act of 1918.

The Webb-Pomerene Act was written ostensibly to allow small firms to combine in the export trade in order to compete with the larger German and English selling and buying combinations.[33] Before 1914, at any rate, certain American specialty exports such as copper, silver, cotton and other unfinished commodities were, according to American leaders, subject to European buying combinations which forced down the prices of these commodities in export markets. German buying cartels controlled copper prices and the English Silver Board controlled the world price of silver (especially the price which American producers received for it).[34]

Of even more importance in balancing American trade deficits was the price of American copper. Two countries controlled the price of copper. In England, what was called the "fixing board" bought much of the American product and therefore dictated limits on the price. Germany, as the

33. U.S. Senate, Committee on Interstate and Foreign Commerce, *Promotion of the Export Trade, Hearings on H.R.* 17350, 64th Cong., 2d sess. (Washington, 1917), 35–41. (Hereafter cited as *Promotion of Export Trade.*)

34. Federal Trade Commission, *Cooperation in Export Trade*, I, 359–60. In recent years, especially during the fall of 1965, the United States government has effectively accomplished part of the goals of American metal producers and fabricators through using the strategic stockpiles, which it owns, to influence and even control commodity prices. In this sense American copper or aluminum stockpiles have much more influence over prices paid to American producers than does any single national market. The American government has taken upon itself many of the functions once envisioned as the proper functions of the Webb-Pomerene Associations.

chief center of the copper fabricating industry, controlled the price of the fabricated product, which in turn affected the cost of American raw copper. Germany was able to do this because of the strength of its electrical manufacturing industry, which used copper as a primary raw material in its products. German buyers exercised more control over copper prices than did the British "fixing board." In most other cases, however, England controlled metal prices.[35]

American business leaders argued that so long as British and German buying combinations were able to "rig" international commodity bidding, American sellers must be allowed to cooperate in bolstering those prices the buying combines would otherwise successfully depress.

While American corporation leaders invariably argued that the antitrust laws had to be waived for the export trade in order that small business corporations involved in commodity exports might have protection against European buying combinations, the paradoxical fact remained that a very high proportion of the interest in and support for an export trade act came from large American corporations. The European experience implied that if American firms were to compete successfully in foreign markets, then they too needed a general pattern of combination among raw material producers, financiers, manufacturers, and shippers.

By 1916, much vertical and horizontal integration had been achieved in the iron and steel industry, in electrical and farm equipment manufacture, and in other industries. But any further steps in this process were subject to prosecution under the restraint-of-trade laws until passage of the Webb Act. Under the Webb Act, General Electric could combine with the Guaranty Trust Company, the W. R. Grace shipping concern, and other firms to compete effectively with

35. *Ibid.*, 357–60.

German or English development projects. This was at least as important, as far as the supporters of the Webb-Pomerene Act were concerned, as allowing small producers to combine to enter markets in competition with European cartels. No European steel cartel could match the power of the United States Steel Corporation. Similarly, no electrical equipment cartel equalled the power of General Electric. It was the ability of bankers, manufacturers, and shippers to combine and coordinate their efforts that made the European cartels more effective competitively than the American trusts. In many cases, the cartels had been formed in the face of the power of the individual American corporation.

The problem for American foreign trading interests was to establish a miniature United States economic system in foreign countries. The solution to the legal ban on combinations to implement such projects depended upon repeal of the antitrust laws as they related to international commerce. This was what the Webb-Pomerene Act accomplished. But the establishment of an American system in foreign countries created a new financial problem. Over the long run, the remodelers of American foreign trade policy would have either to sell the securities for such operations to the American public or pressure the government to allocate taxes collected from the public to finance such expansion. In the short run, American security buyers, mostly banks and corporations, were acquiring European foreign investments, in this way "taking proven properties" and thereby "eliminating the risk and delay usually attendant upon investments in new fields."[36]

36. See address entitled "Investment in South America" by Percival Farquhar, President, Brazil Railway Co., New York, in National Foreign Trade Council, *Proceedings of the Fourth Annual Convention* (New York, 1916), 28. (Hereafter cited as NFTC Convention *Proceedings*.)

Most sections of American business, along with the Federal Trade Commission and other government agencies, recommended the passage of the Webb-Pomerene Act.[37] The Webb Act, along with the pertinent sections of the Federal Reserve Act, were believed by business and government leaders to provide the basis for expanding and rationalizing American foreign trade. If utilized effectively, and if combined with a tariff policy protecting the American exporter against unequal discrimination, the acts would enable American business to meet and defeat European competition.[38]

The Paris Economic Conference increased Congressional concern with such economic problems. On July 10, 1916, Senator William Stone of Mississippi moved, with unanimous consent of the Senate, to have the decisions of the conference and any information in the hands of the Wilson Administration relative to the meeting published as a Senate document. Stone maintained in his speech that the proposed European alliance "may not be in accord with the interests of this country," even though it seemed directed mainly against Germany. He thought there was probably a larger program underway than mere commercial war against Germany, and worried that it might be directed against the United States as well as Germany.[39]

Senator Lodge was the only other senator to speak on the subject. He advocated publication of all pertinent documents on the subject of commercial policy planned by both the Allies and the Central Powers. In the event of the victory of

37. *Promotion of Export Trade*, 1–61. Letters of endorsement of Webb-Pomerene Act by Federal Trade Commission and business interests of various kinds.
38. *European Economic Alliances*, 8–9, 15–17; *Promotion of Export Trade*, 50–55.
39. *Trade Agreements Abroad*, 5.

either, the United States had to consider what to do. Lodge believed victory by either side would present economic problems for the United States:

That they will try to close the gates of trade and commerce upon us in many directions I regard as highly probable, although the aim and extent of the effort must remain at present a matter of speculation. But if we are to meet this situation, successfully, we must be prepared economically and industrially as I believe we should be prepared physically and in arms. To this end the essential thing is so to organize our industries that they will be strong, independent, and ready for the conflict when and if it comes. . . .

The greatest element in any defense against such an economic offensive, Lodge held, was the great domestic market. The ability to deny an exporting nation access to that was a potent weapon.[40]

The economic program the Allies forged at Paris in April 1916 did not come as a complete surprise to leading American businessmen who were attempting to remodel American foreign trade policy. In January 1916, Alba B. Johnson, President of the Baldwin Locomotive Works and President of the National Foreign Trade Council (NFTC), predicted, in a talk before the 1916 NFTC convention, a postwar economic alliance which would be "broader than the British Empire" and which would "take the form of preferential trade among the Allied nations." Though not "created in any spirit of hostility" to the United States, "such arrangements would increase the difficulties of our [American] struggle for foreign trade." Already in January 1916 the British Board of Trade had called a conference of "all the representatives of British Trade organizations" to consider

40. *Ibid.*, 8.

the question of a postwar Allied trade alliance.[41] Willard Straight, Vice-president of the American International Corporation, seconded Johnson's warning to the 1916 convention and argued that a "tariff agreement between the United Kingdom and her colonies, and special concessions under this scheme of Imperial Preference as part of a general reciprocal arrangement between France, Russia, Italy and Belgium and their various dependencies, would create an entirely self supporting commercial unit which would cover a well balanced exchange of raw products for manufactured articles."[42] Straight understood that such an internally balanced trading area would have small need to respect the traditional American stake in the general European market.

As a result of a study in 1916 of the projected European alliance, the NFTC advocated prompt adoption of the program already developed to remodel the American foreign trade system. In addition, it called for enactment of the Wilson Administration's shipping bill, the addition of a strong antidumping provision to the revenue act to protect the American domestic market, and the development of an effective bargaining tariff.[43] The NFTC expressed its willingness to work with the Tariff Commission on framing an adequate act. The NFTC also recommended that rates on manufactures should be as low as "radical prudence permits," suggested a section enabling concessions to be granted in exchange for equal treatment, and urged the invoking of retaliation in cases of discrimination. Such a

41. Presidential address of Alba B. Johnson to the Fourth Annual Convention of the National Foreign Trade Council in NFTC Convention *Proceedings*, 1916, 15–16.

42. Address entitled "Relation of Tariff to World Trade Conditions after the War," by Willard Straight in the Fourth Annual NFTC Convention *Proceedings*, 1916, 64.

43. *European Economic Alliances*, 11–13.

tariff would enable the United States to secure favorable commercial treaties and give enough flexibility to the American tariff to make it serviceable in a fight against European discriminations.[44] This idea of the tariff as an offensive as well as a defensive weapon in the campaign to expand American trade was to be embraced by Republicans and Democrats alike.

British leaders gave assurances to the United States that the system devised at Paris was aimed at the Central Powers and that the United States and other neutrals would be exempt. Nevertheless, hearings on the Webb-Pomerene Act revealed that the United States Congress was deeply concerned about the effects of the developing system on American foreign trade.[45] British press and parliamentary debates indicated, despite official disclaimers, that the system would be used against the United States. On July 12, 1916, Lord Asquith of the British Board of Trade announced to the House of Commons the appointment of a commission to study the recommendations of the Paris Conference. Both tariff reformers and free traders were represented on the commission, whose purpose was to determine the British form of the implementation of the Paris resolves.[46]

The commission was asked to determine (1) industries essential to the safety of the nation and steps that should be taken to establish them; (2) measures needed to recover home and foreign markets and to secure new markets; (3) what should be done to develop the resources of the Empire and the extent to which they should be developed; and (4) to what extent and by what means imperial sources of supply could be prevented from falling under foreign control.[47]

44. *Ibid.*, 11–13.
45. *Promotion of Export Trade*, 34–58, 62–64.
46. *European Economic Alliances*, 35–36.
47. *Ibid.; Trade Agreements Abroad*, 46–49.

In addition, there was extensive discussion in the British press on postwar British policy. Theoretical attempts were made to relate commercial policy to practical needs and desired social ends. The reasoning strongly resembled pre-nineteenth century mercantilist thought. (Nineteenth century economic thought assumed the expansibility of markets, but pre-nineteenth century mercantile doctrine assumed markets to be nonexpansible.) Nonexpansible markets meant intense and fierce commercial rivalry for the relatively small pie labeled World Trade. Nineteenth century thinkers, following Jean Baptiste Say, assumed that growing markets based on the freest possible trade and the greatest growth of specialization and division of labor, provided the primary guarantee of market expansion. The concept of expansibility of world markets was simply the application of the domestic market division of labor to the world market.[48]

The British commercial press showed less and less confidence in British ability to compete in world markets, and a stronger tendency to rely on political-military power as a means of market allocation.[49] *Fairplay*, a British journal devoted to shipping and finance, pointed out on August 10, 1916, that no matter who was to win the war, the Allies or the Central Powers, no nonsense was to be taken from the neutrals. The winning combatants, said *Fairplay*, would be the main armed force in the world; also, the Allies intended to put up a tariff wall against the neutrals wherever it suited them. They meant to restore themselves as self-supporting nations, "at some expense it may be while the operation lasts, but certainly not for the benefit of neutrals."[50]

48. *European Economic Alliances*, 21–25.
49. *Ibid.*, 46–64.
50. Quoted in *European Economic Alliances*, 57.

On July 19, 1916, Ernest J. P. Benn outlined in the *London Evening Standard* the reported views of the British Board of Trade on problems demanding government attention after the war. These included the need to raise twice as much annual revenue as before the war; the need to repair material damage done by the war; the need to find employment for British soldiers and munitions workers; the need to fill up the empty warehouses of the world; the need to take Germany's place in France, Italy, and Russia; the need to pay higher wages than ever before to English workers; and the need to cheapen production in order to compete with Germany and the United States in neutral markets.[51]

These objectives, which the British press ascribed to the Board of Trade, were defined in neomercantilist or state capitalist terms. Prime Minister Hughes of Australia, one of the official British delegates to Paris, in an interview published in the *London Times* on June 21, 1916, analyzed the meaning of the Paris Agreements as follows:

Their potential effects are almost infinite. They indicate a way by which the great rivers of commerce can be diverted from those channels along which, before the war, Germany had with masterly cunning contrived to guide them, to the great advantage of herself and the detriment of the allies, to others controlled by the allies which will distribute the benefits more evenly.[52]

Britain proposed nothing less than the reconstruction of world trade relationships on the basis of explicit political preference in place of the laissez faire principles advocated by the United States. Germany had been the leading investor in Russia, and its financial interest in Russia was expanding at a faster rate than was the French; hence the reconstruction of Russia was to become in large measure a

51. Benn, quoted in *ibid.*, 48–49.
52. Quoted in *Trade Agreements Abroad*, 50.

British project. In this way, and under English tutelage, Russia was to be integrated into the Entente system.[53]

For all these reasons American business leaders saw the British plans as a distinct threat to their commercial interests. During World War I, the United States exported to Europe without being paid in commodity imports from Europe. The Allies made their payments by reselling securities they owned in American industries and by exporting gold to the United States. This gold was in turn used to construct a credit structure about eight times the value of the gold. Upon the basis of this credit structure the United States further expanded its foreign trade. Recovery of a portion of this gold reserve by the Allies, said Frank Vanderlip, President of the National City Bank of New York, "is essential to the recovery of European prosperity after the war." To defend the American credit structure against a European export offensive, Vanderlip urged a campaign to increase American exports to take up the expected decline in munitions sales. A successful export drive, he reasoned, would eliminate the necessity for the United States to export gold.[54]

Just as the United States was ready to enter world markets as a serious competitor in manufactures on the basis of is own ability to expand in a world without unequal discriminations, Europe was heading toward state capitalism and a policy of discrimination in commercial relationships that would allocate world markets politically. Put into operation, the Paris program would have created an exclusive European economic community based on joint development of neutral markets by the Allied governments, and an alliance of European state capitalisms against Germany (and, implicitly, against the United States). In place of this,

53. *European Economic Alliances*, 57–58.
54. F. A. Vanderlip to the Fourth Annual Convention of the National Foreign Trade Council in NFTC Convention *Proceedings*, 1916, 430–35.

American industry and government wanted a restoration of political and commercial peace and an economic community encompassing the United States, as well as the European victors and vanquished. The widest possible world markets were in America's interests. Germany's admission to the family of nations without commercial discrimination was a key factor in such a world. Preventing the formation of geographical or political blocs based on trade preference became the *sine qua non* for a return to nineteenth century economic ideology—and for protecting the material interests of the United States. In another sense, the failure to readmit Germany to the family of trading nations implied either permanent military occupation of Germany, which France seemed nearly willing to assume, or a new commercial war which would lead to a renewal of the same military conflict between Germany on the one side and France and England on the other.

In the narrow sense, state capitalism[55] meant discrimination against American commodities, particularly manufactures, at a time when foreign markets were necessary to the

55. The term "state capitalism" is used in this study to denote a partnership between the state and the private business corporation, based on the state's use of the tax power to sustain the economic activities of the corporation because that corporation is defined as an instrument of public policy. Specifically with respect to the organization and development of foreign markets, the state assumes a special obligation to finance such activities because it is assumed by government and corporate executives that the increase in the nation's share of world trade is in the general interest of the society. Use of the term "state capitalism" as a label for the general rules the Paris Conference established for developing an exclusive world trading system under the control of the Allies seems to this writer justified both because these rules make world market allocation highly political and because the means proposed to develop that exclusive system for the first time since the Napoleonic wars ended are based on the state's taxation of the whole of society to finance an economic end politically defined as desirable in the general interests of society.

stabilization of American industry and to the employment of American workers. The United States had two choices. It could adopt state capitalist measures on its own, or it could build a defense based on its own economic strength and on the use of that strength (by way of production, raw material resources, and the size of the domestic market) as bargaining weapons against discrimination. American leaders chose the second alternative. Their position was enhanced by the weakness of the Allies. Europe had to turn to the United States for capital with which to reconstruct devastated industry. In addition, there existed a relative diversity of interest between the British, French, and Japanese.

CHAPTER III

❧ *Cooperation or Competition?*

SHORTLY AFTER Armistice Day, 1918, American and British businessmen and politicians began to consider the nature of the economic and political postwar relations between their two countries. Because of conflicts of interest between Britain and its continental Allies and the relative weakness of Britain in relation to the United States, the program worked out at Paris in April 1916 could not fully be brought into force. Partly for this reason Britain tried to come to grips with the problem of how to protect its interests in the face of considerable American will and power to frustrate British efforts. Before World War I, Britain was not prone to make any considerable concessions to American world trade interests. After the War, it proposed what was in effect an economic alliance and a sharing of the responsibility and advantage of world economic development.[1]

Britain owed its late nineteenth and early twentieth century preeminence in world trade to its position as financier of the world. Beginning in the 1890's England's costs of production per unit, as distinct from its costs of distribution,

1. "Summary of Great Britain's After-the-War Attitude on Trade and Finance," Philip B. Kennedy, American commercial attaché in London, to State Department, November 22, 1918, printed in U.S. *Senate Document No. 86*, U.S. Senate, Committee on Judiciary, *Loans to Foreign Governments*, 67th Cong., 2d sess. (Washington, 1921), 36–37. (Hereafter cited as *Senate Document No. 86*.)

were significantly higher than those of Germany or the United States. But its finely-tooled system of collecting and investing the capital of its citizens abroad enabled it to hold markets against lower-cost competitors. Indeed, Britain was the world's largest foreign investor and the overall financier of half the world's foreign trade. Even a great proportion of the trade of its two major competitors, Germany and the United States, was financed in London. During World War I, however, England was forced to borrow extensively in the United States to obtain raw materials, food, and munitions. Prior to American entry into the war, the British paid for their imports in two ways. Private capitalists first sold their international investment securities to American investors for dollars. This informal means of securing dollars was employed from the outbreak of the war until January 1917, when the British government sequestered securities having a dollar market. The total of British foreign investments liquidated from 1914 to March 1919 was about $2,655 million. Roughly $500 million of this amount represented British investment in the United States, and was sold to Americans by the British government. Private investors sold at least an equal amount of American securities before the government nationalized foreign securities. In addition, approximately $705 million in Latin American securities were sold to Americans by private investors or the British government.[2]

2. There is no single source available which details the liquidation by geographical area, industry, or type of investments. However, both the total of British foreign investments and the subtotal for such investments in Latin America (defined as Mexico, Cuba, the West Indies, and Central and South America) can be gleaned from a number of sources. Total British investments in Latin America in 1910 were $3,090 million (a figure I arrived at by multiplying £618 million by the average rate of exchange for the period 1914–1919 of five dollars to the pound). For statistics on this see E. Victor Morgan, *Studies in British Financial Policy, 1914–1925* (London, 1952), 328–30. Morgan also shows that

In this manner the securities formerly representing British claims on the American economy were in great measure returned to the United States. However, the income from these investments had been the means by which England, prior to the war, had paid for a large part of her imports from the United States. Their loss posed a serious problem.

Having paid off much of its indebtedness to England, the United States was in a position to enter postwar economic competition as a long-term foreign investor. Domestic industries were also producing increasing surpluses for foreign trade. Two possibilities were open to American economic-political leaders: they could lower the tariff and permit more imports to be exchanged for exports, or they could make an effort to become a large-scale foreign investor. A tariff low enough to allow sufficient imports to balance current exports was not contemplated seriously by either party in Congress.[3]

Hence the real problem for England was not whether the

the total of British liquidations, by private enterprise and government, was about $2,655 million, in *ibid.*, 331. At the same time, American acquisitions of direct investments outside the United States, those giving management control of the properties, was about $1,227.2 million. In Latin America, American direct investments increased by about $705.6 million. My statistics on American direct investment expansion in Latin America are derived from Cleona Lewis, *America's Stake in International Investments* (Washington, 1938), 605–06, Tables I, II, III. In view of two significant facts—(1) it appears that no new investment projects were initiated by American investors in Latin America in the years 1914–1919 (nor were they attractive or possible in view of American exports being directed toward Europe, and the availability of "risk-free" British investments); and (2) there was no other major international investor capable of purchasing existing English investments in Latin America—it seems fair to conclude that British liquidations were roughly equivalent to American acquisitions of $705.6 million in Latin American direct investment securities.

3. League of Nations, Economic, Financial, and Transit Department, 2d Ser., Economic and Financial, *Commercial Policy in the Interwar Period: International Proposals and National Policies* (Trenton, N.J., 1942), 126; see also Chapter VIII, this volume, on the tariff.

United States was going to become a world investor, but whether American world commercial policy would be consistent with British management of world finance and trade. The British had a world trade organization centering on the London bill discount market. This market was tied to the five big British banks, which had foreign branches throughout the world. This was the financial mechanism British industry used to collect capital at home to invest abroad in order to secure world markets. English manufacturing industries were in turn connected with the banks through interlocking directorates and industrial trade associations. At the close of the war, shipping lines were involved with the banks and industrial corporations in a similar fashion, and by direct mergers.[4]

British industrial and political leaders feared that the United States, once relieved of its debt-service burden, and possessing an enormous exportable surplus, might attempt

4. The extent to which British banking, shipping, and manufacturing interests conducted integrated operations is disputed in American and British sources. British sources generally understate and American sources overstate the degree of integration. No matter what the extent, it is clear that such operations were more integrated in Britain than in the United States; it is also clear that such integration undercut the open door. There is also ample evidence that the British government encouraged and at times forced such integration. On forced integration see Norman H. Davis to U.S. Treasury Mission in Belgium, January 9, 1919, and Mission's reply to Davis, January 18, 1919, in *Senate Document No. 86*, 30–31.

For the American argument for extensive commercial integration in Britain, see U.S. Senate, Committee on Judiciary, *Trade Agreements Abroad*, Senate Document No. 491, 64th Cong., 1st sess. (Washington, 1916); National Foreign Trade Council, *European Economic Alliances, A Compilation of Information on International Commercial Policies after the European War and their Effect upon the Foreign Trade of the United States. Also An Analysis of European and United States Commercial Inter-Dependence and Treaty Relations* (New York, 1916). British denial of such integration is sketched in the *Report of the Committee on Finance and Industry (MacMillan Report)*, Cmd. 3897 (London, 1931).

to replace London as the primary financial center of the world. Making New York the financial hub meant establishing a branch bank system comparable to the British system, but European reconstruction presented an excellent opportunity for the United States to construct such a financial network. To counter such a development, the British proposed cooperation in the development of world markets. According to Philip B. Kennedy, American Commercial Attaché in London, the British view of cooperation meant that American goods and capital would be fed out through "the machinery largely in the control of British banks and financial houses."[5] Such an arrangement would preserve for the British their middleman status, as well as the income derived from that position. Thus world trade and market development would be shared by England and the United States, and the British financial empire protected against the creation of a competitive American system which would lower gross and net income for both countries.[6]

Britain was also afraid the United States was trying to take over world shipping. Historically, shipping power had been connected very closely with banking and had provided Britain with income—in profits for the transport of goods— as well as functioning as part of the integrated prewar system of securing and maintaining foreign markets. British fears were initially aroused when Edward Hurley, head of the United States Shipping Board, proposed an integrated transportation policy tying American railroads with shipping in such a way as to provide a government subsidy for American shipping. Not unnaturally the British concluded that subsidized American self-sufficiency in shipping was the Board's goal.[7]

5. Philip B. Kennedy to State Department, November 22, 1918, *Senate Document No. 86*, 36.
6. *Ibid.*, 36, 37–40.
7. *Ibid.*, 37–39.

A subsidized American mercantile marine was connected in British minds with the wartime American penetration of Latin American markets. According to British leaders, American press and business circles were claiming specific trade routes, which meant that the United States was particularly entitled to the Latin American market, to which British ships had carried British goods before the war. British ships had actually dominated *all* trade routes. As the nation with the largest fleet, it could not agree that any routes could be particularly American. In order to preserve British shipping in general, England moved to merge and consolidate its operations into great national lines. In addition, British shipping interests were willing to enter into ship pooling arrangements with American shippers. According to a note of September 9, 1918, from President Wilson to Edward Hurley, Chairman of the United States Shipping Board, Lord Reading of the British Admiralty had proposed a "conference . . . about pooling" American ships with the British.[8] This proposal implied a division of business and profits.

In export trade, as in finance, England was willing to come to an agreement with American operators. The principal field of cooperation proposed by the British concerned underdeveloped areas such as Latin America. Sir Arthur Steel-Maitland, Secretary of the Department of Overseas Trade, suggested that instead of engaging in competition, the two nations "might get together and divide contracts in South American and in other places."[9] In finance, trade, shipping, and the development of underdeveloped areas, therefore, England was willing to enter into partnership

8. Wilson to Hurley, September 9, 1918, in William Diamond, *The Economic Thought of Woodrow Wilson* (Baltimore, 1943), footnote 68, 188; Philip B. Kennedy to State Department, November 22, 1918, *Senate Document No. 86*, 38–39.

9. Philip B. Kennedy to State Department, November 22, 1918, *Senate Document No. 86*, 40.

with American interests in order to protect British management of world trade, a control which had been built up over
the years.[10]

For the privilege of entering the British-managed system
as an important partner, the United States was expected to
make several concessions to the British point of view. The
sine qua non of American entry was an understanding that
America would not construct an independent system of its
own, and that the existing elements of an independent system would be integrated into the British mechanism. Britain
would feverishly rebuild its system, while America was to
halt such activity. Wilson's concept of "no economic barriers" would have to be "whittled down" for a period in
which British industries established during the war might
consolidate control of their own domestic market. The automobile industry was considered a prime example of this
requirement.[11]

"The [British] Overseas Trade Department and commercial interests generally" looked upon an imperial preference
tariff as a "matter of domestic policy"; hence the United
States was expected to accept preference as comparable to
the American tariff.[12] The United States was also to go along
with Allied economic control over Germany in order that
reparations might be taken to finance the reconstruction and
modernization of British industry. As a corollary to this part
of the deal the United States was not supposed to insist that
the Allies allow Germany to enjoy the commercial benefits
of most-favored-nation treatment during a temporary reconstruction period; that would protect essential English industries against more efficient German competitors. Finally,
the British and American governments were to come to an

10. *Ibid.*, 39–40.
11. *Ibid.*
12. *Ibid.*

agreement on the control and allocation of raw materials.[13]

The first order of business under this program, developed by the British in 1918, was to obtain long-term reconstruction credits from the United States. Priorities were to be assigned, as they had been during the war, to shipping and manufacturing. Even to begin the execution of the British plan of reconstruction, the American government's agreement was necessary on two elementary problems: interest and principal payments on British government debts to the United States had to be postponed in lieu of outright cancellation, and new loans from the United States government on a long-term basis had to be obtained. John Chamberlain, Secretary of the British Treasury, in a note of December 8, 1919, to Albert Rathbone, Assistant Secretary of the United States Treasury, argued for postponement of principal and interest payments to the United States on the grounds that payments added to British "difficulties in dealing with the immediate problem of financing necessary imports from the United States."[14]

From the end of 1918 through the end of 1919 the State and Treasury Departments tried to work out a policy which would return international economic relationships to private channels as soon as possible, while at the same time shoring up the economies of continental Europe sufficiently to prevent civil disorders.[15] But in 1919 at least, the twin goals seemed irreconcilable. American leaders agreed upon the

13. *Ibid.*, 40.
14. Albert Rathbone to Hardiman Lever of the British Treasury, December 8, 1919, in U.S. Senate, *Special Committee on Investigation of the Munitions Industry*, 74th Cong., 2d sess. (Washington, 1936), 9475–76. (Hereafter cited as *Munitions Industry Hearings*); Carter Glass to Norman H. Davis, January 20, 1919, *Senate Document No. 86*, 34–35.
15. Glass to Davis, January 20, 1919, *Senate Document No. 86*, 34–35.

necessity (and desirability) of returning capital lending to private hands. But the issue was when and how to so return international investment to private banks.

In late 1918, before his resignation, Secretary of the Treasury William G. McAdoo asked Congress to authorize further government lending in order to expand the commerce of the United States. Since the war had ended, such loans could not rest on the authority of the first four Liberty Loan Acts, which granted to the Administration authority to lend for prosecution of the war. Specifically involved, and what McAdoo wished to use, was the $1.5 billion which had been legally appropriated by Congress under the fifth Liberty Loan Act, but which had not yet been collected either through bond sales or taxation. Carter Glass, who replaced McAdoo, asked Congress for the same authority in order to maintain United States exports. Congress refused Glass as it had McAdoo. According to Representative Claude Kitchin, Chairman of the House Ways and Means Committee, "The committee was unanimous in the opinion that this certainly was not the time for the government to loan a billion and a half dollars more to the allies, especially when we had to go out and get it from taxation . . . or by selling bonds. . . . To say the least," Kitchen explained, "we felt that to provide for such a loan at this time was premature." But Congress did give the Treasury permission to sell equipment already in Europe; in addition it appropriated $1 billion to help finance the export of American grain. The Treasury did not receive the broad authority it had sought. Therefore, government loans to the Allies after the Armistice were limited to financing grain and commodity surpluses already in Europe.[16]

16. Don M. Hunt, counsel for the Senate Committee on Judiciary, quoting Congressman Kitchin's remarks on Congressional reaction to the request in *Senate Document No. 86*, 6; U.S. Congress, *Proceedings and Debates*, 65th Cong., 3d sess. (Washington, 1919), House Debates, LVII, February 25, 1919, 4273.

During the winter of 1918–1919, the British government requested large government-to-government loans from the United States. Even before February 15, 1919, when Congress refused the authority to grant government loans, Secretary Glass had decided to limit any such loan to Britain to a total of $250 million and to pressure the British to combine this with a request for funds from American bankers in New York. On January 20, 1919, Glass urged that course in a reply to Undersecretary of State Norman H. Davis, who had forwarded to him the request of the British Treasury official, John Maynard Keynes, for additional loans. In a meaningful passage in his reply to Davis, Glass remarked that he considered the British situation "governed by entirely different considerations from those relating to [the] continental situation where [the] question of maintaining order [was] paramount."[17]

In sum, Glass's letter revealed the State Department's position on foreign loans. On the Continent, where the danger of revolution was serious, liberal government loans were to be made for reconstruction. But aside from the $250 million that was approved, the British were to obtain their reconstruction credits from private American bankers. Thus the American Treasury rejected that part of the postwar British program which sought long-term government loans from the United States.

This decision had in part been reached a few days before the Glass letter, when private American bankers found the British were using American government loans to undermine American private capital. The specific incident occurred while bankers were negotiating a loan with the Belgian government. The British government simultaneously offered $45 million to the Belgians, pending repara-

17. Glass to Davis, January 20, 1919, *Senate Document No. 86*, 34–35.

tions, to aid the "government of Belgium in placing orders for the manufactures and produce of the United Kingdom necessary for restoring Belgium. . . ." According to Davis, British government loans had already hurt private American business with Belgium. On January 18, 1919, Albert Rathbone of the American Treasury Mission to Belgium wrote Davis that the Belgians had called off the negotiations with the New York bankers about the time agreement with the British Treasury was reached. Any additional United States government loans to Britain of a long-term nature would further enable the British Treasury to continue to undermine American private capital in Europe. In addition, the terms of the British-Belgian agreement tied the loan to purchases from the United Kingdom. Thus American money would be used to obtain a profitable market for British manufactures in Belgium.[18]

In correspondence between Leland Summers, who was in Europe investigating uses to which American government loans were being put, and his superior, Bernard Baruch of the Raw Materials Board, Summers explained that Britain and France were using American government loans to buy raw materials in the United States and fabricate them into goods that were being shipped to continental European countries. In short, England was using the loans, not for what was considered legitimate reconstruction purposes, but to achieve a postwar trade advantage—with the United States footing the bill.[19]

Nevertheless the British tried by various means throughout the course of 1919 to obtain further extensions of their long-term debts to the United States, and to exchange short-

18. Norman H. Davis to U.S. Treasury Mission in Belgium, January 9, 1919, and Mission's reply to Davis, January 18, 1919, in *ibid.*, 30–31.

19. Leland Summers to Bernard Baruch, September 13, 1918, *Munitions Industry Hearings*, 9416.

term debts for long-term ones. In the first week of December 1919, John Chamberlain of the British Treasury, in a note to Albert Rathbone of the American Treasury, maintained that any attempt on the part of the British government to pay interest on its debt to the United States would make it "more difficult for the United Kingdom to contribute assistance to the general restoration of Europe." In their formal request to the United States Treasury, the British openly asked for a general cancellation of debts; at the same time, they requested conversion of short-term maturities into long-term debts and postponement of any interest payment. Before it would consider the latter, the United States Treasury demanded that the British send a separate request for simple postponement and conversion into long-term debts, hoping to avoid any implication to Congress that postponement implied eventual cancellation.[20]

In his note of December 8, 1919, Chamberlain for the first time tried to develop an institutional arrangement for a continuation of government loans. He maintained that a long-range program of European reconstruction was necessary; in the British view, "the requirements of the situation exceed the limits of private enterprise and private resources, and it would exceed the power of any single nation to deal adequately with it." While the eventual goal of Britain and the United States was to restore private initiative, a period of comprehensive international cooperation was necessary to create the conditions under which private enterprise might succeed. Some, though not limitless, funds would be needed from the United States, and the British government expressed willingness to discuss such a program.[21] This fore-

---

20. Chamberlain to Rathbone, December 8, 1919, in *Senate Document No. 86*, 70–71.
    21. *Ibid.*

shadowed the abortive international financial conference in Brussels in 1920.

Before the Brussels Conference, Secretary Houston on February 20 sent Wilson a memorandum prepared by Norman H. Davis that analyzed the British debt-loan position, and added his own and Davis's explanation of why they opposed any move toward cancellation. According to the Davis memorandum, Europeans believed cancellation would open the way for them to undertake private borrowing in the New York financial market. According to Davis under Article XI of the Treaty of London of April 26, 1915, the British had promised Italy a financial "contribution corresponding to her strength and sacrifices." Davis believed this pledge related directly to "the obligations of the Italian government now held by the British government, and it may well be that the British desire a cancellation of intergovernmental war debts as a means of discharging secret treaty obligations. If such is the case, the British might thus in great part at our expense discharge their treaty obligations." In the broader sense Britain was pressuring the United States for cancellation as a means of solving the difficulties of making payment. "While the allies have never bluntly so stated," Davis explained, "their policy seems to be to make Germany indemnify them for having started the war and to make us indemnify them for not having entered the war sooner."[22]

Despite American opposition to government loans and to government influence on international financial affairs, the British and the continental powers proceeded to organize their conference at Brussels, scheduling it for September and October. On April 3, Secretary of State Bainbridge Colby outlined the American response to Hugh C. Wallace, American Ambassador to France. Washington's view, said

22. Norman H. Davis to Wilson, February 21, 1920, and covering letter from Treasury Secretary Houston to Wilson, February 26, 1920, *Senate Document No. 86*, 76–78.

Colby, was that government-to-government loans should cease. Therefore the Brussels Conference of government representatives was inappropriate. Only private initiative, assisted by government moral support, could work out credit problems. A meeting of the business interests of the various countries would be in a position to make recommendations —which governments might not be free to make—and to recommend to governments such measures as might be necessary.[23] Colby suggested exactly the steps which were finally taken when the Allies accepted the Dawes Plan in 1924.

In its general instructions to American diplomatic and consular officers dated February 3, 1920, the State Department stated that no more government loans were to be made in peacetime. Reference was made to the Edge Act as the proper instrument for integrated foreign lending.[24] On March 15, Acting Secretary of State Frank Polk emphatically rebuffed pressure from European politicians for a United States government loan to Germany to stabilize German foreign exchange. "The time for government assistance has passed," he maintained. The key to exchange stabilization in Europe lay in balancing the German budget. This would make loans to Germany attractive to American bankers. Once the German budget was balanced, private capital would flow to Germany under the Edge Act, which, Polk stated flatly, would be the only government assistance forthcoming to facilitate foreign loans.[25]

Most American investment bankers reacted somewhat dif-

23. U.S. Department of State, *Papers Relating to the Foreign Relations of the United States*, 1920, 29 vols. (Washington, 1925–1944), 2 vols., I, 90–91.

24. General instruction, Norman H. Davis to State Department, June 15, 1920, in State Department files, National Archives, Record Group 59, 800.5151/3FW. Unless otherwise labeled, decimal number will indicate Record Group 59 in State Department files, National Archives.

25. Polk to American Mission in Berlin, March 1, 1920, 800.5151/3a.

ferently to British pressures for government-to-government
loans. While they wished to return international lending to
private channels as rapidly as possible, they argued by the
summer of 1919 that this was not very easily arranged. A
proposed syndicate of American banks to float reconstruction loans to Europe failed to initiate operations. Its failure,
according to J. K. Towles, chief of the Division of Commercial Attachés of the Bureau of Foreign and Domestic
Commerce, led to a "strong demand on the part of many exporters and banks to have the United States government
advance or guarantee . . . credits," but the United States
Treasury and the Federal Reserve Board emphatically rejected all such suggestions.[26]

The position of the large New York banks in the fall of
1919 was outlined by Thomas W. Lamont of the House of
Morgan in a letter to Russell Leffingwell, Assistant Secretary of the Treasury. The problem, at least to Lamont,
appeared to be that investment houses could not sell foreign
issues to American investors. He maintained that high taxes
discouraged the big investors from buying. The forced reli-
ance of the New York banks on small investors made every
foreign flotation a gamble. United States Treasury loans
were legally blocked. Lamont pointed out that "unless some
other machinery is devised . . . there may come a bad time"
when private investors would not be able to make loans in
the interest of public policy. Lamont proposed "as a hedge
against any such possible contingency" that the Treasury
"consider . . . some enlargement of the powers of the War
Finance Corporation. Such affirmative action, which would
be semi-governmental, would have an excellent psychologi-

---

26. J. K. Towles, Chief, Division of Commercial Attachés in the
Bureau of Foreign and Domestic Commerce, to Chester Lloyd-Jones,
commercial attaché in Madrid, September 18, 1919, in Commerce Department files, National Archives, Record Group 151, Bureau of Foreign
and Domestic Commerce, indexed 640, File No. General.

cal effect," since, said Lamont, "it would serve to build up some confidence in the minds of the investment community."[27]

Lamont was in effect trying government financing by the back door after it had been turned away at the front entrance. Activating the War Finance Corporation meant that exporters would be paid by the United States government, which would also assume the job of collecting from foreign importers. Such arrangements would have been government foreign loans. The Europeans would have won a key victory. But Leffingwell rejected any expansion of the activities of the War Finance Corporation. Even if it had the power, it could not do much good in the foreign investment field, he argued, since it could not borrow in the New York market on terms sufficiently good to allow it to take a constructive role.[28]

The response of the American banking community to the British proposals was also conditioned by divisions within its own membership. There were two main financial powers in New York: first, the House of Morgan and its related interests; second, the National City Bank (the largest single commercial bank in America) and its associated interests. Between the two banking groups there was occasional cooperation, and at least respect for the other's principal spheres of activity. The House of Morgan honored the National City Bank's primacy in the commercial banking field; the National City Bank accepted the overlordship of the House of Morgan in the investment banking field.[29]

The House of Morgan had long-term connections in Lon-

27. Thomas Lamont to Russell Leffingwell, assistant secretary of the Treasury, November 18, 1919, *Munitions Industry Hearings*, 10472–73.
28. Leffingwell to Lamont, November 24, 1919, in *ibid.*, 10473; Lewis, *America's Stake in International Investments*, 364–68.
29. Frank A. Vanderlip and Boyden Sparkes, *From Farm Boy to Financier* (New York, 1935), 246–48.

don through its affiliate, Morgan & Granfell (an investment bank), and in Paris through its affiliate Morgan-Harjes (also investment). One of the London partners, Edward Granfell, was on the Board of the Bank of England. All the partners of the House of Morgan in New York were Americans. In London and Paris some of the partners were American, while others were French or English. These European affiliates involved the House of Morgan in cooperative ventures with English and French finance in floating some European securities on the American market, and also in floating American securities in European markets. In the stock and bond business, Morgan was also involved in cooperation; in a more limited way, it had worked through the British financial mechanism even before the outbreak of World War I.[30]

In that prewar period, the British Treasury had established a correspondent relationship with the Federal Reserve Bank in New York. Its funds were deposited there, and its banking business was done through the New York Reserve Bank. But the House of Morgan was the purchasing agent for all British government buying in the United States. Somewhat the same relationship existed with the Bank of France. On November 8, 1919, the British Treasury wrote to the Federal Reserve Bank of New York and closed out its account.[31] Concurrently, its officials announced that J. P. Morgan & Co. had been appointed as the agent in the United States for transactions between the British government and

30. Phelps, *Foreign Expansion of American Banks* (New York, 1927), 8–9; Benjamin Strong, Governor, Federal Reserve Bank of New York, to R. H. Tremen, member of the board, Federal Reserve Bank of New York, January 2, 1917, *Munitions Industry Hearings*, 9549–50.

31. "Purchase Arrangements for England and France," depositions from files of J. P. Morgan & Co., *Munitions Industry Hearings*, 9228–29.

the American Treasury.[32] This was one of the principal steps in strengthening and extending the House of Morgan's cooperation with the British banking system. The transfer of the British Treasury agency from the Federal Reserve Bank of New York was a blow struck at the American government program, an attempt to gain United States capital through Morgan without meeting the demands outlined by Colby and Polk, and later affirmed by Charles Evans Hughes, to settle reparations and begin reconstruction of Europe on the basis of agreements between private business in the United States and Europe.

After British government and banking circles had apprised him of their desire to enter into cooperation with American banking groups in the development of world trade, the American Commercial Attaché in London, Philip B. Kennedy, tried to ascertain the attitude of American banks to such a proposal in conversations with Archibald Kains, President of the American and Foreign Banking Corporation. This corporation was organized before World War I by one Canadian and 32 American banks to do branch banking business abroad. The most important New York bank in the complex was the Chase National Bank, which was the second largest commercial bank in the United States, following closely in total business behind the National City Bank.[33] Chase had a close relationship with the House of Morgan.[34] It opposed foreign expansion competitive with the British. Its position illustrated the fact that Morgan and associates opposed rivalry with the British world banking system. Kennedy pointed out to Kains the

32. J. E. Crane, Federal Reserve Bank of New York to R. C. Leffingwell, November 8, 1919, *Senate Document No. 86*, 60.

33. Phelps, *Foreign Expansion of American Banks*, 6–32, 36, 149, 156–57, 163.

34. Lewis Corey, *The House of Morgan* (New York, 1930), 416.

advantages of establishing an American branch bank in Australia rather than making connections with existing British banks. The banker replied that the world was coming to America for financing and that America had plenty to do without going out for business. He also indicated that it was ridiculous for American banks to try to compete openly with British banks.[35]

For a variety of reasons, however, the National City Bank did enter into open competition with the British. First of all, the City Bank was connected with the Rockefeller family. The president until 1904 had been James Stillman, two of whose daughters were married to sons of William Rockefeller. Before 1918 Rockefeller, as the largest stockholder, owned 52,000 shares of National City stock.[36] If it is assumed that the House of Morgan relied on its primacy in the investment banking business for financial power, then in an analogous sense the National City Bank derived much of its commercial importance from strong Standard Oil connections. At the close of the war, British industry was busily closing the open door to petroleum resources in areas mandated to it by the League. This was being done through the operations of the Royal Dutch Shell Petroleum Company, a complex partly a state trading company and partly a private enterprise. It was an extremely important element in British state capitalist plans. Control of raw materials was a significant part of these plans, and oil was the key raw material after World War I. Thus Standard and Shell stood diametrically opposed, especially in the Middle East oil lands. In that area, as Frank Vanderlip, President of the National City Bank, noted in 1918, the British and French did not

35. Philip B. Kennedy to State Department, November 22, 1918, *Senate Document No. 86*, 36–37.
36. Vanderlip and Sparkes, *Farm Boy to Financier*, 272–73.

believe in the open door but instead held to a regime of special concession.[37]

But even prior to the great oil rivalry at the close of World War I, the National City Bank stood in a competitive relationship to British banking and exporting interests. On April 10, 1916, David R. Francis, American Ambassador to Russia, in a letter to Secretary Lansing, analyzed the House of Morgan-National City Bank conflict in Russia:

J. P. Morgan and Company are so thoroughly English in sentiment that they look with solicitude, and in fact with suspicion, if not fear, upon any movement to promote commercial relations, or even closer social relations, between Russia and the United States. In other words their desire and plan is to have whatever Russian financing is done in this country to come through London. They also seem to think that any direct commercial relations between this country and Russia is an approach on their preserves. I have also talked with the National City Bank people who thoroughly agree with my plan to promote direct commercial relations between Russia and the United States without the intervention of any other country or influence. Mr. Vanderlip, President of the National City Bank, will send to Russia during the present month two of his vice presidents, whose mission he did not make known to me, but Mr. Vanderlip assured me that he would second any efforts that I would make to establish direct commercial relations with Russia.[38]

The first National City Bank loan to the Russian government was made in April 1916. In June, a syndicate of American banks headed by the National City Bank made an additional loan of $50 million. And in December 1916, a third loan was made by the same syndicate, this time for $25 million. But almost all Russian purchases in the United

37. Frank A. Vanderlip, *What Next in Europe?* (New York, 1922), 70.

38. David R. Francis, U.S. ambassador to Russia to Secretary of State Lansing, April 19, 1916, and Francis to Wilson, April 8, 1916, 711.612/247½.

States during the war until the Bolshevik revolution were
made through J. P. Morgan by the British with British
financing. Even so, the National City Bank, under the leadership of Vanderlip, had established branches in Russia
competing with Morgan for business. In doing this, moreover, it had built, in embryo, a branch bank system which
could effectively undermine London's position as the world
financial center and strengthen New York as such a center if
it was ever expanded in an all-out campaign.[39] That the
National City Bank lent to Russia independently of the British, and established branches in Russia, demonstrates that
this part of the American banking community decided in
favor of establishing an independent commercial network in
Russia. National City, like the State Department, was eager
to eliminate the British middleman from American commercial relations with Russia.

Vanderlip, Rockefeller, and the National City Bank group
were committed to developing an independent American
world mechanism largely because of their industrial approach to banking. On the other hand, the House of Morgan
practiced investment banking that was not directly integrated with actual industrial construction and production.
The postwar profits of the House of Morgan did not come
from arranging the export of American goods, but from
floating securities for development projects under the overall
control of the integrated British financial mechanism. By
cooperating with the British to distribute goods (whether of
American or British production) through the British world
financial organization, Morgan helped the British win a
share of the profits from world trade incommensurate with
England's productive efficiency. Morgan seemed to agree

39. Staff memorandum for Under-secretary of the Treasury R. C.
Leffingwell, June 28, 1919, *Senate Document No. 86*, 92; Vanderlip,
What Next in Europe?, 170–71.

with the British argument that Anglo-American banking cooperation would yield the highest possible income to both economies. From the American point of view high profits would be obtained for a negligible investment, since the American banks would use the British financial system. From the British point of view the decrease in profit accompanying, a long, drawn-out competitive struggle could be avoided. From the point of view of both, markets could be divided and prices stabilized.

The attitude and outlook of the individuals making up the leadership of the National City Bank was somewhat different. On the simplest level, it is possible to explain this difference as the result of the preponderant influence of the Rockefeller-Stillman-Standard Oil bloc on the board of the National City Bank. Standard Oil was an industrial producer. It was not concerned with floating British securities in order to secure commissions on such sales. Standard was interested in finding new oil fields overseas, and in distributing Standard Oil products in all oil markets. Standard was in bitter competition with the British oil giant Royal Dutch Shell in all the oil lands. It would receive no markets for oil through cooperation in a British system. But an independent American corporate giant engaged in extensive development of underdeveloped areas could complement the expansion of Standard Oil by building railroads, enlarging seaports, and introducing American commodities and technology. In this sense, an American overseas development corporation was a natural complement of Standard Oil interests.

That it was Vanderlip instead of Rockefeller who originated the development project affiliate of the National City Bank in 1914 does not undermine this analysis. Rockefeller gave enthusiastic support when Vanderlip organized the American International Corporation (A.I.C.). He even wanted to take a larger share of the American International stock than Vanderlip was willing to give him. For that matter, the idea of a worldwide economic development corporation first came to Vanderlip from two railroad builders, Charles A. Stone and Edwin F. Webster, who felt there was no longer any sustained call to build railroads in the United States. They told Vanderlip that thickly populated and un-railroaded China was the place of the future for past builders of American railroads. To Vanderlip it was all quite intoxicating.[40]

As it was organized in 1915, before the World War had induced the British to propose a cooperative American-British policy, the American International Corporation had on its board a Morgan representative, Charles H. Sabin of the Guaranty Trust Company. Vanderlip "felt very good" about getting Sabin. Guaranty Trust was "the most active competitor . . . in the field" and it was "of great value to get them into the fold in this way."[41] Describing the A.I.C. some years later, Vanderlip indicated its geographical breadth of interest and the large number of prominent industrial spokesmen participating:

. . . it was to be interested in all manner of promising enterprises in foreign lands, in the Orient, in South America; over the face of the whole earth. The very idea of the thing was exciting in Wall Street. We made C. A. Stone the president and had a remarkable Board of Directors; James J. Hill, Theodore Vail, P. A. Rockefeller, Stone, Edwin F. Webster, Otto Kahn, Ambrose Monell, James A. Stillman [Sr.], Beekman Winthrop, Henry S. Pritchett, R. A. Lovett, Joseph P. Grace, Cyrus H. McCormick, Charles H. Sabin, W. E. Corey, J. Ogden Armour, and C. A. Coffin [of General Electric].[42]

Kahn's presence on the Board of the A.I.C. showed that all three major banking groups, Kuhn, Loeb (Kahn), National

40. Vanderlip and Sparkes, *Farm Boy to Financier*, 266–67.
41. *Ibid.*, 268–69.
42. *Ibid.*, 268.

City (P. A. Rockefeller), and the House of Morgan (Sabin) were represented in this proposed corporate giant. Its potential frightened the British, as Sir Arthur Steel-Maitland told Philip B. Kennedy in November 1918.[43]

Morgan's participation in the A.I.C. shows that despite its regional cooperation with the British in Western Europe and Russia, the House of Morgan was nevertheless interested in an independent American system. Morgan cooperation with the British was based on the belief that the best way to achieve an independent American banking system was, in the words of Jason Neilson of the Mercantile Bank of the Americas, to "Americanize" the British banking system. Neilson maintained that this would "create an American instrument which has all the elements contained in the systems of other nations."[44] Broadly speaking then, both major elements in the American financial community had the same long-term objective. The difference was essentially over approach.

Additions were made in 1916 to the board of directors of American International. After consulting his own board, for example, James A. Farrell of United States Steel joined. When Vanderlip explained the project to the previously doubtful James J. Hill, the railroad leader enthusiastically joined the board, bought stock in American International, and also asked for a block of stock in the National City Bank. Vanderlip's experience with Ogden Armour, of Armour Packing, was similar.[45]

The extent to which the National City board, and especially Vanderlip, were competing with England and trying to make New York the financial center of the world was

43. Philip B. Kennedy to State Department, November 22, 1918, *Senate Document No. 86*, 39–40.
44. National Foreign Trade Council, *Proceedings of the Fifth Annual Convention* (New York, 1917), 148.
45. Vanderlip and Sparkes, *Farm Boy to Financier*, 268–69.

shown clearly in Vanderlip's "West Point" for training
branch bankers. One of the most severe handicaps to an
American branch system around the world was simply the
lack of trained personnel not only willing but also able to
staff branches abroad. Vanderlip established a school in
Brooklyn to train young men for the system. In justifying
the approach to Stillman, Vanderlip maintained that existing recruitment was haphazard and feeble.

> The way banks have been run, in feeding their executive force
> with uneducated office boys, trusting here and there to a develop-
> ment of some exceptional mind, is about on a par with the old
> fashioned way of farming, where a man used the small potatoes
> for seed, and sold the larger ones. The modern farmer gives as
> much attention to his seed . . . as he does to cultivation after
> the crop is in the ground. That is just what we are doing. . . .[46]

Vanderlip went to the colleges and made arrangements to
give summer employment to picked young men at the end of
their sophomore year. They were then taken into the bank
during their last semester of college. These selection and
training procedures were designed to "furnish a picked lot of
men, particularly for foreign service."[47]

In a letter to Stillman in February 1915, Vanderlip indicated the extent to which National City had gone into the
branch bank business. A group of vice-presidents of National City held daily meetings to discuss the branch bank
situation. The committee was considering seriously a whole
network of branches in Europe as early as February 1915.
Denmark, Spain, and Switzerland were under consideration,
with Italy as a possibility.[48] These projected branches were
successfully in operation by December 1916.[49]

46. *Ibid.*, 261–62.
47. *Ibid.*, 262.
48. *Ibid.*, 259–60.
49. Federal Reserve Board, *Third Annual Report Covering Operations
for the Year 1916*, 12 vols. (Washington, 1917–1928), 147. (Hereafter
cited as Federal Reserve Board, *Annual Report*.)

At the end of World War I, the National City Bank-Standard Oil industrial complex continued its program of developing an integrated world finance and trade system independent of the British through the American International Corporation and the International Banking Corporation. Vanderlip asserted in 1918 that the United States could indeed become the financial center of the world; and it was clear that the National City group thought within that framework. Other American banking interests, including the House of Morgan and the associated Chase National Bank, chose instead to work with and through the British system.[50] As Archibald Kains explained to Philip B. Kennedy, "for American banks to try and compete openly with British banks reminded [him] of the small boy who tried to teach his grandmother to suck eggs." Such competition just did not make sense.[51]

The American government's response to the proposed partnership with Britain was generally negative. One key element in the projected partnership was shipping. When informed that Lord Reading of the British Board for Overseas Trade had suggested that the United States and Britain pool their shipping, President Wilson wrote Edward Hurley, Chairman of the U.S. Shipping Board, on September 9, 1918, that it was "an extraordinary proposition" and Hurley should tell Reading that "it will not be possible for us to make special arrangements with any one nation, in as much as it is our fixed policy and principle to deal upon the same terms with all."[52] Wilson refused to pool American and British shipping.

The British suggestion that raw materials be allocated by

50. Corey, *House of Morgan*, 416.

51. Philip B. Kennedy to State Department, November 22, 1918, *Senate Document No. 86*, 37.

52. Wilson to Hurley, September 9, 1918, quoted in Diamond, *Economic Thought of Wilson*, footnote 68, 188.

inter-Allied joint decision meant, in substance, British control of markets and prices for raw materials produced in America. This was also rejected early in the Peace Conference. In an instruction to his subordinates of the American Relief Commission in Paris, Herbert Hoover in November 1918 stated that "this government will not agree to any program that even looks like inter-allied control of our economic resources after peace. . . . The same applies to raw materials. Our only hope of securing justice in distribution . . . and proper return for the service that we will perform will revolve around complete independence of commitment to joint action on our part."[53]

A third major component of the British plan was the continuance of long-term government loans for European reconstruction. In a letter to Wilson on April 23, 1919, Lloyd George argued that "in the financial sphere, the problem of restoring Europe is almost certainly too great for private enterprise alone and every day puts this solution further out of court. . . . Apart from private enterprise his majesty's government see only two possible courses—direct assistance and various forms of guaranteed finance." Lloyd George urged acceptance of the Keynes Plan, which would have renewed European economic activity on the basis of a United States government guarantee for loans made by private American bankers. Security for the loans, according to the Keynes Plan, would have been long-term bonds based on future German reparation payments to the Allies.[54]

Wilson responded, "It would not be possible for me to

53. U.S. Department of State, *Papers Relating to the Foreign Relations of the United States*, 1918, *The World War*, Supplement I, 2 vols. (Washington, 1933), I, 616–17.

54. Lloyd George to Wilson, April 23, 1919, reprinted in Ray Stannard Baker, *Woodrow Wilson and World Settlement*, 3 vols. (Garden City and New York, 1923), III, 336–38.

secure from the Congress of the United States authority to place a Federal guarantee upon bonds of European origin. . . . Our Treasury also holds the view (and in this again I concur) that to the very limit of what is practicable such credits as it may be wise to grant should be extended through the medium of the usual private channels rather than through the several governments." The key to renewing European economic life was Germany's need for "working capital." But the reparations clauses of the Treaty, Wilson wrote further, stripped Germany of "practically the whole of her liquid asset. . . . Simultaneously, the suggestion is in effect made that America should in a large measure make good this deficiency, providing in one form or another credit, and thus working capital to Germany. . . . How can anyone expect America to turn over to Germany any considerable measure of new working capital to take the place of that which the European nations have determined to take from her?"[55] Wilson in effect refused to extend government credit to the Allies. For, as he pointed out, guaranteeing loans based on long-term bonds tied to reparations was the same as a long-term loan.

Indirectly, Wilson's refusal to guarantee such bonds also modified any effective cooperation between the American banking community and its British equivalent. For, as Lamont argued to Leffingwell, private capital was afraid to loan to Europe without some form of government guarantee of such loans.[56] The refusal to guarantee European bonds tied to war debts meant that Britain would have to liquidate more of its foreign investments to obtain American loans. This was a constant theme, sometimes implicit, as in Wil-

55. Wilson to Lloyd George, May 5, 1919, in Baker, *Wilson and World Settlement*, III, 344–46.

56. Lamont to Leffingwell, November 18, 1919, *Munitions Industry Hearings*, 10472–73.

son's advice to Lloyd George, sometimes explicit, as when
Albert Rathbone advised Hardiman Lever of the British
Treasury on December 31, 1918, that the British government had "American and neutral securities available for
sale," which might be utilized in "defraying the cost of raw
materials" from the United States.[57]

On May 16, 1919, ten days after Wilson rejected the
Keynes Plan, Thomas Lamont and Norman H. Davis, members of the American Commission to Negotiate Peace at
Paris, submitted a counterproposal at the suggestion of the
President. They recommended that "credits to Europe . . .
be extended through normal channels of private enterprise."
But in the interim, while conditions were unstable, "some
United States government aid, on a limited scale" might be
extended. "A condition precedent to America's active cooperation, is that there shall exist no tariffs or secret trade under-
standings between or among the European nations, the
effect of which will be discriminatory against America and
the lesser nations." Similarly, the Europeans would have to
agree to equality of opportunity in the matter of concessions
as another condition of the extension of American credit.[58]
To oversee the "general scheme of Credits," the English and
French governments should agree to the formation of a
"small Special Committee made up of bankers and men of
affairs."

Thus once again during the Wilson Administration a
system very similar to the later Dawes Plan was suggested.
This committee of experts "should keep in close contact"
with the managers of a "proposed investment group in
America."[59] Since the leading European Allies, Britain and

57. Rathbone to Lever, December 31, 1918, *ibid.*, 9475–76.

58. Lamont and Davis to Wilson, May 15, 1919, in Baker, *Wilson and World Settlement*, III, 352–61.

59. *Ibid.*, 360–61.

France, refused at this time (May 1919) to accept the key American conditions involving nondiscrimination in tariffs and equal opportunity in concessions, even temporary United States government loans were not forthcoming. But arrangements for "investment mobilization in America" through the medium of private capital went ahead when an institutional basis was established by the passage of the Edge Act on December 24, 1919.[60] The United States did accept, however, the right of Great Britain to institute Imperial Preference and agreed to treat it as a domestic British concern. During the Peace Conference the United States pursued equality of opportunity (the open door) only as it applied to the territories which had changed hands as a result of the war and the Peace Treaty.[61]

The United States government rejected the Anglo-American partnership plan to develop world markets through the British system when it refused to agree to inter-Allied control of raw materials and shipping, and when it refused to grant further long-term government loans. Wilson's rejection of the Keynes Plan at the Peace Conference reaffirmed the policy of halting government loans; it was also a means of applying pressure to ease the reparations burden on Germany. This meant that Wilson refused to allow the Allies to keep Germany under their control. Therefore, another British condition for partnership, Allied control of Germany, was rejected by the United States. Instead, the Wilson Administration suggested a solution to German reconstruction broadly similar to the Dawes Plan, which was finally implemented in 1924 under Harding, Hoover, and Hughes.

The three remaining components of the British proposal were rejected by the United States because agreement could

60. Federal Reserve Board, *Annual Report*, 1920, 23–24.
61. H. W. V. Temperley, ed., *A History of the Peace Conference of Paris*, 6 vols. (London, 1921), V, 65–70.

not be reached on the extent to which the principle of equal opportunity (the open door) was to be applied to world commercial relations. In essence, the Wilson Administration refused partnership in the development of Latin America, rejecting an American-British shipping pool while continuing to subsidize an American merchant marine. Similarly, the demand for equality of opportunity in the "newly constituted states, mandatories and [other] territories" which had "changed hands as a result of the war and [the Peace] Treaty"[62] meant not partnership but competition, with commercial victory going to the most efficient competitor. The sole case in which the government accepted the British conditions for partnership was in its willingness to consider imperial preference as the legitimate equivalent of the American domestic tariff. The United States thus excepted, for the time being, existing preferential arrangements from the demand for equality of opportunity.[63]

This whole series of government decisions limited the extent to which Anglo-American cooperation could take place at the banking level. As Lamont outlined the problem to Leffingwell, extensive foreign loans had to be supported by the government if the bankers were to corral the capital from American investors.[64] While it was true that the banking community split, with the Morgan group willing to cooperate and the National City-Standard Oil group refusing cooperation, the Morgan agreement with the British was largely ineffective. But the road to a different sort of Anglo-American partnership could still be opened if the British would accept the American proposals for German

62. Davis to Rathbone, May 12, 1920, *Munitions Industry Hearings*, 9490.

63. Temperley, *History of the Peace Conference*, V, 65–70.

64. Lamont to Leffingwell, November 18, 1919, *Munitions Industry Hearings*, 10472–73.

reconstruction and the application of the open door policy to new states and mandatories resulting from the war and the Peace Treaty. At the conclusion of the Peace Conference, therefore, the only recourse remaining to Britain was to negotiate with private business interests to obtain American capital. To facilitate the accumulation of sufficient capital to meet European needs, Congress passed the Edge Act, to which American leaders were to turn in their efforts to create an American system.

CHAPTER IV

🦅 *Attempts to Corral Capital for an American System: The Edge Corporations*

WITH THE cessation of most government lending in September 1919, American manufacturers were confronted with the problem of how to finance their exports. In a letter to Wilson on September 11, 1919, Secretary of the Treasury Carter Glass pointed out that "Governmental financial assistance in the past and talk of plans for future government or banking aid to finance exports has apparently led our industrial concerns to the erroneous expectation that their war profits, based so largely on exports, will continue indefinitely without effort or risk on their part." He warned that "those industries which had been developed to meet a demand for great exports, paid for out of government war loans, will be forced to close plants and forego dividends unless they maintain and develop an outlet abroad. The industries of the country must be brought to a realization of the gravity of this problem, [they] must go out and seek markets abroad, [they] must reduce prices at home and abroad to a reasonable level, and create or cooperate in creating the means of financing export business."[1]

1. U.S. Senate, *Special Committee on Investigation of the Munitions Industry*, 74th Cong., 2d sess. (Washington, 1936), 10470–71. (Hereafter cited as *Munitions Industry Hearings*.)

The Administration's decision to discontinue loans was a reversal of the wartime situation under the Liberty Loan Acts, when Congress appropriated money to finance the exports needed by the Allies to prosecute the war. Through the War Finance Corporation and the Capital Issues Committee the capital accumulated through the sale of government bonds was funneled to industry.[2] In that manner the government (as well as the Allies) acted as a large and almost guaranteed consumer of the products of American industry. In addition, the government made direct grants for plant expansion. From a position of enjoying almost guaranteed markets, the manufacturers were suddenly told to exercise their freedom to go out and win their own business. But freedom with expanded capacity and shrinking markets was a precarious freedom.

Under these conditions the manufacturers had four ways in which they could seek financing for their exports. First, they could exert enough pressure to reverse the government decision not to underwrite exports. Second, they could accept whatever financial support the investment bankers were willing and able to offer. Third, they could finance their own exports. Fourth, they could interest the bankers in a joint program.

Before the war the investment banks had financed industrial plant expansion for many large corporations such as United States Steel, General Electric, and International Harvester. In exchange, the investment banks had often required that the corporations surrender partial control of

2. National Foreign Trade Council, *Proceedings of the Eighth Annual Convention* (New York, 1920), 20. (Hereafter cited as NFTC Convention *Proceedings*); see remarks of James A. Farrell, President, United States Steel Corporation, in opening the 7th annual convention; Eugene Meyer, Jr., "Financing Our Exports," NFTC Convention *Proceedings*, 1919, 183–85. Meyer was managing director of the War Finance Corporation.

their executive functions to representatives of the banks.[3] In great measure government purchases during the war had freed the industrial corporations from investment banking control.[4] What the bankers had to offer in 1919, therefore, was for the most part unsatisfactory to the manufacturers.

Three factors influenced the amount of capital the bankers extended to expand American technology into foreign markets. First, the Morgan-British partnership; second, the shortage of capital available to the banking community; and third, an economic judgment made by most bankers that long-term investment was not the most profitable employment of their limited capital.

The partnership between the House of Morgan and British banking established something approaching an agreement on investment priorities between American lenders and British borrowers. The British and other European economies urgently needed American agricultural and other raw materials to supply their manufacturing industries. Britain and most other European states maintained a system of import regulations in order to consume their short supply of foreign exchange by emphasizing the purchase of essential raw materials and limiting the import of manufactured consumer goods. The latter were generally defined as nonessential.[5] The raw material needs of the British economy

3. This analysis and the data for it are taken from Thomas C. Cochran and William Miller, *The Age of Enterprise* (New York, 1951), 194–202; Lewis Corey, *The House of Morgan* (New York, 1930), 247–63.

4. See address of John Gardin, Vice-president, International Banking Corporation, "Financing Foreign Trade Through Credits and Investments," NFTC Convention *Proceedings*, 1920, 141–42.

5. Henry F. Grady, *British War Finance, 1914–1919* (New York, 1927), 62–63; F. Abbot Goodhue, "Acceptance Syndicates to Finance Export Trade," *Acceptance Bulletin*, August 1921, 3–4. Goodhue was the president of the International Acceptance Bank.

complemented the desire of American producers to continue exports of agricultural and other raw material surpluses.

But the amount of capital available to the bankers was sharply limited by the fall of 1919. Even that part of the American banking community interested in the installation of American technology abroad, the National City-American International group, restricted its technological export program due to the capital shortage. For example, a subsidiary of the American International Corporation, G. Amsinck & Co., built a dock in the seaport of Buenaventura, Colombia, in 1919. But it did not extend a long-term loan for the Cauca Valley project. Instead, it took as payment $1,205 million in short-term government obligations.[6] American International was operating to keep its capital liquid. Only limited expansion of American technology overseas was possible under such credit conditions. In similar fashion the capital shortage was also a factor influencing the Morgan group to keep most of its capital liquid. Capital shortage in the midst of plentiful capital was due to the fact that the savings of the country lay in the hands of the American middle-class public. Such people had exchanged their modest savings for United States Government Liberty Bonds during World War I. But they were now unwilling to buy government obligations of European nations, fearing that the political and economic difficulties of Europe would make investments insecure. Since the Morgan group, and American bankers generally, could not sell large issues of European government bonds to the real owners of America's surplus capital, the bankers proceeded to lend their own capital in the form of short-term credits. Such credits were attractive for two reasons: they were redeemed quickly and brought relatively high rates of

6. Cleona Lewis, *America's Stake in International Investments* (Washington, 1938), 372–73.

interest. The risk of default or loss of capital was thought to be minimal because in most cases short-term credits were extended for the export of raw materials. These went to foreign manufacturers, who turned the raw materials into finished products which they then exported. The proceeds from the exports were used to repay the American bankers.[7]

Since in 1919 the foreign exchange regulations of most European states discriminated against the import of American manufactured consumer goods, the exports of American manufacturers were at that time largely limited to sales of capital goods. Europe favored the import of capital goods because such imports increased the capacity of European manufacturing industries to supply export markets, which in turn earned scarce foreign exchange. But short-term credits were of no assistance in financing capital goods exports. Unlike raw materials, capital goods imports required credit terms of five years or more to enable Europeans to earn the income to pay for them. From the European point of view no alternative to long-term credits existed, for Europe suffered from extensive capital obsolescence and capital destruction as a result of the war. In late 1919 and early 1920 investment capital from the bankers to finance the export and installation of American technology (capital goods) abroad was almost completely unavailable. The investment bankers were unwilling to take the smaller income implicit in a policy of investing their own meager capital for five-year and longer periods when they had the alternative of financing relatively high-yield, low-risk raw material exports.[8]

In 1919 and 1920 some corporations financed their own exports in order to compensate for their recently curtailed production by expanding export markets. The Baldwin Lo-

7. Goodhue, "Syndicates to Finance Export Trade," *Acceptance Bulletin*, 3–4.

8. *Ibid.*

comotive Works (of the American Locomotive Corporation), which cut its payroll from 16,500 in 1918 to 10,000 in 1919, engaged in some self-financing. Large markets for railway rolling stock existed in Europe, China, and South America; the means of financing the sales were provided by both the Baldwin Works and the parent American Locomotive Corporation. "Starting with sales to Belgium in 1919 that amounted to 11.6 million dollars, Baldwin and American sold engines to Poland, Rumania, Argentina, Mexico, China, and Colombia." By 1922 American Locomotive (and its Baldwin Works) held $24.3 million of foreign government treasury notes as payment for the exports. "Some of these notes were paid off from the proceeds of loans publicly offered in the United States, but in the main they were repaid by the debtor governments in relatively small annual amounts without recourse to the American security market." In at least one case, that of Rumania, partial payment was made on a virtual barter basis when American Locomotive accepted Rumanian oil for its locomotives.[9]

The other major way in which corporations financed their own exports was through direct investments abroad. For example, in 1920 the International Telephone and Telegraph Corporation acquired control of one telephone company in Cuba and one in Puerto Rico.[10] A General Electric subsidiary, Electric Bond & Share Co., had begun acquiring foreign investments before 1915. Negotiations for foreign acquisitions proceeded, and by 1923 Electric Bond & Share held foreign properties in Cuba, Guatemala, and Panama.[11] Other American firms acquired considerable direct investments in existing properties in 1920[12] (although such expan-

9. Lewis, *America's Stake in International Investments*, 371–72.
10. *Ibid.*, 327.
11. *Ibid.*
12. *Ibid.*, 367–75.

sion was minor when compared to similar activity during the
war and after 1922). These direct investments installed
American technology abroad and represented corporate
self-financing of exports. The International Telephone and
Telegraph Corporation, for example, manufactured telephone equipment in the United States, which it exported to
expand and modernize its foreign properties.[13] Corporations
which supplied their own credits for exports by either or
both of these two methods could obtain the capital from
internal surpluses or by floating their own issues to the
American public in the absence of investment banking
connections to funnel the capital from the investing public.
Relatively few corporations, however, could in 1919 and
1920 undertake their own financing.[14]

By the winter of 1919–1920 the whole international trade
picture had become a nearly stagnant pool of unused goods
and unfulfilled needs. European industrialists were unable
to export enough manufactured goods to obtain the means to
repay American bankers for the short-term credits which
had been extended to them. According to John McHugh,
Chairman of the Commerce and Marine Division of the
American Bankers Association (ABA), European buyers
owed American sellers about $4 billion in short-term bills of
exchange which had to be exchanged for long-term investments if American exports to Europe were to be resumed.

13. *Ibid.*, 326–27.
14. Leland Rex Robinson, *Investment Trust Organization and Management* (New York, 1924), 240–42. Robinson's data shows here that
sometimes even corporations with strong banking connections, such as
General Electric, in effect floated their own paper through corporate
controlled investment trusts. Electric Bond & Share, which later became
American & Foreign Power Co., performed exactly this function for GE.
Nonetheless, it must be borne in mind that GE, International Telephone
and Telegraph, and W. R. Grace, the leaders in the self-financing
movement, were almost inactive from 1919 to 1922.

"Dollars," argued McHugh, had to be "placed at the disposal of the foreign debtor of the American business concern with which to pay the latter and thus open up again the flow of our [American] goods [to Europe] where they have now ceased to flow."[15]

Both investment bankers' short-term credit operations and manufacturers' self-financing of exports proved to be insufficient to provide the credit needed to export American-produced surpluses and to supply those nations of Europe which were attempting to restore their war-shattered industries. Since both Congress and the executive branch of the government were unwilling to make government-to-government loans, or to offer a government guarantee for private loans to Europe,[16] the manufacturers turned to the only remaining alternative: they attempted to interest the bankers in a joint program to tap the capital in the hands of the general American public. To do so, they turned to the Edge Act, which was enacted on December 24, 1919, to establish a legal basis for the cooperation of American banking and manufacturing interests in the development of American foreign commerce.

15. American Bankers Association, *Journal of the American Bankers Association*, XIII, January, 1921, 460–61. Reported proceedings of the Foreign Trade Financing Conference held in Chicago, December 1920. (Hereafter cited as ABA *Journal.*)

16. Thomas Lamont to Russell Leffingwell, assistant secretary of the Treasury, November 18, 1919, Leffingwell to Lamont, November 24, 1919, *Munitions Industry Hearings*, 10472–73; Wilson to Lloyd George, May 5, 1919, reprinted in Baker, *Woodrow Wilson and World Settlement*, 3 vols. (Garden City and New York, 1923), III, 344–46. Some government lending continued after the war, but almost all of it was on the Continent and was clearly designed to relieve actual suffering in physically devastated areas. Much of the material sold was composed of war surplus and grain already in Europe and controlled by the United States Grain Corporation. See Lewis, *America's Stake in International Investments*, 364–65.

The Edge Amendment to the Federal Reserve Act provided for the national incorporation of two types of foreign trade financing corporations: short-term acceptance (banking) corporations, and long-term (investment) debenture issuing corporations. The object of Congress in the former case was that it "should be possible for several banks to combine in the ownership of . . . corporations doing an acceptance business, and operating in foreign countries, either through branches or through ownership of subsidiary corporations."[17] Congress was aware that without the right to combine "only very few of the very strongest banks would be able to engage in foreign [acceptance] banking."[18] In effect, then, this part of the Edge Act provided for the unification and combination of banking capital interested in foreign acceptance banking, tending to increase the amount of such capital in active operation and making more acceptance credit available. The immediate result of provisions allowing American bankers to combine to establish acceptance banks was the organization of two foreign (acceptance) banking corporations, the American and Foreign Banking Corporation and the Mercantile Bank of the Americas.[19]

A more significant section of the Edge Act provided for the federal chartering of corporations with the power to extend long-term loans to foreign governments and corporations. Banks combining to form long-term investment corporations were required to have a capital stock of at least $2 million. Only member banks of the Federal Reserve System were permitted to hold stock. Such a bank was given the power to borrow from the American investing public up to

17. Federal Reserve Board, *Annual Report Covering Operations for the Year 1923*, 12 vols. (Washington, 1917–1928), 464.
18. *Ibid.*
19. *Ibid.*, 464–65.

ten times its capital and surplus by issuing "debentures, bonds, and promissory notes."[20] According to Fred I. Kent, President of the Bankers Trust Co. of New York, it was "for the purpose of enabling the huge investment fund of the United States to take a safe and satisfactory part in the foreign trade of our country that the idea of a debenture issuing Edge Corporation was born."[21] Banking and industrial spokesmen such as Kent, Vanderlip, and William C. Redfield (of the American Manufacturers Export Association) believed that the Edge investment corporations would attract the savings of small investors because the debentures sold would be issued by corporations under the regulation of the Federal Reserve Board. Leaders of the Edge corporation movement hoped that investors would get the impression that the government approved these debentures, and that they were somehow similar to the Liberty Bonds with which they had been made familiar during World War I.

An Edge investment corporation, then, could make long-term loans in any amount up to ten times its capital and surplus. With the capital it acquired from the investment public the Edge investment corporation would be able to buy the bonds and shares of foreign governments and corporations. According to Leland Rex Robinson, in his *Investment Trust Organization and Management*, "The framers of the Edge Act . . . were eager to facilitate American exports by arranging long term financing, and by encouraging the active development of agencies for the foreign penetration of American capital, accompanied by American enterprise."[22] If successful, such an effort would create large islands of American-controlled enterprise abroad, which

20. Robinson, *Investment Trust Organization*, 26–28.
21. NFTC Convention *Proceedings*, 1921, 12–13.
22. Robinson, *Investment Trust Organization*, 29.

would guarantee consumption of American products and increase the nation's share of world markets. In this way the Edge investment corporations would assume the role played by the government during World War I. American industry—and hence, the economy—would be stabilized at a high level of productivity without any unusually heavy use of the federal tax power.

The first public call for a long-term investment corporation under the Edge Act came from the Seventh National Foreign Trade Council (NFTC) Convention in May 1920. Through its Committee on Financing Foreign Trade (Convention Group II), the NFTC proposed a joint committee composed of the American Bankers' Association (ABA), the United States Chamber of Commerce, and the NFTC to develop a system of long-term trade finance.[23] In the course of discussion on foreign investment, manufacturers revealed their conception of how such a program should work. Eugene P. Thomas, President of the United States Steel Products Co., drew analogies from the past experience of British manufacturers. "Her manufacturers not only sold machinery and equipment, but sent out skilled labourers to install and operate it. To a large extent, the British investor, or his compatriots to whom he advanced the money retained proprietary control, so that the head offices of enterprises operating in all parts of the world were to be found in London. The companies, managers and workmen were resident representatives abroad of British industry and enterprise. They introduced and advertised British goods; they accustomed domestic mechanics to the use of British tools, and in a hundred ways they served as connecting links between the community of their residence and their origin."[24] Such an

---

23. NFTC Convention *Proceedings*, 1920, 744–45.
24. *Ibid.*, 70. Thomas's address was called "Increasing Exports."

integrated foreign investment program was a frequent proposal made by large American manufacturers. It was their vision of the Edge system in operation.[25]

In an attempt to coordinate the attitudes and the activities of the bankers and manufacturers and to define a specific relationship to, and develop a program for implementation of, the Edge Act program, the ABA made a study of the foreign credit situation in the early spring of 1920. John McHugh, Chairman of the Commerce and Marine Division of the ABA, explained that no machinery for long-term capital investment had been established, because the United States was then owed nearly $4 billion in short-term bills

25. NFTC Convention *Proceedings*, 1919, 418. In an address entitled "Direct Selling in South America," B. S. Steenstrap, general manager of the General Motors Export Co. argued:

> Loans to South America for municipal and national improvements should be encouraged in this country. It was customary for European banks, when making loans of this kind, to specify that the materials should be purchased from, and the work supervised by, citizens of their countries. When the Germans loaned money on a railway, they furnished the rails, locomotives and equipment and even the motormen and guards. If we are to take full advantage of our opportunities in South America we must provide the capital for the development of transportation and other urgently needed improvements.

At the same meeting William E. Peck, President, Wm. E. Peck & Co., argued the same thesis. In an address entitled "Can American Fabricated Products Hold Foreign Markets?" in *ibid.*, 151, he pointed out:

> We must not only invest in foreign securities, but we must also send our capital there and develop public utilities just as the English and Germans have been doing for many years, buying the materials and machinery at home and thereby creating a permanent market for supplies and repairs. We have not done this in the past because the home market has been too inviting, but we cannot expect to maintain our trade without an investment of capital which would also mean employment for our young men who would permanently settle in South America and further increase the demand for home products.

See also James A. Farrell, "An American Foreign Trade Policy," NFTC Convention *Proceedings*, 1922, 576.

acquired during 1919 and 1920. These credits were frozen, and the banks had no more capital which could be safely extended. According to McHugh, commercial banks were at the end of their rope. So much foreign credit had been extended that the domestic credit structure had contracted.[26]

Under the leadership of McHugh, the Commerce and Marine Division of the ABA made plans for a Foreign Trade Financing Conference to be held in Chicago in the fall of 1920. The executive council of the ABA approved the plans. Represented at the conference in Chicago on December 10–11, 1920, were the ABA, the NFTC, the United States Chamber of Commerce, the American Manufacturers Export Association, and the American Manufacturers Import and Export Association.[27] Speaking as a banker with particularistic outlook, as well as the chairman trying to obtain consensus out of divergent manufacturing and banking interests, McHugh led the discussion of the trade situation with a view of laying a basis for a conference consensus on a program of action encompassing as nearly as possible the interests of both groups.

He proposed an Edge corporation organized as a debenture bank. It was to deal with European corporations and governments in financing worthwhile projects of a nature which would reconstruct and expand European economies. The procedure would be initiated when a European government outlined a specific project, and would become an actionable project when the board of the Edge bank approved it. Then the Edge bank would sell its own debentures in the American market, offering security in the form of first mortgage bonds on the project guaranteed and deposited by European governments. In the sale of the debentures, an

26. ABA *Journal*, XIII, January 1921, 458.
27. *Ibid.*, 459–60.

attempt would be made to place them with every bank and industrial enterprise in the country.[28] McHugh hoped that in this way depositors in banks outside the main centers (New York, Chicago, Cleveland, Detroit, and San Francisco) could be induced to use their savings to purchase Edge debentures. That would effectively tap the wide pool of national savings, over which the big banks and industrial corporations involved in foreign investment had no control.

McHugh continued his analysis with a sharp attack on timid businessmen who preferred having the government undertake a foreign investment program. Once in the foreign investment business, he maintained, the government might never get out. Even if it did finally start to withdraw, it might move too slowly. He further argued that the government, while operating in the foreign investment field, would create political problems which could only hurt business. Up to that point, McHugh spoke as a chairman. He then went on to say, as a banker, that the projected Edge corporation, once it came into existence, could eliminate much of the existing commercial debt (the $4 billion of "good" but as yet unpaid bills of exchange acquired by American banks in the shortlived boom of 1919). It would accomplish this desired end, he explained, by converting short-term European obligations into long-term investment that would provide Europeans with funds to pay off their previous debts. He concluded with the statement that Europe would continue to be the main market for American goods for some generations in the future.[29] On the whole, McHugh proved to be remarkably foresighted in his prognostications about America's future markets. Aside from Canada, Central America, and Northern Latin America, the leading markets for American

28. *Ibid.*, 460.
29. *Ibid.*, 460–61.

exports have been mainly in Europe. But American manufacturers did not like the bankers' concentration on the European market. They dreamed of the underdeveloped
countries as areas needing and welcoming American technology. Many of them did not fully understand that unless
Europe was prosperous enough to buy from expanded production in the underdeveloped nations, stimulated through
exports of American technology, the world shortly would be
unable to consume new commodities.

William C. Redfield, Wilson's former Secretary of Commerce, who had since become President of the American
Manufacturers Export Association, expressed the point of
view of the manufacturers. He began by agreeing with all
that previous speakers had said. Unlike McHugh, however,
he addressed himself to the period that would follow the
immediate emergency. The conference ought to consider,
said Redfield, the problem of building up a permanent foreign trade. "Unfreezing" frozen credits was an emergency
measure. "Perhaps these things are now to be done," he
hesitantly agreed, referring to short-term financing of food
and clothing. "But not for long," he continued, "because if
that is all that is to be done, we shall have failed." Redfield
saw a distinct danger that unless the United States "could
step further than financing current transactions, unless we
pass beyond the merchandising stage and become constructive, til the American flag is known as that which builds up
to stay, all around the globe," the United States would
become a second-class power.[30]

Clarifying what he meant in his desire for America to
have "vision" and "courage," Redfield described in glowing
terms the great British foreign trade machine which had
evolved out of world conditions after 1860. In Redfield's

30. *Ibid.*, 464.

view, all parts of the English trade machine meshed beautifully: English standards, equipment, citizens, and technology—in short, all aspects of English foreign investment—exerted a very powerful pull in favor of British industry in world markets. Redfield argued that the British system had arisen naturally out of world conditions in the nineteenth century. But if it were deliberately conceived by "Englishmen who were playing the long game for their country's eternal future, it would have been a great stroke of business genius."

Redfield implied that Americans should plan for their "eternal future" by entrenching themselves in the ownership of railroads and factories. "The difficulty with us [the United States] as manufacturer," he continued, "is not in our lack of competing power. That is an insult to our intelligence of the common facts of the day." The difficulty lay in the fact that the United States had no branch banks of its own. "All our drafts went out through banks owned by our competing countries. . . ." These banks reported home on any American orders that were important. Americans were in the habit of giving commercial knowledge to their competitors. Redfield's remedy for the malady he described was to Americanize the "foreign" tools of trade already in use by the United States. There was no limit to the world which he saw opening before Americans if they had but the "vision and courage to do a very simple thing. . . . Put American money into American owned and American run and American controlled industries and institutions around the globe."[31]

Herbert Hoover delivered the major address to the conference. His remarks were based on assumptions even broader than those of McHugh or Redfield. There were traces in it of

31. *Ibid.*, 463–64.

the efficient engineer planning the future of his society, and of the politician worrying about the future of a society which had been good to him, and for which he had a deep patriotic attachment. He seemed aware that American power was threatened, ironically enough, by the great efficiency which bankers like McHugh, manufacturers like Redfield, and engineers like Hoover had helped it attain.

The crux of the problem, at least in its early stages, appeared to Hoover to be European reconstruction. He believed that any failure to revive Europe meant that the United States would be brought down to Europe's low living standards. America had done enough short-term lending to Europe. That approach merely postponed the problem. A real solution to Europe's recovery problem, and to America's problem of finding the road to long-range prosperity, lay in "the systematic, permanent investment of our surplus production in reproductive works abroad." In this manner, he thought, the United States would reduce the return on exports that came back as imports to the amount of profit on long-term investment, "as the states in Europe [had] before the war." He also pointed out that the United States "must take compensation for the labor of our people in the accruement of our assets outside of our borders."[32] In other words, Hoover advocated that the United States be paid for its exports by obtaining ownership of long-term investment in Europe.

Hoover arrived at this prescription from a comparison of the American and British experience. He saw the United States in the position in which England found itself after 1860, when it could no longer take full value for its growing exports in the form of imports. If the English were to con-

32. *Ibid.*, 462–63. Hoover's speech was called "Momentous Conference."

tinue to expand and progress, they had to invest the profits from the sale of those commodities abroad. In that way "they not only extended the capacity and the absorption of British goods, but they lifted the standard of living of the entire world."[33]

From the necessity of investing surpluses abroad, Hoover moved imperceptibly to the definition of such a step as "the most beneficent operation that can be done to humanity." "Service" and "need" marched happily arm in arm. A completed circuit between American surplus production and unsatisfied foreign markets, according to Hoover, would lay the basis for carrying out service and implementing necessity. But the United States had only a small part of the financial machinery and the personnel so necessary to provide such a link. Americans interested in building such structures could not hope to be successful until the United States government was willing to give "protection and support to Americans interested in the development of American enterprise abroad." But this was a different matter from government investment banking, which, he said, would enable foreigners to obtain capital cheaper than Americans seeking United States capital.[34]

On the other hand, direct loans from the American government to foreign governments, such as were arranged by the War Finance Corporation, were pronounced "good" by Hoover. But these loans should be temporary, and for emergency purposes. They were not for reproductive investments. Government-to-government loans should only be resorted to in the last event, after all private means had been tried. Hoover concluded his talk with a plea for cooperation among the great organizations of bankers, merchants, employers, and workers which had grown up in America

33. Hoover, "Momentous Conference," *ibid.*, 463.
34. *Ibid.*, 462–63.

between 1895 and 1920. If these competing economic groups would eschew cooperation and instead press their claims for special favor "in the community into a great conflict with each other, then the whole fabric of our national life has gone by the board." If steps toward cooperation developed out of the Chicago meeting, the United States "will have laid the foundation of a new economic era," and "will have solved the ills of our economic system in the last century in the only fashion that democracy can solve its troubles, and that is by the initiative of the individual and by the sense of service to the community as a whole."[35]

In a sense Hoover synthesized the most perceptive elements in the social thought of Theodore Roosevelt and Woodrow Wilson. Hoover agreed with Roosevelt's observation that society was dividing into special interest groups threatening the stability of America. But he rejected Roosevelt's view that the state should coerce the groups into artificial coordination. Like Wilson, Hoover believed that the way out of the dilemma was for the special interests to join in an effort to develop foreign markets. To Hoover the Chicago conference could be the instrument that would allow American society to avoid social conflict at home and at the same time negate any need for the state to coerce the various groups in the style of Roosevelt's "New Nationalism."

The major action of the conference was to establish a permanent committee of some thirty members representing "geographical districts and the various lines of agriculture, industry and finance." The purpose of the committee was to create a long-term Edge corporation with an authorized capital of $100 million. Under provisions of the Edge Act, this firm would have the power to lend up to a billion dollars.

35. *Ibid.*, 463.

This corporation was supposed to be ready for action by January 1921.[36]

The committee was composed of representatives of both manufacturing and banking interests. Its membership included John McHugh, Chairman, Marine and Commerce Division of the ABA; Paul M. Warburg of Kuhn, Loeb; Louis E. Pierson of the New York Bank of Commerce; Fred I. Kent of the Bankers Trust Company, New York; Thomas B. McAdams, Vice-president of the ABA; John S. Drum, a San Francisco banker; and, from the House of Morgan, Charles H. Sabin. Agriculture was represented by Julius H. Barnes, a grain broker from Duluth, Minnesota; and by Thomas E. Wilson, President of Wilson and Company of Chicago. Herbert Hoover, still a prominent figure in the Wilson Administration, was also on the committee. McHugh served as chairman.[37]

Named the Foreign Trade Financing Corporation, the firm was chartered by the target date. But 25 percent of the total capital, the legal amount necessary to do business, had not yet been subscribed. The bankers wanted to combine both short and long-term functions in one Edge institution. The Federal Reserve Board, however, ruled that no one bank could perform both functions.[38] Undoubtedly the Federal Reserve Board wished to avoid combining long-term and short-term investment in one institution because the existing practice of British investment trusts was to keep the two separated. The Reserve Board probably also wanted one institution devoted solely to long-term investment because

36. *Ibid.*, 469. Remarks by McHugh, chairman of the Foreign Trade Financing Conference, in opening the meeting.

37. *Ibid.*, 456.

38. Philip B. Kennedy, "The Foreign Trade Financing Corporation," NFTC Convention *Proceedings*, 1921, 458–59.

that was the element of foreign investment that needed most strengthening. The bankers then moved in February 1921 to organize another Edge corporation for short-term acceptance financing.

Redfield reiterated in April the position he had expounded at the Chicago conference. He indicated that manufacturers expected a limited amount of the activity of the Edge bank to be devoted to long-term loans designed to refinance unpaid short-term loans. At the same time, he argued that the main function of the bank should be the sale of long-term securities of the Foreign Trade Financing Corporation to transfer capital abroad without attempting to sell unfamiliar European securities to Americans.[39] In his May 1921 report to the executive council of the ABA, McHugh, chairman of the conference's permanent committee, pointed out that the corporation had its inception two years before the frozen credits were a factor in the foreign trade situation. "Commendable as such a purpose would be," said McHugh, it was "no part of the Corporation's purpose to 'thaw out' . . . 'frozen credits.' "[40]

McHugh's remarks indicate that despite the difficulties of the firm itself, there was broad agreement between manufacturing and banking interests as to the primary purpose of the corporation. A further expression of this agreement appeared in the February 1921 issue of the ABA *Journal*, in which John H. Williams, a professor at Northwestern University and top economist for the ABA, analyzed the purposes of the long-term Edge corporation. He suggested that

39. William C. Redfield, "There Are Other Factors Yonder," ABA *Journal*, XIII, April 1921, 661–62.

40. John McHugh, "Report of the Commerce and Marine Division to the Executive Council of the American Bankers Association," ABA *Journal*, XIII, May 1921, 733. McHugh was chairman of the Commerce and Marine Division of the ABA.

the Edge corporation would in the long run render most effective service by financing American trade with the non-European world. His argument hinged on the fact that European nonproductivity was temporary, whereas the need for foreign investment in the non-European world was to be "permanent and growing."

As a corollary, Williams saw the financing of agricultural commodities as a need that would last only until the American agricultural price structure was corrected. He implied that agricultural price changes would bring supply and demand into balance. "In the normal future," he said, "manufactures will be the main export financed by the Edge Corporations."[41] After this analysis, Williams discussed the Edge corporations in terms of European parallels (English, Scottish, and Dutch investment trusts) and domestic American parallels (such as bonds taken by American electrical manufacturers in exchange for street railway equipment which they sold to American municipalities). Williams saw the Edge corporations as the means by which industrial corporations would distribute their commodities overseas in the same manner as they did at home.[42]

In a circular letter sent to various American banks in March 1921, John McHugh tried to explain the evident failure of the bankers to do anything about getting the long-term Edge bank into operation. They had "purposely delayed an intensive campaign to acquire subscriptions to the capital stock [of the Foreign Trade Financing Corporation] because of the evident need for more education and further publicity in order to arouse the business people to get further legislation, both state and Federal." To expedite this, McHugh promised that the permanent committee would be

41. John H. Williams, "Our Foreign Trade Balance Since the Armistice," ABA *Journal*, XIII, February 1921, 572–73.
42. *Ibid.*

enlarged so as to get strong representation from every state and every line of industry.[43]

At some point between May and November 1921, however, the bankers' interest in the ideas and principles of the Edge system waned, or at least cooled. In the face of this diminution of banking interest in the previously agreed upon objectives, the manufacturers quickly became suspicious. At the May 1921 convention of the NFTC, Willis H. Booth, former member of the Federal Reserve Board and a prominent banking spokesman, was questioned closely by S. L. Weaver of the Los Angeles Chamber of Commerce. To Weaver's query why the banks did not invest in the long-term Edge bank debentures, Booth was evasive. He maintained that state laws prevented state-chartered banks from buying that kind of stock. The bankers, said Booth, were in the process of winning changes in those laws.[44]

In its final declaration, the 1921 NFTC convention called for the sale of Edge corporation debentures in every community. The 1922 convention repeated this demand and, in addition, went on to complain that little or nothing had been done to move the Edge corporations into action. The convention called for investigation of the relationship between Edge corporations and the Ter Meulen scheme, a European proposal that American investment bankers extend long-term loans to European governments in exchange for bonds. If it were found necessary, the declaration continued, an amendment to the Federal Reserve Act ought to be passed to allow member banks of the Reserve System to invest in the Edge corporations.[45] The manufacturers were growing more

43. Letter of John McHugh in American Acceptance Council, *Acceptance Bulletin*, March 1921, 3.
44. NFTC Convention *Proceedings*, 1921, 251.
45. "Final Declaration," NFTC Convention *Proceedings*, 1922, ix, x, xi.

and more impatient. Little or no financing was being arranged for them.

In November 1921, McHugh modified the tone of his interpretation. In order to export the American surplus, and to liquidate part of the frozen credits, he thought it necessary to import "approved" foreign securities "under the plan contemplated by the Foreign Trade Financing Corporation."[46] Also, in an address before the 1921 convention of the ABA in November, Sir Drummond D. Fraser, a leading figure in the London financial community, spoke on the relationship of the Edge banks to the Ter Meulen scheme to revive Europe. The Edge banks, he said, should convert the short-term credits (still frozen) into long-term credits. These short-term credits should be transferred to American investors. "Thus the old financial machinery would be lubricated and a new machinery created," said Fraser.[47]

After the ABA convention, the sale of debentures issued by the Foreign Trade Financing Corporation stood at about the same point as it had when the institution had first been chartered. Very little had been done. While the long-term Edge bank did little under the stewardship of American bankers, the other division of the Edge corporations, the short-term acceptance banks, were quickly organized and had been put into operation by August 1921. In addition to the American and Foreign Banking Corporation and the Mercantile Bank of the Americas, a third short-term Edge Bank, the International Acceptance Bank, was organized in February 1921. Paul M. Warburg was chairman, and F. Abbot Goodhue (Vice-president of the First National Bank, Boston) was president. P. J. Vogel (of the Chase National

46. "Report of the Commerce and Marine Division to the Executive Council of the American Bankers Association," ABA *Journal*, XIV, November 1921, 240.

47. ABA *Journal*, XIV, November 1921, 251.

Bank, New York) and E. W. Davenport (Vice-president, First National Corporation, New York) were vice-presidents.[48]

The purpose of the bank was to finance America's foreign commerce and world trade, largely through the device of granting acceptance credits for 60 to 360 days. It was organized in such a way as to be noncompetitive with European banks. Foreign interests were allotted a total of one-third of the capital. The division of the foreign share was made between Swiss, Dutch, Swedish, and English operators (the latter through the National Provincial and Union Bank of England Ltd.). As a complement to, or perhaps a condition for, this European cooperation, the International Acceptance Bank agreed not to establish branches of its own abroad. Instead, it was to work through correspondents under European control. In addition, a European advisory council was contemplated to "give the American officers the benefit of their counsel and cooperation." Among the prominent subscribers of stock were representatives of Kuhn, Loeb (through Paul Warburg) and the National City Bank (through the American International Corporation). Morgan was also represented through F. A. Goodhue of the Chase National Bank. Morgan seems also to have been involved in the venture on the American side through some of the firm's non-New York affiliates. The prospectus assured its audience that the new bank would in no way compete with the Foreign Trade Financing Corporation (the long-term Edge bank).[49]

While a major propaganda campaign was carried on in 1921 in favor of the Foreign Trade Financing Corporation, little came of it. Its $100 million capital remained largely

48. "International Acceptance Bank, Inc.," *Acceptance Bulletin*, February 1921, 9, unsigned article.
49. *Ibid.*

unsubscribed. Bankers indicated that they would not tie up their capital in nonliquid loans so long as conditions in Europe were insecure. Gradually the long-term Edge bank was converted into a short-term acceptance bank. By the beginning of 1922 the plan to use the Edge system as a means of feeding American capital out in long-term investments faded and degenerated into the financing of so-called finishing credits, which were connected mainly with the export of raw materials to supply European manufacturing industries.[50]

F. A. Goodhue, President of the International Acceptance Bank, explained in August 1921 that the bankers could not afford to take any chances. They were hesitant to finance any ventures save those involving small amounts of capital, and even those for only short periods with the loans rigidly secured. Raw and semimanufactured exports finished in the importing country for domestic sale or for re-export were the only class of exports readily handled by the banks. The banks regarded American participation in that sort of transaction as absolutely necessary if United States banking was "to continue to play an important role in international banking," and if it were to "assist the distribution of our surplus products."[51]

To the leading manufacturers it seemed the bankers were using the foreign investment program to benefit sectarian interests, because they were using whatever capital they had available to finance agricultural exports. Manufacturers did not think that acceptance credits did much, if anything, to finance the share of the surplus which they produced. They

50. Robinson, *Investment Trust Organization*, 27–30; William Howard Steiner, *Investment Trusts and American Experience* (New York, 1929), 48–49.

51. Goodhue, "Syndicates to Finance Export Trade," *Acceptance Bulletin*, August 1921, 3–4.

suspected that the bankers had betrayed their commitment to a long-term Edge bank. Industrial spokesmen grew more and more impatient with the unwillingness of the bankers to begin operations of the long-term bank and to finance the export of the American industrial surplus in a systematic way.

At the NFTC convention in May 1921 some of the resentment appeared on the record and in public. William H. Knox of Knox and Co., New York, reemphasized the necessity of an investment trust-type Edge bank. He also accused the bankers of betraying the national economic interest by floating foreign-controlled bond issues outside the Edge bank structure. "Why," Knox asked, "with all our wealth and resources, we should find it more profitable to put our money in foreign loan, rather than in great American banks, and thereby directly use our own capital for the purpose of increasing and controlling our own foreign trade, is somewhat of a mystery to the average foreign trader."[52]

Manufacturing spokesmen, of whom Knox was typical, were mistaken in their interpretation. It was true that the leading element in the banking community, the House of Morgan, had long-established ties with British banks, which tended to make them leery of any direct export development campaign British banks might interpret as hostile; but this was not the reason why they failed to put the Edge investment institution into operation. The bankers concentrated on acceptance credits mainly to finance export of American agricultural and other raw materials to Europe because these were the products the Europeans needed to revitalize their industry, and because as late as 1922 there were not sufficient markets for existing industrial capacity. Any such

52. William H. Knox, "Financing Export Shipments," NFTC Convention *Proceedings*, 1922, 438.

new industrial expansion would have to await the reconstruction of European production and commerce. Otherwise
it would simply add to the existing problems of agricultural
and industrial surplus. In this sense the bankers took a more
long-term view than did the manufacturers.

It is quite possible, however, that the bankers might have
been more audacious about an immediate foreign investment
program to install American technology if they could have
obtained United States government guarantees for the capital involved. They had been seeking such guarantees since
discussion of the China consortium of 1913. Losses suffered
under a government-guaranteed program would not necessarily undermine a long-range investment program. Indeed
the result of losses might simply be to stimulate more direct
government subsidies for foreign trade, which would effectively eliminate the risk to private investors. But the Harding Administration, like that of Wilson, totally rejected this
concept.

In the broadest sense, then, the death by disuse of the
long-term Edge bank in 1922 reflected a policy decision by
the House of Morgan that under existing circumstances—
symbolized by the still unsettled German reparations problem—any long-term investment in Europe would be dangerous. The risks were so great in 1922 that even had the
bankers floated debentures for investment in Europe they
probably could not have sold them. But had they succeeded,
the consequences might have been more ominous for the
future if the debentures finally proved worthless. If the
American public got "burned" on purchases of debentures
they would probably be a long time in buying new issues
floated by American bankers. The investment program
planned at the Chicago Conference was not designed to be a
one-shot deal. In fact to use the Edge system successfully
investors had to be induced to continue and expand the flow

of their investment. Hence the charge that the bankers were acting only out of selfish interests was inaccurate. The bankers did want an American system abroad, but they did not believe that 1922 was the proper time to create it. In a subsidiary way they wanted to avoid conflict with the British system, but only partly for narrow interest-group reasons. They believed the United States could proceed to build its own system only in cooperation with Britain in the rebuilding of Europe, and that a precondition for reconstructing Europe was the settlement of political disputes over German reparations and the extent to which the open door was to be the governing principle of world economic development.

CHAPTER V

🦅 *The Struggle to Make New York the World's Financial Center*

AN EXAMINATION of the objectives sought by American industrialists and bankers between 1914 and 1920 reveals that both these groups thought the best method to make the United States the financial center of the world was to duplicate the process by which Great Britain had established its financial supremacy. Defining the world-wide system of British branch banks as the key institution which enabled the British to dominate world markets and to establish their technology in a major part of the world, American leaders propagandized for branch banks.

The industrial corporations, however, were dissatisfied with the amount of American technology established abroad, and pressured the bankers throughout this period to increase the pace of branch bank expansion with particular emphasis on Latin America. In part, the desire to compete with the British in long-term investment had led to the passage of the Edge Act. It was not until the end of 1920, however, that American economic leaders began to realize that simple duplication of British institutions would not yield the desired results. New complications arose which the British, in their rise to economic supremacy, had never encountered. Britain reached its economic and financial peak in a period of unified world markets held together by a common gold standard and without the need to face major industrial competition. The United States, on the other hand, faced a disintegrated world market without a common monetary standard, and major industrial competition. Because of these changed conditions, neither branch banks nor Edge Act investment trusts could be successful in installing American technology abroad.

These factors led the industrial corporations to rely on their own direct investments abroad in the form of branch factories and subsidiaries to export American technology. This means of exporting technology, combined with the resumption of the gold standard and a limited system of branch banks, provided the basis for the expansion of American foreign trade in the 1920's.

American business was content before 1900 to have American banking function as a junior partner in British world finance. American and British interests were considered basically compatible in world markets. The most important American exports were agricultural commodities, and they were noncompetitive. No strong banking connections were needed to sell American wheat, cotton, and tobacco. By the turn of the century, however, manufactures had become a major component of American exports. This trend continued, and by 1913 the percentage of manufactures in American exports rose to 49 percent.[1] The change in the nature of American exports evoked a movement in business to construct an international financial system to market American manufactures.

This need was discussed for at least a decade before the Federal Reserve Act was passed in 1913.[2] The commissions

1. Clyde Phelps, *The Foreign Expansion of American Banks* (New York, 1927), 89–90; William Adams Brown, *The International Gold Standard Reinterpreted, 1914–1934* (New York, 1940), I, 146–48.
2. Brown, *Gold Standard Reinterpreted*, I, 146–48.

paid by American business to London bankers to finance United States foreign trade came more and more to be labeled "tribute." In the narrow sense, of course, the tribute metaphor was an exaggeration. British bankers financed American trade more cheaply than New York bankers could.[3] But in the broad sense, as the manufacturing component of exports grew, it began to seem to American manufacturers that the cheap commissions provided by the British system also operated to narrow their markets, because American commercial secrets passed through the hands of British bankers to British exporters. Also, this criss-cross financing—New York to London and back to New York—meant that American exporters paid two commissions, one to a London banker and one to a New York banker.[4]

One of the key pressures behind the passage of the Federal Reserve Act was the widespread desire to facilitate the creation of banking institutions which would enable American interests to finance foreign commerce.[5] Paul M. Warburg of Kuhn, Loeb noted shrewdly in 1909 that the fundamental weakness of the American banking system,

3. Phelps, *Foreign Expansion of American Banks*, 102.
4. Harold L. Reed, *The Development of Federal Reserve Policy* (Boston and New York, 1922), 156–58.
5. Cleona Lewis, *America's Stake in International Investments* (Washington, 1938), 191. Lewis points out, "Reports of the National Monetary Commission, published in 1910, had also stressed the need for American Banks abroad." The Monetary Commission Reports were the working papers on which the Aldrich Bill (Republican version of the Federal Reserve Act) was based. See also G. Butler Sherwell, "American Branch Banking in Latin America," *Journal of the American Bankers Association*, XVI, December 1923, 365–66. (Hereafter cited as *ABA Journal*.) Sherwell argues that one of the main purposes of the Federal Reserve System was to provide a better means to develop the export trade. Under the National Banking Act, national banks could neither "accept bills," nor establish branches abroad. The Reserve Act removed these prohibitions and hence facilitated the creation of an American bill discount market.

compared to European systems, was that it rested "upon stocks and bonds as its foundation."[6] The European system rested "upon discounts as its foundation." The National Monetary Commission accepted Warburg's analysis. His analysis resulted in section thirteen of the Federal Reserve Act, which allowed the Reserve Banks to discount " 'notes, drafts, and bills of exchange arising out of actual commercial transactions.' "[7] Section thirteen, and subsequent rulings of the Federal Reserve Board, encouraged the growth of foreign bill acceptance and a market for accepted bills in New York. The use of bills and the growth of a market for bills developed a trend to bypass London's services. Hence the exchange risk, implicit in currency fluctuations, was removed. This in turn tended to stabilize costs, and to remove the need to pay an extra commission to London banks to rediscount bills drawn on foreign customers.[8]

As a necessary complement to a discount market for trade acceptances in the United States, section twenty-five of the Federal Reserve Act gave national banking associations (with capital and surplus of more than a million dollars) authority to create foreign branches. As minimal requirements, branches were necessary to act as agents to collect foreign bills, to issue letters of credit, and to collect credit information for American industry.[9] Impatience with the pace of the formation of an independent American branch bank system soon developed among American manufacturers and exporters.

At the 1915 convention of the NFTC, widespread dissatisfaction was expressed with the foreign branch situation.

6. Reed, *Development of Federal Reserve Policy*, 107, 110.

7. *Ibid.*, 110.

8. Federal Reserve Board, *Federal Reserve Bulletin*, May 1, 1915, 53. (Hereafter cited as Federal Reserve *Bulletin*.)

9. Reed, *Development of Federal Reserve Policy*, 175–76; Phelps, *Foreign Expansion of American Banks*, 57.

John J. Arnold, First Vice-president of the First National Bank of Chicago, pointed out how the "three cornered arrangement" whereby London banks financed American foreign trade could "and should be eliminated" under the Federal Reserve Act. If the Act were utilized properly and foreign branches established, then the United States would shortly create "a direct dollar exchange market" between the United States and South America and the Orient. This procedure would deny London "the undue advantage which that center has had in the past."[10]

Arnold maintained that the key obstacle in the way of growth of foreign branches was the legal inability of banks to cooperate with one another in foreign business. Permission to cooperate, Arnold contended, would place the bankers "in a position where they can, if they will, take some of the capital and start the ball rolling." Arnold believed that, once established, these cooperative banks would attract capital from manufacturers.[11] At the same meeting, Murray Carleton, Chairman of the Board of Carleton Ferguson Dry Goods Co. (St. Louis), advocated that American business take advantage of Europe's preoccupation with war to establish an independent American branch bank system; it was "the duty of the American business man to make himself independent in the markets of the world. . . . If branch banks [were] established . . . immediately," Carleton reasoned, they could be established "without suffering from the competition they would have to meet under normal conditions." This was the way for America to take its "proper place in the international trade of the world."[12]

Louis Goldstein of the New Orleans Chamber of Com-

10. National Foreign Trade Council, *Proceedings of the Third Annual Convention* (New York, 1915), 40–41. (Hereafter cited as NFTC Convention *Proceedings*.)
11. *Ibid.*, 109–10.
12. *Ibid.*, 48–49.

merce pointed out that few banks were in a position to give foreign credit service; few possessed "the resources . . . required."[13] Fred B. Whitney of the Lake Torpedo Company, Bridgeport, Connecticut, argued that the banks that had the resources, those in New York, Boston, Pittsburgh, and Chicago, could provide the necessary services, but failed to do so because of their conflicting interests. What was needed was a system under which people "in Chicago in the packing industry, in Minneapolis in the flour industry, in Pittsburgh in the steel industry, and in the South in cotton, can have their banks in those localities get together and form a foreign trade bank to meet foreigners successfully."[14]

The most explicitly hostile response to Arnold's proposals came from Fred I. Kent, Vice-president of the Bankers Trust Co., a leading spokesman for the New York banks. Kent expressed strong opposition to any changes in the American law on foreign banking. He held that the real economic position of the country did not warrant changes in banking laws to force the pace of foreign bank expansion. Kent maintained that it was particularly dangerous to invest in Latin America while the United States was still a debtor to Europe, for that would be a case of borrowing from Europe in order to lend to Latin America. Branches based on such complex and uneconomic commercial relations might very well fail.[15]

Another international trade banker, George H. Kretz, manager of the Foreign Department of the National Park Bank of New York, expressed skepticism about the feasibility of cooperative foreign banking. He favored banks with foreign departments continuing to operate on an individual basis. Kretz doubted enough banks could be pulled together, especially in the interior of the country. Branches were for

13. *Ibid.*, 112.
14. *Ibid.*, 114.
15. *Ibid.*, 41–44.

the future. "What South America needs now, and what it has had from England, Germany, France and other countries," Kretz pointed out, "is permanent capital, fixed capital, that will build railroads, develop their industries; not capital that will have to come back [to the United States] in sixty or ninety days. . . ."

In the future, Kretz thought the United States might "inaugurate a system permitting us to make permanent investments whereby capital stays out for years to come and grows up with the country; this would naturally require that the customers deposit their funds with the banks as a long time investment without the privilege of withdrawing on short notice. Such a system we [the commercial banks] have not at present, although private firms like . . . J. P. Morgan & Company can do that kind of business."[16] An interior banker, George Woodruff, President of the First National Bank of Joliet, Illinois, agreed with Kretz that "any American bank operating in South America should keep its own assets in short-time obligations. . . ." He argued, however, that long-term American capital could be invested in South America since South American bonds could "undoubtedly be sold in the North American market, provided they are handled by strong people [such as the House of Morgan], and providing the security back of them is understood in the United States."[17]

Edward Ewing Pratt, chief of the Bureau of Foreign and Domestic Commerce, came out strongly for an increase in branch banks overseas. The Commerce Department official, like the manufacturers, saw cooperation between banks in different cities as a likely means of encouraging the development of both foreign exchange (short-term financing) and long-term security investment. He was critical of Kent's

16. *Ibid.*, 111, 115.
17. *Ibid.*, 116.

pessimism over the future of branches and disagreed with his contention that the debtor status of the United States operated against long-term investment overseas. He acknowledged that part of the problem was that the Federal Reserve Act tended to concentrate banking capital in "the hands of New York bankers." Some changes in the Federal Reserve Act were necessary, Pratt implied.[18]

Generally, it was the manufacturers, interior bankers, and exporters who at the 1915 convention supported the idea of an amendment to the Federal Reserve Act to permit cooperation to create foreign branches. Bankers already involved in foreign finance opposed the projected aggressive innovation.[19] But in his address, Governor David Rowland Francis of Missouri unofficially committed the Administration to support combinations in export trade, and pointed to the Clayton Act as an example of such exemptions from the basic antitrust legislation.[20]

At the 1916 convention of the NFTC, the continuing discussion of the foreign branch question revolved around the need for branches (especially in South America), and the need for a flow of orders for American manufactured goods from importers in South America to make economic use of the projected branches. The institutional basis for the growth of branches was laid in a bill sponsored by the Administration in 1916 (and endorsed by the Federal Reserve Board and the Federal Advisory Council of the Board) to allow certain types of banks to cooperate in the formation of foreign branches.[21] Rightly assuming success in the legis-

18. *Ibid.*, 121.
19. *Ibid.*, 110–18.
20. *Ibid.*, 169.
21. Federal Reserve Board, *Third Annual Report Covering Operations for the Year 1916*, 12 vols. (Washington, 1917–1928), 137–38. (Hereafter cited as Federal Reserve Board, *Annual Report*); NFTC Convention *Proceedings*, 1916, 406, 422.

lative chambers, the delegates went on to discuss ways and means of putting the expected branches to use in the planned development of markets, particularly in Latin America. A realization of the interrelation of a discount market for foreign exchange bills, foreign branches, and the long-term investment of American capital permeated the discussions.

The branch bank movement attained wide proportions in 1916, largely stimulated by the activities of the National City Bank and its newly acquired affiliate, the International Banking Corporation (IBC). National City opened branches in Brazil, Argentina, Chile, Russia, and Italy.[22] The Mercantile Bank of the Americas (a Morgan affiliate) followed with its own plans for expansion.[23] Pierre Jay, Chairman of the Board of the Federal Reserve Bank of New York, reported to the convention that the volume of bills created (and in use) in 1916 would have taken years to create in peacetime.[24] Also in 1916 the first statistical evidence appeared that the long-term investment balance, so disturbing to the bankers in 1915, was shifting rapidly in favor of American foreign investment. Despite the pessimistic view of the banking community in 1915, Jay reported enormous progress in reversing the long-term investment balance in favor of the United States. The total of loans abroad for 1915 had been approximately one billion dollars, but a billion dollars of long-term American securities had been repurchased from abroad.[25] Indications were that the United States would be a net long-term creditor by 1917.

Export leaders began to view long-term foreign investment as the element which integrated all the other aspects of

22. Federal Reserve Board, *Annual Report*, 1916, 147; NFTC Convention *Proceedings*, 1916, 308–09.
23. NFTC Convention *Proceedings*, 1916, 57.
24. *Ibid.*, 406.
25. *Ibid.*, 407.

an independent American trading system. James A. Farrell, Chairman of the NFTC and President of United States Steel, argued before the convention delegates that without expanded foreign investment, the wartime commercial expansion would be lost when peace returned.[26] He reasoned that such investment was not merely the basis of economic Pan-Americanism; that without it the United States could never become the world's banker. According to Edward J. Berwind, President of Berwind-White Coal Mining Company, European preoccupation with the war presented the opportunity "to acquire on advantageous terms, the ownership, or control of railroads, public utilities, and industrial enterprises" which had been dependent on England (and Europe) for their "financial support." These opportunities, Berwind suggested, dramatized the "need for better machinery" to finance foreign investment. He saw the newly-formed American International Corporation (A.I.C.) "as an intermediary between the investor and the opportunity."[27]

The American International Corporation aroused considerable enthusiasm both as an entity designed to expand long-term investment and as a model to be imitated by other interests to multiply such investment.[28] American International was held to provide an excellent way of linking the large but scattered supplies of capital in the hands of the American public with the banking and manufacturing interests.[29] Maurice A. Oudin (Manager, Foreign Department of General Electric) described the A.I.C. as an institution showing "the way toward satisfying our present necessities. . . . Its striking example should be the forerunner of many similar enterprises with like aims." But, "pending the removal of the incubus of fear of the application of

26. *Ibid.*, 36–37.
27. *Ibid.*, 40–41.
28. *Ibid.*, 17–18.
29. *Ibid.*, 17–18, 40–41, 265–66.

the anti-trust law to . . . foreign trade," he cautioned, "we can expect few or no additional associations to be formed, nor any decided and general cooperative movement on the part of our manufacturers," to take place.[30]

One of the problems discussed in NFTC conventions was how to gather sufficient investment capital to install American technology abroad. Many of the medium-sized corporations, and some large ones, did not in 1916–1917 have such capital to invest at long term. These manufacturers hoped that the construction of branch banks would somehow induce investment bankers in the United States to sell the bonds of South American governments, in this way financing the installation of American technology. Even large corporations, which did have access to capital either in the form of internal surpluses or through strong banking connections, wanted an export trade law that would allow them to combine legally in order that groups of corporations engaging in complementary activities could associate together in a pattern of operations, combining banking, shipping, and finance.

By June 1916, the A.I.C. was contemplating several Latin American municipal loans. But again, in this case as in others, what stood in the way of an extensive development was the need for an export trade law exempting manufacturers from the antitrust laws. National City Vice-president William S. Kies told Vanderlip on June 13, 1916, that all that blocked the A.I.C.'s organization of many export companies was the fact that the projected Webb-Pomerene Act had not yet passed.[31]

30. Maurice A. Oudin, "A New Domain of American Effort," NFTC Convention *Proceedings*, 1916, 265–66.

31. William S. Kies to F. A. Vanderlip, June 13, 1916, in F. A. Vanderlip Manuscripts, Butler Library, Columbia University, New York City (box labeled American International Corporation). (Hereafter cited as Vanderlip MSS.) Unless otherwise labeled, all citations from Vanderlip MSS will be from American International box.

On September 7, 1916, Congress amended the Federal Reserve Act to allow banks to cooperate in the organization of foreign branches, and at the same time exempted bank directors engaged in cooperative foreign branch building from the provisions of the Clayton Act, which regulated business combination.[32] But manufacturing corporations were not so exempted; they remained barred, at least formally, from cooperating with banks in the establishment of branches.

The same issues were again discussed at the NFTC convention in 1917: how to obtain the desired foreign investment, and the extent of the need for an independent United States foreign banking system to guide the hoped-for investment. Manufacturers continued to praise the virtues of foreign branches, and to lament the lack of action on the part of American bankers to further their growth.

During these years when the manufacturers were agitating so persistently for an American system (1916–1919), the House of Morgan had been pursuing a policy of Americanizing the British banking system. Before the war, it held a subordinate relationship to English banking and helped to arrange jointly with British banks the distribution of foreign capital issues in the American market. Gradually, however, the House of Morgan increased its share in such joint ventures. Joint international flotation meant that British branch banks, their personnel, and the trade information gathered by them became more and more available to Morgan. The Morgan interests expected that as the American economy generated capital surpluses, the share of American participation in long-term foreign investments would increase sharply; as the American share of joint investment increased, the British foreign banking system would in effect

32. Federal Reserve Board, *Annual Report*, 1916, 138–39.

become an American commercial property.[33] This partnership implied that the Morgan group was unwilling to challenge Great Britain except in Latin America and China (by changing the rules of a new consortium). Elsewhere, Morgan interests were willing to agree to British banks continuing to finance the export of a high percentage of British technology.

Meanwhile, the foreign expansion of American banks gained momentum after approval of the 1916 legislation to remove potential Clayton Act prohibitions and the legal obstacles to cooperation among banks in foreign commerce. By the end of 1916, for example, the Federal Reserve Board had authorized the formation of eight branches and 38 sub-branches of National Banks abroad: 26 of these were located in Latin Amercia; 12 in Russia and eight in Italy. All but two of these were affiliated with the National City Bank of New York. The other two, planned for Latin America, were tied to the Continental and Commercial National Bank.[34]

The pattern continued through 1917. National City opened eight additional branches and sub-branches, while the Morgan-affiliated First National Bank of Boston opened

33. On the expectation of the Morgan interests that they would achieve control over the British foreign banking system, see the NFTC Convention *Proceedings*, 1917, 139–48. After a wide-ranging discussion of foreign investment and foreign banking, Jason A. Neilson, Vice-president, Mercantile Bank of the Americas, explained to the delegates that the Morgan interests, for which he spoke, were, "endeavoring to Americanize the English and German commercial banking systems and create an instrument which has all the elements contained in the systems of other nations." The theoretical basis of the Americanization aspect of their effort undoubtedly rested on the belief that the nation dominant in international long-term investment would make general use of the world banking facilities of all nations. There was not much new about this broad approach. British investors had done much the same thing with the French international branch bank system before World War I.

34. Federal Reserve Board, *Annual Report*, 1916, 147.

only one.[35] In 1918, three additional Morgan institutions joined the fray: the American and Foreign Banking Corporation established four branches in Latin America; the Mercantile Bank of the Americas established eight affiliates (all in Latin America); and the Asia Banking Corporation announced plans to expand into Asia.[36]

The National City complex was the fundamental element in this foreign expansion. In 1916, the National City Bank had acquired control of the International Banking Corporation (IBC) and its extensive system of branches largely concentrated in Asia. By 1918, the IBC and National City were well integrated; their foreign branches totalled 45, more than the rest of the banking community combined.[37] The state banks affiliated with the House of Morgan—Guaranty Trust Co., Equitable Trust Co., and the Farmer's Loan and Trust Co.—maintained offices in England and France and used European banks as agents throughout the world.[38] This was apparently what Morgan meant by "Americanizing" the European banks.[39]

The Federal Reserve Board recommended in 1918 a number of changes in section 25 of the Federal Reserve Act to make regulations for state and nationally chartered banks uniform. The problem was that "many national banks" had "become stockholders in banks . . . organized under state laws" for international banking business. This meant such groups were subject to both state and national Federal Reserve Board regulations. These enterprises were now viewed by the Board as "national"; hence the Board contended they were entitled to national charters. One of the reasons the Board desired "uniformity" was to match the extensive development of financial facilities for foreign trade apparent in

35. Federal Reserve Board, *Annual Report*, 1917, 187.
36. Federal Reserve Board, *Annual Report*, 1918, 59–61.
37. *Ibid.*
38. *Ibid.*, 60–61.
39. NFTC Convention *Proceedings*, 1917, 148.

recent projects of the British Board of Trade. National charters would clear up ambiguities and allow American banks to compete on equal terms with the British banks. The Board hinted that one weakness in the American position involved the inability of United States banks to participate in syndicates as their British counterparts could.[40]

No expansion of branch banks was reported in 1919. Two partnership arrangements with foreign banking systems, however, were registered with the Reserve Board: the Morgan-affiliated National Bank of Commerce and the First National Bank of Boston joined the Comptoir National D'Escompte of Paris to form the French American Banking Corporation, which in turn planned no branch expansion, preferring to rely on the existing branch connections of the Comptoir National. The National Park Bank of New York joined the Union Bank of Canada to form the Park Union Foreign Banking Company. Both of these mergers illustrated the Morgan policy of cooperating, rather than competing, with foreign banking systems. The Union Bank of Canada was tied to Lloyd's Bank of London through interlocking directorates.[41]

Significant expansion in independent United States branches was reported for the last time in 1920. The American and Foreign Banking Corporation, a short-term Edge institution with Morgan ties, created thirteen new branches. All were located in Latin America, however, and were therefore only regionally competitive with the British banking system. Six other branches were established in 1920, four of these by National City.[42] By the end of 1920, therefore, there was a grand total of 181 American branch banks and affiliates (see table).[43]

40. Federal Reserve Board, *Annual Report*, 1918, 61–62.
41. Leland R. Robinson, "British Banking—The Foreign Policies of the London Big Five Banks," *Acceptance Bulletin*, October 1923, 7.
42. Federal Reserve Board, *Annual Report*, 1920, 26–27.
43. Phelps, *Foreign Expansion of American Banks*, 131.

AMERICAN BRANCH BANKS ABROAD AND THEIR
DOMESTIC AFFILIATION, 1920*[44]

Country	National City or IBC affiliate	Morgan affiliate	Total in each country
Argentina	3	2	5
Belgium	2	1	3
Brazil	5	3	8
Chile	2		2
China	8	9	17
Colombia	3	14	17
Costa Rica		2	2
Cuba	25	3	28
Dominican Republic	6	7	13
England	2	4	6
Ecuador		2	2
France	1	4	5
Germany		1	1
Haiti		1	1
Honduras		6	6
India	3		3
Italy	1	1	2
Japan	2	2	4
Java	2		2
Nicaragua		5	5
Panama		5	5
Peru		7	7
Philippine Islands	2	2	4
Puerto Rico	2		2
Russia	2†		2
South Africa	1		1
Spain	2	2	4
Straits Settlement	1		1
Trinidad	1		1
Uruguay	2		2
Venezuela	3	5	8
	81	88	169

* *Sources:* Federal Reserve Board, *Bulletin*, December, 1920, 1299, and Cleona Lewis, *America's Stake in International Investments*, 197.

† These branches listed as temporarily closed in 1920 in Federal Reserve *Bulletin*.

44. The table does not show the location of twelve branches affiliated to the Morgan group. It proved impossible to find the location of those

No sooner had the peak been reached, however, than the boom began to contract. No new branches were reported in 1921; National City discontinued five branches, three in Colombia and one each in Trinidad and the Union of South Africa.[45] The Federal Reserve Board reported no activity registered in 1922.[46] This was a year of serious difficulties for any American banks operating overseas. In Latin America it was a disastrous year: the number of branches and agencies declined from 75 in 1921 to 46 in 1922; subsidiaries decreased from 32 in eight countries to 26 in seven countries.[47] In some areas the situation became so bad (as in Cuba, where "stupendous losses" were incurred) that in 1923 the Federal Reserve Bank of Boston was considering setting up a branch in Cuba to stabilize "the currency and banking situation" there.[48] Cuba was a nation where the most extensive American branch bank system had been undertaken, yet Cuban banking was in a complete turmoil by May 1923. From 1923 onward the contraction of American branch banking increased its momentum. The Morgan foreign branch institutions led the retreat. In 1924, the Morgan Asia Banking Corporation liquidated, selling out to the International Banking Corporation.[49] One year later the House

---

because they were affiliates or branches of private banks. Private banks were not legally required to report their foreign expansion to the Federal Reserve Board, for their branch activity was not legally regulated under section 25 of the Federal Reserve Act. Wherever I have located branches of private banks, such as the London and Paris branches of the Guaranty Trust Co., I have included them in the regional breakdown in the table. In view of the general pattern of Morgan expansion, it seems likely that the branches of unlisted private banks were mostly in western Europe, functioning as part of the second aspect of Morgan strategy "Americanizing" the branches of European banks.

45. Federal Reserve Board, *Annual Report*, 1921, 84–85.
46. Federal Reserve Board, *Annual Report*, 1922, *passim.*
47. ABA *Journal*, XVI, January 1924, 462–66.
48. Federal Reserve Board, *Annual Report*, 1923, 460–63.
49. Federal Reserve *Bulletin*, June 1920, 606–07.

of Morgan sold the bank of Central and South America to the Royal Bank of Canada,[50] which was in turn a part of the British-controlled world banking system.[51]

Though both the National City and Morgan groups suffered losses, and were forced to close some branches during 1921 and 1922, their contraction did not have disastrous consequences for the total effort to develop guaranteed markets for American commerce. Branches were significant in only one aspect of the American program: the attempt to substitute dollar acceptances for sterling bills in the short-term, day-to-day finance of world commerce. The contraction of branches diminished the institutional facilities for drawing short-term acceptances in dollars on New York commercial banks. This aspect of the effort to make New York the primary international financial center suffered a reverse, and American contraction gave the British the opportunity to expand the use of sterling drafts in short-term financing.

But economic conditions brought about by the war had modified the importance of trade acceptance as a primary element in export market development and control. Exchange markets were unstable partially because most nations had gone off the gold standard. "Branches of all financial institutions, both those existing before the war and maintained thereafter, and those newly established . . . found themselves seriously handicapped by the exchange uncertainties which . . . prevented them from making advances to traders and producers in the countries in which they were situated. In these circumstances American . . . bankers . . . have been disposed to avoid losses which might be incurred through the making of large commitments ex-

50. Phelps, *Foreign Expansion of American Banks,* 159–60.
51. Robinson, "British Banking—The Foreign Policies of the London Big Five Banks," 7–8.

pressed in the [commercial] paper of the countries where their branches might be located."[52] In addition to exchange difficulties related to the breakdown of the gold standard, the shortage of investment capital in Europe after the war limited the importance of foreign branches as a method of transferring permanent investment from developed to under-developed countries.[53] Instead, the activities of foreign branches of European banks after the war were confined to financing raw material imports to the metropolitan countries. The American branch bank system as of 1922, concentrated as it was in Latin America, in combination with direct investment of American corporations, was sufficient for the raw material needs of the American economy.

The contraction of American branch banks had little effect on the expansion of capital investment abroad. One significant element in foreign investment was capital issues floated by American (and semi-American) corporations to expand existing, or to create new foreign facilities. In the world depression year of 1921, for example, such investments totalled $72 million, an increase of $4 million over 1920,[54] when the expansion of American banks was at its peak. Even these figures understate the total of direct investments by American corporations. New York shipping interests purchased an interest in the Hamburg American lines in 1920; similar arrangements were made between American and German tire manufacturers. Since the corporations did not go to the capital market for these transactions, they were

52. "Foreign Trade Banking," Federal Reserve *Bulletin*, September 1920, 908, unsigned editorial item.

53. *Ibid.*

54. Ralph A. Young, *Handbook of American Underwriting of Foreign Securities*, Trade Promotion Series No. 104, Bureau of Foreign and Domestic Commerce, Department of Commerce (Washington, 1930), Tables 6, 17. (Hereafter cited as Young, *Commerce Department Handbook.*)

not included in the direct foreign investment totals for American corporations for 1920.[55] The total of all kinds of foreign capital issues in 1921 was $692 million,[56] some $90 million more than the total of foreign long-term investment had been in the peak prosperity year of 1920.

Before World War I, the foreign branches of English, German, and (to a lesser extent) French banks had been the key elements in exporting technology and thereby developing controlled export markets. European industries did not as a rule establish manufacturing subsidiaries abroad. But American firms had begun the practice of establishing foreign manufacturing subsidiaries around 1900.[57] This method of exporting technology largely eliminated the need for branch banks. The International Telephone and Telegraph Company did not need a banking intermediary to buy a Latin American telephone company. The whole financial side of the operation could be covered as a domestic business transaction with bonds floated in the domestic market; the capital obtained in this manner was simply used to purchase the foreign enterprise. A bank might be subsequently established in the country where the new investment was located, but it would not be necessary because the communications equipment affiliate of the International Telephone and Tele-

55. "American Investment Abroad," Federal Reserve *Bulletin*, August 1920, 777–78, unsigned editorial item; Young, *Commerce Department Handbook*, 161.

56. Young, *Commerce Department Handbook*, 11.

57. This is an arbitrary date which I have selected because 1900 was the first year in which the total value of American-owned factories abroad reached $100 million. Real origins are impossible to trace. While it is true, for example, that between 1875 and 1879, twenty-three branches of American factories were established in Canada, no statistics indicating their value and therefore their relation to export trade became available until 1900. For a discussion of branch factories, origins, and geographical locations see Lewis, *America's Stake in International Investment*, 293–97.

graph Company would export to its foreign affiliate without the need of a branch bank to supply commercial information on the credit rating of the buyer. The buyer would be International Telephone and Telegraph itself. In short, the corporation would act as its own branch bank because of its dual role as buyer and seller to itself.[58]

American branches were still important, however, in relation to loans to foreign governments, and in loans to foreign-controlled corporations guaranteed by foreign governments. Branches were significant in these cases because they could and did function as agencies to collect credit information on borrowers and because foreign borrowers could draw from them dollar drafts to remit dividends and interest of American lenders. But, in connection with the job of supplying credit information, the importance of branches declined because of changes in the activities of the United States Commerce Department. Herbert Hoover initiated the practice of having the growing number of American Trade Commissioners abroad gather credit information for American lenders. The basic need for foreign branches then, was to service loan repayment in areas where loans to foreign governments were being made.

Since much of the lending of this type was concentrated in Latin America and Canada,[59] it would seem then that a

58. In 1924 the International Telephone and Telegraph Co. purchased the government-owned telephone company in Spain. When the purchase was made there were 90,000 phones in use in Spain. By 1931 the total had increased to 231,000. See Lewis, *America's Stake in International Investment*, 326. No branch banks were necessary for IT&T to export phone equipment to Spain, for it was exporting to itself. It was both buyer and seller. In this sense IT&T was more concerned about a stable currency, hence resumption of the gold standard, than about branch banks.

59. Loans to foreign governments, and to foreign corporations whose obligations were guaranteed by foreign governments, were larger than American direct foreign investments from 1919 to 1929. See Young,

well-developed system of foreign branches was really needed only in these two areas. Even after the contraction of the American foreign branch bank system in 1921, 72 branches and subsidiaries were still located in Latin America. Since investment continued to expand in 1921 it is logical to assume that this number of branches was sufficient to meet the needs of American investors in this area. Similarly, though the branch bank movement never attained any substantial dimension in Canada, the needs of American corporate and individual investors for banking services were adequately cared for through the partnership which the House of Morgan maintained with British banks operating in Canada.[60] In addition, Canadian and American dollars were directly convertible. Manufacturing exporters had habitually complained that the lack of branch banks in Latin America impeded their attempt to develop those markets, but few (if any) similar complaints were ever made with respect to banking facilities for foreign trade in Canada.

The American international financial system was composed by 1924 of three parts: the National City-IBC complex with branches in Latin America and Asia; the House of Morgan's branches in Latin America and its connections with the British and French banking networks; and the practice, small but growing, of American corporations to act

Commerce Department Handbook, Tables 4, 14. These portfolio investments in the obligations of foreign governments reflected the cautious attitude of many American investment banking houses. Government guaranteed loans seemed to minimize the risks which the investment banker incurred.

60. The National Park Bank of New York, a Morgan associate bank, joined in partnership with the Union Bank of Canada to form the Park Union Foreign Banking Company, according to Federal Reserve Board, *Annual Report*, 1920, 53–54. During the same period the Union Bank of Canada was tied to Lloyd's Bank (of London) through interlocking directorates. On this see Robinson, "British Banking—The Foreign Policies of the London Big Five Banks," 7.

as their own bankers as well as exporters and manufacturers through the establishment of foreign subsidiaries. The latter method was destined to become the major means of exporting American technology to Canada and Latin America.

Economically then, the fact that both the Morgan and National City groups relinquished some of their postwar expansion of foreign branch networks in 1921 was not of major significance. Of more importance to the American economy as a whole, and to exporters specifically, was the question of whether or not world markets could be expanded any further without reconstruction of the European economies. This problem dovetailed with the government policy of trying to reduce German reparations and win the readmission of Germany to the world economy under conditions less onerous than imposed by the Versailles Peace Treaty. The basic issue of where to commit capital, in Europe or in the underdeveloped countries, was discussed by bankers and professional economists in 1920 and 1921.

At the 1920 meeting of the American Economic Association, for example, two economists operating in the banking community, John H. Williams (American Bankers Association), and Benjamin F. Anderson (Chase National Bank), debated the issue of whether Europe or the underdeveloped areas should be the primary target for American capital. Anderson maintained that the fundamental need was to create markets in the underdeveloped areas for Europe—not for the United States. Williams took the opposite point of view: he argued that the underdeveloped areas should be the recipients of American investment, and that such investment should be used to finance the export of American manufactures rather than agricultural commodities.[61]

61. American Economic Association, *American Economic Review Supplement*, March 1921, XI, No. 1, *Papers and Proceedings of the Thirty-third Annual Meeting* (December 1920), 31–45.

Policy-makers in the New York banking community also discussed this issue. In his presidential address to the American Acceptance Council in 1921, Paul M. Warburg argued that restoration of Europe was necessary before the United States could use its lending power for "world trade and development."

> If I were to translate America's position with regard to the economic problems into plain business language, I should say: we are substantial creditors to the Old World Corporation, which is our best customer and which is facing great financial difficulties. Is it to our interest to let this corporation go into insolvency and disintegration, or shall we encourage and further a reorganization?[62]

Warburg's analysis touched more than the obvious issue of the need to reconstruct Europe as a market for American raw materials and agricultural commodities. In addition, European production had to be expanded if the Latin American nations were to sell their raw material surplus to Britain and continental Europe. An unreconstructed western Europe weakened Latin American economies by depriving them of traditionally large markets. And small markets for Latin American exports prompted American investors to be fearful of long-term investments in those countries. While the volume of American investments in Latin America was large in 1920, 1921, and 1922, the inability of European banks to finance imports from Latin America weakened the total Latin American economy.

Some investment bankers, such as Hans C. Sonne, of Hugh & Company (New York), argued that American bankers should operate as merchandise brokers "moving the produce and merchandise of the South American countries," no matter whether the produce ultimately went to America,

62. American Acceptance Council, *Acceptance Bulletin*, December 1921, 4.

Europe or to "any other part of the world. . . ." The experience of 1921 had showed that it was "useless to attempt to further develop our own country until a satisfactory market is created for our own surplus products." Until such markets were developed, Sonne thought, "we must invest our capital surplus abroad. . . ." Latin American merchandise banking was the proper area in which to invest the capital surplus.[63] Men like Sonne were arguing that, in the broadest sense, markets for both American agricultural surplus and any large-scale expansion of opportunities for secure capital investment in Latin America were dependent on European reconstruction.

The relative unimportance of the dollar acceptance system (except in the financing of South American merchandise exports to Europe), as exhibited in the tendency of American manufacturers to act as their own branch banks, as well as the depression of 1921, were the basic reasons for the cessation of the foreign expansion of American banks. The result was that the campaign to displace sterling drafts with dollar drafts in the day-to-day finance of world trade was largely unsuccessful; the important qualification was that most American short-term exports, and a large part of Latin America's merchandise exports, were financed by means of dollar drafts.

George E. Roberts, Vice-president of the National City Bank, demonstrated in 1921 that dollar acceptances declined proportionally more than the sterling acceptances during the economic depression of that year.[64] Indeed, the *Acceptance Bulletin* maintained that sterling bills had reached a postwar peak in May 1921, while dollar drafts had declined by

63. Hans C. Sonne, "South American Trade Prospects," *Acceptance Bulletin*, January 1922, 8–10; see also a speech by Harold J. Dreher, head of an Edge bank, *Acceptance Bulletin*, April 1922, 10.

64. *Acceptance Bulletin*, June 1921, 3–4.

two-thirds.[65] In April 1922, Harold J. Dreher, Vice-president of the Federal International Banking Corporation of New Orleans (an Edge Act corporation), warned that London was regaining the financial leadership of the world. Dreher cautioned against "competitive struggles" at home, lest they give victory to the British.[66] And in May 1922, William P. G. Harding, Governor of the Federal Reserve Board, indicated that the Board planned to change its regulations so that dollar drafts could be sold in New York at a rate competitive with sterling drafts sold in London. If such changes were not made, he argued, even Americans would shift from dollar drafts to the more economical sterling bills.[67]

Sir Ernest Harvey, a partner of the leading London discount house of Allen and Harvey, dismissed fears that New York would displace London as the bill-accepting center of the world. He seemed in July 1923 to regard the contest as over. "There has been considerable speculation as to the extent to which New York might take the place of London as an acceptor of bills and the consequences of the displacement of sterling by the dollar," he noted in an article in the *Times* of London. "New York has made serious efforts to create an equivalent to the London discount market, but, in spite of the advantage of still being on an effective gold basis, the experience must have been discouraging because money has been lost. . . . It is permissible to hope that . . . the accepting houses, the Big Five and other deposit banks, with the collaboration of the bill broker, may, for the benefit of the world, re-establish the supremacy of the London money market."[68]

65. *Acceptance Bulletin*, May 1921, 2–3.
66. *Acceptance Bulletin*, April 1922, 10.
67. *Acceptance Bulletin*, May 1922, 9–10.
68. *Acceptance Bulletin*, July 1923, 5–7.

Hartley Withers, an expert in the affairs of the City, explained the relative failure of New York's offensive in the acceptance field on the dual grounds that the New York Stock Exchange competed with the New York discount market for cash, which encouraged instability, and because Federal Reserve policy did not help the New York bill market to the same extent that the Bank of England assisted the London market.[69] Despite the fact that acceptances were no longer a key factor in the export of American technology after World War I, the acceptance bankers as an interest group continued to urge expansion of dollar acceptances.

The attempt to create an independent, world-wide American branch bank system prompted British bankers and industrialists to undertake after the war a concerted campaign to retool their system in order to meet the challenge, and at the same time take over the largest part of the prewar German sphere of economic influence in Central and Southeastern Europe, the Middle East, and Latin America. The major steps in this process were: the coordination of the activities of British business and government; the centralization and unification of banking and industry in the United Kingdom; and the integration of the German trade and payments system, thrown open by the German defeat, into the reorganized British system.[70]

Though it had always existed, the tie between the British government and the banking community (The City) became even closer during World War I. Operating through the Bank of England and the Treasury, the government accomplished this by controlling foreign capital issues. This

---

69. *Acceptance Bulletin*, September 1925, 30.

70. Robinson, "British Banking—The Foreign Policies of the London Big Five Banks," 6–8. See also Leland R. Robinson, "Foreign Credit Facilities of the United Kingdom," *Acceptance Bulletin*, December 1923, 15.

authority was maintained and extended after the war through Defense of the Realm regulations.[71] Perhaps in exchange for an element of control, the government also began to render assistance to the private managers of overseas investment. The Trade Facilities Act made government capital available to overseas bankers for risky credit ventures. And, at the instance of the Board of Trade, the British Trade Corporation was organized in 1917.[72] It received indirect government financial support through the Trade Facilities Act credits extended to its subsidiaries.[73]

At its first annual meeting in 1918, the Governor of the British Trade Corporation outlined its three major purposes: to encourage export trade directly by close links between banking and commerce; to attain the same measure of efficiency as German overseas banks had before the war; and to create subsidiaries to "enter trading fields formerly held by the enemy and to secure them for the British manufacturer. This is particularly the case in Brazil and other south American markets, in the Levant [and] in southern Russia. . . ."[74] The British Trade Corporation organized a number of these subsidiaries, such as the Levant Company in the Middle East, the Anglo Brazilian Commercial Agency in

71. Henry F. Grady, *British War Finance, 1914–1919* (New York, 1927), 51–54. Grady was concerned with his subject matter as an American trade commissioner in London during the war. On prewar ties see Herbert Feis, *Europe the World's Banker, 1870–1914* (New Haven, 1930), 85–87.

72. Robinson, "Foreign Credit Facilities of the United Kingdom," 15.

73. Grady, *British War Finance, 1914–1919*, 231–32. Support was often indirect through consultation of Treasury officials with private bankers, the bankers, in turn, extending credit to the British Trade Corporation. Grady implies that the bankers' knowledge of government interest and encouragement was enough to induce them to join support of the Trade Corporation. On "consultation" see also Brown, *Gold Standard Reinterpreted*, I, 658.

74. Robinson, "Foreign Credit Facilities of the United Kingdom," 15.

South America, and the Portuguese Trading Corporation, to effect the takeover of these former German positions.[75] The British Trade Corporation's ties to the dominant element in the financial community existed through interlocking directorates with three of the "Big Five" banks, Barclay's Bank, the London Joint City and Midland Bank, and the National Provincial and Union Bank.[76]

British interests expanded into key German economic positions in Central Europe by seizing control of the Anglo-Austrian bank. Before the war this bank, though located in Vienna, was a German institution. It possessed an extensive system of affiliates in such countries as Austria, Czechoslovakia, Hungary, and the United Kingdom. Once the war broke out the British government gave the Bank of England the right to appoint four members to the Board of the Anglo-Austrian branch located in London.[77] Seizure of enemy-owned property within the borders of an Allied country was legitimized after the war in Article 248 of the Versailles Peace Treaty. Once the British government had seized control of the Anglo-Austrian records and correspondence in London, British authorities were in a position to know what affiliated institutions in Austria and Czechoslovakia were doing in Central European commercial matters. This knowledge eased the way for private British interests to seize control of the Anglo-Austrian network.[78] J. P. Hutchins, an

75. *Ibid.;* Grady, *British War Finance, 1914–1919*, 231–32.

76. Robinson, "British Banking—The Foreign Policies of the London Big Five Banks," 6–7.

77. *Acceptance Bulletin*, January 1924, 16.

78. See Article 248 of the Versailles Treaty. Seizure by Allied belligerents of enemy-held property in Allied nations was legitimized. Aside from legitimacy, the Bank of England possessed all the records of the London branch of Anglo-Austrian and therefore knew its holdings, interests, and other business secrets. It was thus in a position to "take over" such interests.

official of the American International Corporation, explained
to Vanderlip how the British operated to control enemy
banks in southeast Central Europe and Turkey.[79]

Both the British Trade Corporation and the Bank of England played a considerable role in obtaining control of the
former German banking and industrial sphere in the frag-
mented Turkish Empire. For example, the Bank of England
seized control of the Deutsche Bank's 25 percent share in the
formerly joint British-German owned Turkish Petroleum
Company,[80] while the British Trade Corporation subsidiary,
the Levant Company, "acquired the whole share capital of
the National Bank of Turkey."[81] Since Britain had League
of Nation mandates in much of the area, its acquisition of
such investments appears to have been relatively easy.[82]

In July 1919, the British Overseas Bank began opera-
tions. Many of its activities were concentrated on taking
over former German economic operations in Central and
East Europe.[83] A number of affiliates of the Big Five and
independent British banks were behind the British Overseas
Bank.[84] In Italy, which had been an extremely important
German economic sphere before the war,[85] the British Italian
Corporation was created to supplant German financial influ-
ence in Italian industry and commerce. The British Italian
Trading Corporation received indirect support from the

79. Hutchins to Vanderlip, May 31, 1919, Vanderlip MSS.
80. U.S. Senate, *Oil Concessions in Foreign Countries*, Senate Document No. 97, 68th Cong., 1st sess. (Washington, 1923) 53–54; entry of
March 9, 1920, memorandum of conversation with Herbert Hoover in
Henry L. Stimson Manuscripts, Diary, in Yale University Library, New
Haven, Conn. (Hereafter cited as *Stimson Diary.*)
81. Grady, *British War Finance, 1914–1919*, 236–37.
82. *Ibid.*, 238; U.S. Senate, *Oil Concessions in Foreign Countries*,
53–54; entry of March 9, 1920, *Stimson Diary*.
83. Robinson, "Foreign Credit Facilities of the United Kingdom," 15.
84. Grady, *British War Finance, 1914–1919*, 239.
85. Feis, *Europe the World's Banker*, 239.

British government; and, through its affiliate Compagnia Italo Britannica also won Italian government support. Some twenty-three leading British banks, including Lloyd's and Westminster's, took shares in British Italian.[86]

Between 1919 and 1922 a large number of additional overseas banks were established by British operators. Together with new affiliates (which were largely branches and subsidiaries of the London Big Five) the British financial community had come very near to its stated objective of "affording all British facilities" to British businessmen.[87] By 1923 the British system of overseas banks was reinvigorated, reorganized, and in excellent condition to hold its own as the major center of world wide acceptance financing.

But the British effort to protect its prewar position as the financier of half the world's day-to-day export trade by means of protecting sterling as the major bill of exchange was only partially successful. A considerable and growing part of both United States and Latin American day-to-day exports were by 1924 financed by dollar acceptances. Of even more significance, however, was the fact that the basic American challenge was not in acceptance financing, but in long-term foreign investment. Here New York was the incomparable leader. Whereas London continued to use branch banks and long-term commercial loans to expand British technology abroad, Americans used the dual method of the long-term loan and the foreign branch-factory and subsidiary.

In addition the United States expanded its holdings of investments in Central and South America using its special political position in the Western Hemisphere to force Latin American governments to seize and sell German invest-

86. *Acceptance Bulletin*, November 1923, 19.
87. *Ibid.;* also *Acceptance Bulletin*, January 1924, 15.

ments to the highest bidder, namely the United States. As
early as July 21, 1917, the American Ambassador in Brazil,
Edwin V. Morgan, reported to Secretary Lansing that there
were "326 banks, corporations, firms and individuals" acting
as German-controlled enterprises, or trading with Germany.
Both Britain and the United States wanted to acquire portions of these German interests. By October 1918 the British
had worked out a plan for a joint purchase of German banks
in Brazil by a syndicate of American and British banks. But
U.S. Treasury Secretary William G. McAdoo warned Lansing that the Treasury had "not come to a definite conclusion
as to the method in which the American share of such
German owned banks in Brazil should be taken over." Still,
McAdoo was certain that it was "very undesirable to have a
group of British banks undertake the formation of a Brazilian bank in which they would ask American financiers to
co-operate." McAdoo wanted America's share of German
banks in Brazil to be under sole American control, probably
so that such banking resources would function as part of an
American system of trade expansion, rather than as a joint
Anglo-American venture.[88]

That the American Treasury and State Departments
viewed American aquisition of German investments in
northern Latin America as necessary to the creation of an
American-controlled system of trade, is reinforced by the
strong pressure the United States government used to acquire such German holdings in Peru, Guatemala, and
Ecuador.

88. U.S. Ambassador in Brazil Edwin V. Morgan to Secretary Lan-
sing, July 21, 1917, Morgan to Lansing, October 27, 1917, Lansing to
Morgan, November 12, 1917, McAdoo to Lansing, October 9, 1918. See
U.S. Department of State, *Papers Relating to the Foreign Relations of the
United States*, 1918, *The World War*, Supplement II (Washington,
1932), 340–43, 351–52.

In January 1918 the United States wanted to acquire the German-owned Casa Grande sugar refining plant in Peru. The screws were first turned on the Peruvian government when the United States War Trade Board issued a ruling that American banks could not discount the acceptance drafts of the German-owned corporation. Barring the discount of the drafts meant the corporation could not get paid for its sugar, and could not continue its operations. This in turn meant that its 10,000 workers would be laid off and that one of Peru's major means of earning foreign exchange would end. On January 25, 1918, the Peruvian legation proposed that its government would "exact that the net earnings of the Casa Grande Plant be deposited in Peru until after the war," thus denying to Germany the ability to use such earnings while the war continued. But the United States was unwilling to accept that proposal. On May 6 Lansing agreed to lift temporarily the War Trade Board restriction on American banks, allowing them to discount Casa Grande drafts. "It is understood, however," Lansing told de Freyre, the Peruvian Minister to the United States, "that such a temporary license would be granted pending a prompt decision by the owners of the Casa Grande estate as to whether they would authorize the Peruvian administrator of the estate to make a sale of any or all of the shares of the corporation."[89]

Lansing did not simply want to deny Germany the income from her Casa Grande investment, but wanted to place the investment on the market in a forced sale. Under existing conditions, with all major international investors using their capital to fight the war, only American interests could raise the funds necessary to purchase Casa Grande shares. But

89. Peruvian Legation to Department of State, January 25, 1918, de Freyre to Lansing, February 27, 1918, Lansing to de Freyre, May 6, 1918, *ibid.*, 401–04.

the Peruvian government was not anxious to act as an agent for the United States in this venture.

Lansing responded to Peruvian procrastination by renewing the original United States threat. Lansing warned de Freyre on June 18 that "unless within 15 days from today the owners of the Casa Grande Estate shall have conferred upon the administrator full and complete authority to make an absolute and bonefide sale of the Estate, which was one of the conditions under the terms of my note of June 3 upon which the continuance of the above mentioned temporary license was made to depend, this Government will be obliged to revoke the license already granted." The Peruvians moved part of the way to meet American demands. On July 10 de Freyre told Lansing that "the representatives in Peru of the Casa Grande Estate have delivered to the American Mercantile Bank at Lima a cablegram addressed to the directory of the firm at Bremen, requesting full power to dispose of the estate."[90]

But the Germans stood their ground, refusing, as de Freyre told Lansing on July 27, "to give the Peruvian administrator full power to dispose in the unconditional form required by the Government of the United States."[91] Lansing and American interests lost the contest for Casa Grande.

In certain respects treatment of German investments in Guatemala was even more revealing of how the United States obtained German investments in Latin America. In June 1918 the Guatemalan government offered to appoint an American citizen, Daniel B. Hodgson, as Alien Property Custodian for Guatemala. The American Minister to Guatemala, Leavell, pointed out to Lansing that "the appointment

90. Lansing to de Freyre, June 18, 1918, de Freyre to Lansing, July 10, 1918, *ibid.*, 408–10.
91. de Freyre to Lansing, July 27, 1918, *ibid.*, 411.

would be most desirable." Lansing quickly cabled approval on June 26. Leavell cabled back to Lansing on July 4 that the "Electric Power and Light Co. of Guatemala City, the Electric Light and Power and Telephone Cos. Quezaltenango, and the Vera Paz Railway Co." had been placed in Hodgson's hands "to begin with." Acting Secretary of State Polk then asked on July 12 that Leavell make an effort to shape Guatemala's Alien Property Law in such a way that there would be a provision "in such legislation to invest full powers of sale of German properties in the administration."[92] The "administration" was of course Daniel Hodgson.

Between July and September the United States increased pressure on the Guatemalan government by having the War Trade Board deny export licenses to American firms selling necessary electrical supplies to the still German-owned Guatemala City Electric Power and Light Company. The embargo was so effective that Leavell informed Lansing on September 12 that "unless electrical supplies ordered from the United States some months ago are forwarded at once this city will be in total darkness within six weeks." Six days later Lansing instructed Leavell to tell Guatemala "that when its Alien Property Custodian is given full authority to sell the German property, the War Trade Board will be pleased to license freely supplies for Empressa Electrica de Guatemala." On September 20 Leavell wrote Lansing that President Cabrera of Guatemala assured Leavell "that full authority to sell would be given to the Alien Property Custodian within a few days."[93]

Lansing then acted to see to it that American interests

92. Leavell to Lansing, June 24, 1918, Lansing to Leavell, June 26, 1918, Leavell to Lansing, July 4, 1918, Polk to Leavell, July 12, 1918, *ibid.*, 365–66.

93. Leavell to Lansing, September 12, 1918, Lansing to Leavell, September 18, 1918, Leavell to Lansing, September 20, 1918, *ibid.*, 370–71.

acquired the German investments in Guatemala. He instructed Leavell on September 27 to "inform Hodgson confidentially that the Government of the United States deems it of the first importance that American interests be given every opportunity to offer their bids upon any German properties which might under Guatemala's Alien Property Custodian's ruling be sold." Lansing went on to stress that there "are at present important American groups anxious to enter the Guatemalan field. Request the delay of sale of any German properties until representatives of these United States groups arrive. Wire the moment legislation is passed permitting the sale of German properties."[94]

In the case of German investments in Ecuador the United States used tactics similar to those it had employed in Guatemala, Peru, and Brazil. In the case of cacao plantations in the Ecuadorian province of Los Rios the United States used War Trade Board regulations as an instrument to prevent the viable operation of such German properties. The Ecuadorian Minister to the United States, R. H. Elizalde, complained to Lansing on October 29, 1918, that American actions were causing unemployment and suffering in his country. Elizalde then proposed that his government would be willing to deny the Germans profits from their investments by depositing "in an Ecuadorian or American bank in the name of the Government of Ecuador" such profits until the end of the war. But this did not satisfy Lansing. He wanted Ecuador to take "any course which would effect the permanent elimination of the German interests in the properties in question." Then the United States government would be "more than willing to afford such facilities, financial or commercial, as may be necessary."[95]

94. Lansing to Leavell, September 27, 1918, *ibid.*
95. Elizalde to Lansing, October 29, 1918, Lansing to Elizalde, November 12, 1918, *ibid.*, 363–65.

Given the fact that the United States acquired considerable portions of British as well as German investments in Latin America, and given the fact of a growing American capital surplus after the depression of 1920–1922, the American method of extending long-term commercial loans and creating branch factories and subsidiaries proved superior to that of the British. Step by step New York became the international financial center. This reality was still somewhat obscured in 1923 because of continued British leadership in the extension of world-wide acceptance credits. The American position was dramatized in 1924, however, when American bankers took the leadership in the Dawes Plan loan to Germany. American bankers floated over half the loan. The British took what was left. American leadership in long-term international investment and British leadership in acceptance finance led British financial leaders such as Sir Felix Schuster of the National Provincial and Union Bank of London to propose once again a partnership of "mutually helpful" competition "in the development of world markets" to supplant the unscrupulous competition of the past.[96] When the British and continental Allies accepted the Dawes Plan in 1924, such mutually helpful competition became practicable. But the senior partner in the Anglo-American system of trade payments and investment had become the United States. Ten years after the passage of the Federal Reserve Act the hopes of American businessmen who advocated an independent system of banking and investment were realized.

96. *Acceptance Bulletin*, May 1922, 12.

CHAPTER VI

🦅 *The Lion and the Eagle*

As THE primary source of surplus capital after the war, the United States was in a delicate position. Almost all the victorious Allies in Europe wanted direct access to American capital under conditions which would allow them either to establish closed door empires or to revitalize empires already in existence. Had the United States joined the League of Nations in 1920, the European powers undoubtedly would have been in a position to nail shut the door in many areas of the world, while at the same time adhering to a formal recognition of the open door out of deference to President Wilson. Wilson and his Republican successors thought the open door policy was the only foundation upon which any viable, just, and pacific development of commercial (and hence political) relationships could be established. Differences over American entry into the League of Nations were basically manifestations of divergent interpretations concerning the relative feasibility of the open door within the League structure.

During the Foreign Relations Committee hearings on American entry in 1919, the future president, Senator Warren G. Harding, who had received information about the Anglo-Persian agreements to develop the oil resources of North Persia, expressed hostility to the League on the grounds that such agreements gave England one more vote in the Assembly of the League. This situation, the committee intimated, was one more reason why the United States should absent itself from the proposed League.[1]

According to Henry L. Stimson, Herbert Hoover, in conversation with him in March 1920 "fiercely denounced" the clause in the Versailles Treaty on expropriation of private property. "Citing the case of expropriation of German property in neutral countries," Hoover argued that Great Britain would get "all of the German investments in South America."[2] Wilson had tied the League of Nations Covenant to the Treaty of Versailles; so, in order for the United States to enjoy equal access to such German investments by ratifying the treaty the Senate would also have to approve the League Covenant. Even though he regarded American attempts to acquire these investments as important, Hoover refused to endorse Wilson's League, based as it was on what Hoover regarded as the very dangerous Article 10.

The factor which weighed most heavily in convincing Republican leaders that the League framework would place restrictions on the operation of the open door was the manner in which British diplomats and commercial policymakers handled the questions of oil and the reconstruction of Russia. There was considerable correspondence between Secretary of State Bainbridge Colby and his British counterparts on the clear (to Colby) but unadmitted (by British diplomats) policy of the British government to close the

1. U.S. Senate, *Oil Concessions in Foreign Countries*, Senate Document No. 97, 68th Cong., 1st sess. (Washington, 1923), footnote 89.

2. Entry of March 9, 1920, memorandum of conversation with Herbert Hoover, Henry L. Stimson Manuscripts, Diary, in Yale University Library, New Haven, Conn. The context of the quote is such that Hoover is lamenting failure of the Senate to ratify the Versailles Treaty so that we could bid on such German investments. But even so, Hoover would not accept Wilson's price, acceptance of an Article 10 League. In Hoover's view, this is a much greater liability to the United States than any asset to be gained through the Versailles Treaty in the area of German investments.

door for equality of opportunity in the oil-bearing lands of the Middle East.[3] It was not just the selfish desire of Standard Oil and American statesmen to get their hands on the profitable petroleum resources of the world which made oil important in diplomacy between 1920 and 1924. World oil relations should be considered from several viewpoints, all pointed like spokes on a wheel toward the hub of the open door. The great profit in oil was one spoke. Its military—particularly naval—importance was another. Yet the third spoke, and most significant one, was the relationship between oil (and, by implication, all raw materials) and the effort to adjust commercial conflicts peacefully by means of the open door policy.[4]

Wilson and Colby differed from their Republican successors concerning their respective estimates of the extent to which the open door principle could be implemented within the League framework as a means of assuring peaceful relations. Republicans viewed entrance into the League as acquiescence in a British-managed closed door world, since England had already taken much of the political and economic lead on the Continent, and various clauses of the Versailles Treaty (and politically lesser but significant treaties with Turkey and the Succession States) had given Britain special positions in Central and Eastern Europe and the Middle East. In addition, Article 10 of the League agreement imposed a moral obligation on American statesmen to accept —and even take joy in—a world they had never made, and

3. U.S. Department of State, *Papers Relating to the Foreign Relations of the United States*, 1920, 29 vols. (Washington, 1925–1944), 2 vols., I, 350–51, II, 652–53, 658–59. (Hereafter cited as *Foreign Relations*.)

4. Norman H. Davis to Lord Curzon, May 12, 1920, *Foreign Relations*, 1920, II, 652–53; Van Manning, American Petroleum Institute, to Assistant Secretary of State Arthur C. Millspaugh, August 17, 1921, in State Department files, National Archives, Record Group 59, 800.6363/296. Unless otherwise labeled, decimal number will indicate Record Group 59 in State Department files, National Archives.

which they saw as soil for the seeds of another war. Progressive Republicans argued that the League substituted the principle of force, labeled Collective Security, for the practice of allowing political conflicts, largely held to be based on economic competition, to work themselves out through the principle of the real open door.

Wilson's basic difference with critics of the League was that he thought a concert of power could not be achieved without Article 10. He believed a League based on Article 10 would guarantee that future wars would only be fought to preserve the peace. The mandate principle he regarded as a means of encouraging economic and political independence for underdeveloped countries without resort to revolution. In addition, he thought of the mandate principle as an example that would apply pressure to the world's empires to gradually free their dependencies. Thus Article 10 would insure a concert without keeping the underdeveloped nations permanently dependent. Because Wilson fully expected the mandate principle to work, he was willing to compromise on the pace with which the United States would pressure the world's empires to accept the open door.[5]

5. For example, on December 28, 1918, Wilson explained: "Our thought was always that the key to the peace was the guaranty of the peace not the items in it; that the items would be worthless unless there stood back of them a permanent concert of power for their maintenance." And on January 25, 1919, he again emphasized his view that the process of establishing a permanent concert, which was his view of the League, was vastly more important than the political conditions the concert was to guarantee. "Settlements may be temporary, but the actions of the nations in the interests of peace and justice must be permanent. We can set up permanent processes. We may not be able to set up permanent decisions." See William Diamond, *The Economic Thought of Woodrow Wilson* (Baltimore, 1943), 172, footnote 29, also 165–66, especially footnote 15. Specifically, Wilson believed that a League of Nations would undercut the basis of the development of special spheres; on this see Roy Watson Curry, *Woodrow Wilson and Far Eastern Policy, 1913–1921* (New York, 1957), 289–91.

The attempt to block British plans for a closed door foundation for European reconstruction by means of an international consortium was clearly outlined in the American response to a series of conferences held between 1920 and 1922. The International Financial Conference in Brussels (1920) was the first European attempt, led by England, to impose a combined political-economic reconstruction plan on the United States. The Brussels Conference was closely followed by meetings in Genoa and at the Hague in 1922. The Hague meeting was the last faltering attempt by the British to take a lead in the reconstruction of Europe. The final conference, during which a reconstruction system was finally adopted, involved the Dawes Plan meetings in Paris in 1924. The decisions of this conference were made largely according to American economic assumptions.

On July 31, 1919, in a letter to Assistant Secretary of the Treasury Russell Leffingwell, Benjamin Strong summarized the issues which had to be dealt with before European reconstruction could be undertaken. He outlined six questions: (1) Would the United States accept political responsibility for Eastern Europe and economic responsibility for the whole of Europe? (2) Would the United States Treasury finance reconstruction or would the government simply assist private business in this task? (3) Would the government be willing to adjust the war debts by postponing interest payments in order to make amortization payments easier? (4) Would the government allow Britain and France to write off a part of their debt to the United States equivalent to what other Allies owed those two countries? (5) Would the United States government allow its European Allies to negotiate "the adjustment of the existing debt and arrange a policy for the future, or at any rate give it [the United States] a clear picture . . . of their needs?" (6) Would the United States "join hands with the British in a

reconstruction policy?"[6] Concerned as he was about cooperation between the British and American banking systems,
Strong was prone to cast the problem in somewhat European
terms. Wilson and Colby were much less inclined to do the
same.

The answers to most of these questions depended on
whether or not the British accepted the open door as defined
by the United States. The British decision to take over the
banking structure created by the German Great Banks in
Central and Eastern Europe, and the British attempt to
develop the oil resources of the former Turkish Empire
under a British-controlled system, were stumbling blocks to
thorough cooperation even under Wilson. Of the six questions put by Strong to Leffingwell, Wilson and Colby ultimately answered only one affirmatively. They were willing
only to join a League based on Article 10. This was the
only basic difference between Wilson and his Republican
successors. On January 28, 1919, Carter Glass announced
the discontinuance of government-to-government loans. In
the same year the Edge Act was passed and a program for
private reconstruction credits formulated. The remainder of
Strong's questions were dealt with by Wilson and Colby in
much the same way as they would be dealt with after 1921
by their Republican successors.

Wilson and Colby laid the groundwork when they insisted in 1920 that the Europeans accept the open door in the
"newly constituted states, mandatories and [other] territories which [had] changed hands as a result of the war and
[the Peace] Treaty."[7] The first British move to establish

6. U.S. Senate, *Special Committee on Investigation of the Munitions
Industry*, 74th Cong., 2d sess. (Washington, 1936), 9575. (Hereafter
cited as *Munitions Industry Hearings*.)

7. Davis to Rathbone, May 12, 1920, *Munitions Industry Hearings*,
9490.

European ground rules for reconstruction came when the financial committee of the League of Nations, meeting in Cannes in 1920, considered plans for an International Financial Conference of government officials in Brussels in the fall of 1920. The United States was informally invited to attend the conference, but Secretary Colby refused the invitation. At the same time, he suggested that American Ambassador to France Hugh C. Wallace endeavor to induce one of the neutral nations planning to attend the conference to propose a meeting sponsored by the International Chamber of Commerce, at which representative business groups of the various countries, including the United States, would develop a program for the reconstruction of Europe by private business.[8] This suggestion was a reiteration of the proposal Wilson had made to Lloyd George at the Paris Peace Conference and was the methodology of reconstruction the Europeans finally accepted under the Dawes Plan in 1924. But in 1920 nothing came of Colby's suggestion and the Brussels Conference was held as scheduled.

But Wallace was finally sent as the unofficial American observer. Colby carefully instructed him not to be drawn into any discussions on future United States government loans, cancellation of war debts, or the deferral of payments on obligations owed to the United States by foreign governments. These questions and related ones (such as postponement of interest payments on debts to the United States) were proper subjects for discussion only between the United States Treasury and the treasuries of the countries concerned.[9] Implicit in Colby's instructions of September 17 was the fear that Europe would use the conference to apply multination pressure to obtain some of the above ends without making any concessions to the United States. One such

8. Colby to Wallace, April 3, 1920, 551.A1/1.
9. Colby to Wallace, September 17, 1920, 551.A1/40a.

possible concession would be Allied recognition that the best means for "supplying Europe with the materials requisite for its reconstruction" was "leaving private enterprise free to produce [the] surplus necessary." Colby pointed out to Wallace "that although European Governments are indebted to this Government in [the] amount approaching $10,000,000,000, there remains in [the] hands of European [private] holders investment in property in the United States amounting to several billion dollars."[10] In view of the fact that Albert Rathbone had suggested to Sir Hardiman Lever, in the course of negotiations between the American and British Treasuries in December 31, 1918, that the British could secure American raw materials if they liquidated British-controlled "American and neutral securities,"[11] it is

10. *Ibid.*

11. Rathbone to Lever, December 31, 1918, quoted in *Munitions Industry Hearings*, 9475–76. European leaders felt that their whole economic position was powerfully threatened by the renewed United States pressure for them to dispose of their foreign investments. Indeed, as late as September 30, 1919, Lloyd George and other European leaders tried to get the United States to accept representation on the Supreme Economic Council, so that the co-belligerents might together fix prices and allocate supplies of raw materials, most of which were American produced. While the United States regarded this approach as proof positive that the Europeans, especially the British, were trying to rob us of a "proper return for the service that we will perform," as Herbert Hoover put it in November 1918 before the armistice, the alternative to joint control of American raw materials was unique American control, which in turn implied high prices that the British could not pay without alienating more foreign investments to the United States. Understandably, the British felt that American "Open door" demands were pushing the British to the wall. They responded by looking for non-dollar sources of raw materials which they and their European allies could control as to allocation and price. To get control of non-dollar sources of wheat, cotton, flax, and petroleum, the Europeans, especially the British, had to have special spheres in which American economic interests would be excluded, or at least confined to subordinate status. For documentary evidence of the progression of all these events, see the first American refusal of joint raw material control in *Foreign Relations*, 1918, *The World War*,

clear that Colby was hinting to Wallace that liquidating privately-owned European securities was, from the American view, the desirable means by which Europeans could secure American raw materials.

At the conference Brand Whitlock, United States Ambassador to Belgium, outlined the American position that intergovernment lending was at an end. To interest American private capital, Whitlock pointed out, Europeans would have to convince American investors that Europe was a good credit risk. Political hostility among the European nations, he maintained, was a deterrent to private business participation in European reconstruction. To alleviate the fears of American business some measure of economic cooperation was necessary among the European states. In this connection, he congratulated the League's International Financial Conference "on taking one needed step by inviting representatives of the vanquished countries to the Conference."[12]

The Europeans responded cautiously to Whitlock's arguments. There was no resumption of the Allied campaign to obtain American government or government-guaranteed credits. Officially then, there was recognition of, if not pleasure in, the American decision to discontinue government loans. To meet the American position the Dutch delegation proposed the Ter Meulen scheme, whereby European governments would issue bonds based on assets or revenues controlled by their respective governments. The governments would turn over such bonds to their nationals for use as collateral to import necessary raw materials. Whitlock

Supplement I, 2 vols. (Washington, 1933), I, 616–17; the renewed request for joint control of September 30, 1919, and the reaffirmed American rejection in British Foreign Office, E. L. Woodward and Rohan Butler, eds., *Documents on British Foreign Policy, 1919–1939,* 1st ser. (London, 1947), I, 835–36. (Hereafter cited as *British Documents.*)

12. Brand Whitlock to Colby, September 30, 1920, 551.a1/45.

commented cautiously that assets or revenues used to secure bonds to finance raw material imports would subtract from the ability of a particular government to meet its existing debts.[13] This meant that the Europeans were trying to evade settlement of war debts owed the United States.

Whitlock's report to Norman H. Davis, Acting Secretary of State, revealed that the European Allies were not yet ready to accept the American condition that international credits be extended through private sources. The role of European governments in the projected Ter Meulen scheme meant that no plans could be framed which might violate the objectives of those governments. Therefore nothing practical could be achieved in altering reparations. Until this indemnity was adjusted American investors were not willing to risk their capital to any extent in Germany. The failure of the Brussels Conference strengthened the American diplomatic position because it illustrated that nothing could be done to secure European reconstruction without the consent and active support of the United States.

The Brussels Conference ended in the second week of October. Less than a month later the election of Harding placed foreign policy formation in the hands of Charles Evans Hughes and Herbert Hoover. The election results meant that the United States was not to participate in the League of Nations, but did not mean that the Harding Administration would abandon efforts to shape European political and economic decisions if those decisions were of world-wide importance. A revision of American policy toward the Versailles system had already begun under Wilson.

The Wilson Administration objected to four areas of Allied policy: (1) the European unwillingness to accept a

---

13. Whitlock to Colby, *Foreign Relations*, 1920, I, 100–03.

workable solution to the reparations question;[14] (2) the Allied and Japanese disposal of former German territories, such as the Pacific cable center on the island of Yap,[15] without the approval of the United States; (3) the violation by Britain and France of a pledge to the United States that the oil mandatories in the Middle East would be administered according to the principles of the open door; and (4) the Allied reluctance to settle war debts owed to the United States.

Acting Secretary of State Norman H. Davis had concluded as early as July 8, 1920, that the Allies were not yet ready "to reach a reasonable and sane solution of [the] indemnity problem." In view of this, Davis argued, "it seems that, although it may ultimately be necessary for the United States to participate in [a] solution of the reparations question . . . the present is not opportune . . . and the United States should play a waiting game."[16] In a communique to Wallace on February 10, 1921, Secretary of State Colby also expressed displeasure at the reparations decisions of the Supreme Council of Ambassadors and volunteered the opinion that they were unworkable. He even considered filing a caveat against the Paris plan, though he assured Wallace that the Wilson Administration still favored ratification of the Versailles Treaty.[17] Partly because of the reparations problem and partly because of "the breaking off of negotiations between Rathbone and the British Treasury" on settlement of the debt between the United States and

14. Norman H. Davis to Brand Whitlock, July 8, 1920, *Foreign Relations*, 1920, II, 397–98.

15. Colby to Hugh C. Wallace, February 21, 1921, *Foreign Relations*, 1921, I, 90–91.

16. Davis to Whitlock, July 8, 1920, *Foreign Relations*, 1920, II, 397–98.

17. Colby to Wallace (telegram), February 15, 1921, 462.00 R29/488.

The Lion and the Eagle 149

Great Britain, Wilson refused to attend the Spa Conference of June 21, 1920.[18] The Wilson Administration also communicated its displeasure on the disposal of the island of Yap to Japan in a February 21, 1921, note to the Council of the League of Nations. The objection was based on the ground that no such decision could be taken without the concurrence of the United States, particularly since "the island of Yap necessarily constitutes an indispensable part of any practicable arrangement of cable communications in the Pacific."[19]

But the most significant factor inducing the Wilson Administration to revise its policy toward the Versailles system was the growing tendency of Great Britain and France to violate pledges to observe the open door in the mandates. In a note to the British Foreign Office on July 26, 1920, Colby stated the "opinion of this Government that the treatment of the economic resources of the regions which will be held under mandate by Great Britain or other nations involves a question of principle transcending in importance questions relating merely to the commercial competition of private interests or to control for strategic purposes of any particular raw material." The mandate principle, Colby argued, "was formulated for the purpose of removing in the future some of the principle causes of international differences."[20]

In an aide memoire to Secretary General of the French Foreign Office Paleologue on August 7, 1920, Leland Harrison, American Chargé in France, insisted that the United States had consistently taken "the position that the future peace of the world required that as a general principle any alien territory which should be acquired by the Allied

18. Davis to Colby, June 3, 1920, *Foreign Relations*, 1920, II, 393.
19. Colby to Wallace, February 21, 1921, *Foreign Relations*, 1921, I, 90–91.
20. Colby to John W. Davis, American ambassador to Great Britain, July 26, 1920, *Foreign Relations*, 1920, II, 658–59.

Powers pursuant to the Treaties of Peace with the central powers must be held and governed in such a way as to assure equal treatment in law and in fact to the commerce of all nations."[21] Colby and Harrison were both protesting the San Remo Agreement, made between Great Britain and France on April 24, 1920, which divided the oil resources of former German and Turkish colonies, as well as similar resources in Rumania and Russia.[22] The disposition of mandates, procrastination in settlement of war debts, an unreasonable attitude toward reparations, and violations of the open door stimulated a growing disenchantment with the Versailles system on the part of the Wilson Administration. But English and French violations of the open door were thought to threaten the foundations of future peace, and therefore were of primary significance in leading the Administration to revise its attitude toward Versailles.

Sometime between November 1920 and March 1921, Wilson ordered withdrawal from any participation in both the Allied Powers Council of Ambassadors and the Reparations Commission. The cause of withdrawal was twofold: the failure of the Senate to ratify the Versailles Treaty, and the confirmation of this decision in the November elections, making United States participation in agencies for enforcement of the treaty ambiguous; and second, the growing belief of Colby and Wilson that in "all questions where we [the United States] are accorded a voice the allies show an increasing tendency to ignore our views, as for instance in regard to the ex-German cables, mandates etc., and only consult our views in cases where they look to us for assistance."[23]

21. Leland Harrison to Secretary General of the French Foreign Office, August 7, 1920, *Foreign Relations*, 1920, II, 668.
22. John W. Davis to Colby, April 26, 1920, *Foreign Relations*, 1920, II, 655–58.
23. Colby to Wallace, February 10, 1921, 462.00 R29/420.

With the exception of the question of American participation in the League the continuity in United States foreign policy objectives was confirmed by the instructions of the new Secretary of State, Charles Evan Hughes. Wallace, America's unofficial representative to the Reparations Commission, was told to resume his attendance and to report on decisions affecting the United States while at the same time taking care not to commit the United States.[24]

Four days later, on May 11, 1921, Hughes appointed George Harvey as unofficial United States representative on the Allied Supreme Council. Harvey was ordered to stay out of matters which were of distinct European political concern but to take part in discussions of world-wide importance. To guide Harvey, Hughes informed him that

This government is interested in economic questions growing out of the war. These may relate either to our trade directly or to economic adjustments underlying the recuperation of Europe and therefore affect the prosperity of the United States. The influence of this government should be exerted through you (1) toward effecting economic settlements which will as far as possible promote restoration of normal activities and will encourage the utmost national endeavor without providing escape from just obligations; (2) toward effective recognition of the open door policy of equal commercial opportunity. Conversely the United States maintains its traditional policy in political matters of purely European concern, and must not become involved.[25]

Like Colby, Hughes insisted on the open door and thought that European reconstruction should be dealt with on an economic basis.

With the advent of the new Administration, the European countries, led by Great Britain, resumed their campaign to involve the United States in a conference to adopt a program

24. Hughes to Wallace, May 7, 1921, 763.72119/11130a.
25. Hughes to Harvey, May 11, 1921, 763.72119/135a.

of reconstruction which would place political limitations on the economic open door approach of the United States. Their first move came during a meeting of the Supreme Council in Cannes in December 1921. The Council decided to hold a conference of an "economic and financial character" at Genoa early in 1922. The Allies, Russia, and the belligerents (Germany, Austria-Hungary, and Bulgaria) were to participate. The Cannes program differed significantly from Brussels in that Russia was invited. The conference call rested on several assumptions, the most important of which was the recognition, after three years, that it was difficult to rebuild Western Europe without the development of Eastern European and Russian resources. The Allied Supreme Council, under British leadership, tried to lay down principles whereby trade relations with Russia could be resumed, and under which credits could be extended to Russia. From the British point of view the crux of the problem was the fear of western investors to put their capital in Russia because of nationalization and confiscation of private property. Resolutions were framed which recognized both the right of nationalization *and* compensation, in order to lay a basis for new credits to Russia.[26]

The British policy toward the reconstruction of Russia was based on the concept, more or less fully developed, that the British should lead the process. The Anglo-Soviet agreement of 1921, framed by Lloyd George, was designed to obtain for England first place in Russian development. The combined effort of British policy, and of its private investment trusts and the Royal Dutch Shell combine, was to block the application of the open door to Russia. The instrument chosen to bring about a program of special concessions was the government-sponsored consortium managed by the

26. Hughes to Harvey (instructions), December 27, 1921, 763.72119/11714; Harvey to Hughes, January 6, 1922, 550.E1/4.

British government and joined by France, Belgium, Canada, Holland, Sweden, Norway, Switzerland, Spain, and Denmark.[27] The largest amount of the capital for the consortium

27. As I have pointed out earlier in the text and in note 11 of this chapter, the British (and European nations generally) were in desperate straits with regard to raw material supplies. If they could control the reconstruction of Russia, and relegate America to second place in the process, they could solve their raw material and foreign exchange problems. At a "Meeting of the Heads of Delegations of the British, French, and Italian Governments," in Paris on January 14, 1920, the chiefs of state of the main Allies discussed "Commercial Policy in Russia," on the basis of a memorandum entitled "Economic Aspects of British Policy concerning Russia," prepared by E. F. Wise, a British member of the Supreme Economic Council. After pointing to the very heavy prewar dependence of western Europe on Russian supplies of food and industrial raw materials, Wise explained that the

> cut off [of] these vast supplies from the rest of the world . . . are one of the main causes of high world prices. Europe has been forced to get her breadstuffs and her fats from America at American prices or to starve. . . . The news of substantial exports from Russia would not only bring prices down but might also have the other desirable effect of making the American Government anxious as to a market for some of its surplus and, consequently, much more prepared to supply Europe even on credit. . . . Broadly the opening of Russia to trade would go further than any other factor to reduce the cost of living, to put right the American exchange, to reduce freights, and to ease the general shipping situation. . . . From a purely British trading point of view there can be no doubt that the longer reopening of trade with Russia is delayed the more formidable will be German and American competition. . . .

At the same meeting, Lloyd George argued that the Allies set up a committee (headed by Wise) to outline a specific program. But the British prime minister was careful to note that, "it was no use to go to the United States of America, as this would only increase the difficulty as regards exchanges, and, if possible, the matter should be arranged without them. . . ." Signor Nitti said, "he would accept the whole of Mr. Lloyd-George's proposals . . . Mr. Clemenceau said he was also in agreement." This account is taken from *British Documents*, 1st ser., II, 867–75, 894–96, 898–99. The projected consortium membership was described in Federal Reserve Board, *Federal Reserve Bulletin*, May 1922, 549. (Hereafter cited as Federal Reserve *Bulletin*.)

(International Financial Corporation) was to come from
British government sources. The Trade Facilities Act provided some £20 million.[28] In addition another £15 million,
the unused portion of those funds set aside by Parliament for
the Export Credit Guarantees Department, was available.
More funds could also be obtained if needed. The managers
of the consortium provided carefully that the capital would
be lent to entrepreneurs of the lending countries for investment in Russia, and not to the Soviet government.

United States suspicion of the projected Genoa Conference was aroused when Lloyd George expressed the hope
that the prime ministers of all countries involved would
attend the conference,[29] in this way giving a subtle political
twist to a conference billed as "economic and financial."
Hughes did not receive the official invitation to the conference until January 16, 1922, when the Italian Foreign Minister, Count Ricci, urged United States participation.[30]
Hughes was aware that the principal European Allies
wanted the United States to attend unofficially. Before January 12, however, the still-accredited ambassador of the non-
Bolshevik Russian government in the United States had an
interview with Assistant Secretary of State Fred M. Dearing, during which he argued that the Genoa Conference
was, despite Allied denial, based on principles contrary to
Hughes' declaration of March 25, 1921, that reconstruction
of Russia could take place only on the basis of the open door.
The White Russian ambassador argued that there was a
great danger "that Lenin may give wholesale concessions as
has been done in China. A succeeding government [to the

28. Federal Reserve *Bulletin*, 550; Leo Paslovsky and Harold G.
Moulton, *Russian Debts and Russian Reconstruction*, 1st ed. (New York,
1924), 167–69.
29. Harvey to Hughes, January 6, 1922, 550.E1/4.
30. Count Ricci to Hughes, January 16, 1922, 550.E1/9.

Bolsheviks] would naturally oppose these concessions. It will, therefore, be in the interest of the Powers benefitting from the concessions . . . to keep the Bolshevik Government in power." The ambassador was apparently afraid that Lenin would apply the New Economic Policy in a manner which would feed the Allied desire for concessions.[31]

A few days later the United States Consul General in London, Robert P. Skinner, had an off-the-record talk with Leonid Krassin, the Soviet representative in England. Krassin indicated that Lloyd George had promised the Soviets diplomatic recognition as a result of Genoa. In addition, he stated that Russian oil lands would definitely not be returned to their prerevolutionary owners. As a way of meeting the claims of the original owners, Krassin offered the tempting plum of a grant of oil lands to a consortium of foreign firms. At the same time, he carefully indicated that Soviet authorities preferred the concessionaires to be Americans. The new American operators could then reimburse former holders with shares in the consortium.[32] Skinner's conversation with Krassin confirmed the analysis of the Russian ambassador in the United States.

The tactics Krassin and the Soviet representatives adopted in response to Genoa appeared to be based on a misconception of United States policy. To the Soviets, the objective of the State Department appeared to be an American share in the exploitation of Russian oil fields. This explains Krassin's attempt to interest a consortium of foreign firms in accepting concessions from the Soviet government to develop the oil fields, previously owned by the French Nobel Group and Standard Oil of New Jersey. If an

31. Dearing to Hughes, January 12, 1922, *Foreign Relations*, 1922, II, 386–87.
32. Consul General in London Robert P. Skinner, to Hughes, January 20, 1922, 861.01/367.

American-led group could be induced to develop these properties the American State Department would be forced into a position of neutrality between Standard and the American members of the projected consortium. If State Department policy had been simply to acquire concessions for American firms, then the last major obstacle between the Soviets and western recognition of the Russian right to nationalize would have been removed.

The Soviets were correct in assuming the State Department was interested in American participation in exploitation of Russian oil resources. But they failed to understand the American effort to generalize the open door as the underlying principle governing the economic development of Russia (as well as China). If Hughes failed to protect the vested rights of Standard of New Jersey in Russia, A. C. Bedford (Chairman of the Board, Jersey Standard) argued, "such treatment of private property in any one country would be a dangerous precedent with regard to the treatment of foreign owned property in some other countries."[33] Clearly, failure to defend the Standard-Nobel claims would encourage underdeveloped nations to grant special concessions as a means of obtaining economic development, and in this way undermine the open door. In this respect Standard's battle to protect its vested rights played a key role in Hughes' effort to obtain general recognition of the open door as the principle governing the economic development of Russia.

On January 30, 1922, Richard Washburn Child, American Ambassador to Italy, indicated to Hughes that the rest of Europe was cooling toward Genoa, that the Europeans were beginning to feel as the United States did—that the time for political meetings had not yet arrived. He urged

33. Bedford to Hughes, May 5, 1922, *Foreign Relations*, 1922, II, 786–88.

Hughes to decline participation.[34] Hughes based his refusal to participate (announced on March 8) on the grounds that the conference was not primarily an economic one but was instead of "a political character." At the same time, he said, "nothing should be done . . . looking to the obtaining of economic advantages which would impair the just opportunities of others. . . ." Equal opportunity should be preserved in Russia in the interests of the Russians and all other powers.[35]

In his report on the first day of the conference, Child confirmed some of Hughes' worst fears. Russia was attempting to lay the basis for separate commercial agreements with the various powers. British policy was aimed at securing some kind of overall economic agreement with the Soviets, while the French were trying to block such an agreement. Lloyd George blamed conference difficulties on the absence of the United States.[36] On April 24, Child reported to Hughes that if the conference failed to reach agreement with the Russians, various countries would scramble to make separate commercial and diplomatic agreements similar to those made at Rapallo, where the foreign property question was simply set aside and the Soviets obtained diplomatic and trade relations without settlement with foreign investors.[37]

The German-Soviet agreement of 1922 (Rapallo), though it did not provide for a massive flow of German investment, did make available to the Soviets a large part of the second most advanced fund of technology in the western world. Long-term German investment in Soviet industry was quantitatively small, but credits extended by firms with advanced technology such as Krupp, and the technology

34. Child to Hughes, January 30, 1922, 551.E1/23.
35. Hughes to Child, March 8, 1922, 550.E1/78a.
36. Child to Hughes, April 11, 1922, 550.E1/183.
37. Child to Hughes, April 24, 1922, 711.61/60.

introduced into Russia by means of German-Soviet mixed companies,[38] relieved the Soviets (perhaps decisively) of the need to moderate their position on the right to nationalize foreign investments. This acquisition of German technology during the Genoa Conference undermined Hughes' effort to defend vested rights and the American attempt to apply the open door to Russia. In similar fashion, as Child hinted to Hughes, Rapallo applied pressure on the British to make terms with the Soviet policy of nationalization.[39] Indeed, by the end of April, rumors of just such British moves spread from Genoa to the United States.

Hughes instructed Child on May 2, 1922, to investigate the *New York Times* story that a special agreement between Royal Dutch Shell and the Soviet governnment granted the British a large concession in Russia.[40] Child replied the same day that the British representatives at Genoa assured him that no negotiations had taken place between the British government (or the British-government-controlled Anglo-Persian Oil Company) and the Soviet government. At the same time, however, French and German diplomatic sources indicated that a contract had been signed between Royal Dutch Shell and the Soviet government giving Shell a monopoly on the sale of all exported Soviet oil. Child expressed the view that such an agreement endangered the value of the Standard-Nobel investments in Russia.[41] Bedford of Jersey Standard, in his protest to the State Department on May 5, demanded that the United States protest the British-Russian negotiations. Fair and equal opportunity should be observed

38. Edward Hallett Carr, *German Soviet Relations Between the Two Wars, 1919–1939* (Baltimore, 1951), 54–55.
39. Child to Hughes, April 24, 1922, 711.61/60.
40. Hughes to Child, May 2, 1922, 861.6363/52a.
41. Child to Hughes (telegram), May 2, 1922, 550.E/230.

by all, he maintained. Bedford also referred worriedly to the Italian-Turkish and San Remo agreements.[42]

Before the Genoa Conference the British government, which temporarily controlled the Turkish Petroleum Company, redistributed the stock of that firm. This was significant because the only proved oil resources in Mesopotamia were in the hands of the Turkish Petroleum Company. Before World War I, Turkish Petroleum was a joint venture: 75 percent of the firm was held by British private interests, the remaining 25 percent by the Deutsche Bank. In the scramble for German foreign investments after the war the British took advantage of their control of the firm to redistribute the Deutsche Bank stock to the French oil monopoly, Campagnare Des Petroles France, without consulting the United States and without reference to their pledge to maintain the open door in the mandates. This deal was sealed at San Remo, Italy, on April 24, 1920.[43] Though signed in 1920, the San Remo Agreement was not immediately and everywhere implemented. The division of Mesopotamian oil resources between the French and the British did not take place until early 1922, even though it was a consequence of the San Remo Agreement (which in turn was a partial implementation of the decision taken at the Paris Economic Conference of 1916 to reserve important raw materials to the Allies at the end of the war). San Remo, and the French-British Mesopotamian oil agreement of 1922, were applications of the principles of special concession and trade preferences. The United States recognized the implications of the Anglo-French oil agreement and on February 27,

42. Bedford to Dearing and Hughes, May 5, 1922, *Foreign Relations*, 1922, II, 787–88.
43. The text of the San Remo Agreement is printed in *Foreign Relations*, 1920, II, 655–58.

1922, Acting Secretary of State Henry P. Fletcher informed British Ambassador to the United States Sir Auckland Geddes that the United States refused to recognize San Remo to the extent that it applied "to the disposition of economic opportunities in mandate territories."[44]

The oil conflict was important to the profitability of oil, and to the issues of strategic import, but the conditions of its development were even more important as a symbol of the kind of world economic development which was finally to emerge out of the war. The two kinds of economic development possible were either development based on the closed door of special privilege concession or development based on the open door of equal opportunity. In response to United States accusations that the British were closing the door on the oil resources in the British, French, and Dutch Empires, Lord Curzon on April 21, 1921, made an evasive denial, followed closely by the defense that "even if such a policy was in force it would surely not be difficult to find arguments in its favor in view of the very serious position of the British Empire as regards petroleum supplies."[45]

San Remo, the Anglo-Persian agreements, British oil diplomacy in Mexico, and the restriction of opportunity within the Empire were all part of a trend to place the oil resources of the world under British management. But the British neither desired nor found it possible to exclude American capital from the exploitation of the world's oil fields. The plain fact was (as Hoover was fond of saying) that the general development of world markets—and, by implication, the specific development of oil markets—were dependent on the overseas investment of United States capital. As early as April 13, 1921, a year before Genoa and two years after the oil war had begun, British oil interests put forth a

44. U.S. Senate, *Oil Concessions in Foreign Countries*, 53–54.
45. *Ibid.*, 25–30.

scheme to make use of American capital while at the same time retaining British control of the management of the industry. A. R. Ledoux, a figure who operated on the fringes of the oil industry, tried to convince the State Department of the benefits to be derived from such a program:

Prominent bankers and people close to the present British government assured me that Great Britain is ready to modify its rules for the cooperation or investment by American corporations in British Oil fields, their ideals being that the United States by direct investment in British controlled or British government controlled oil corporations, should become shareholders in them just as France has become . . . in Mesopotamia, and in the Anglo-Persian shares; that just as Great Britain controls the Suez canal by holding the majority of the stock in the canal corporation, so France and America might join in official investment with Great Britain in these British controlled Oil corporations.[46]

Hughes and the State Department remained unimpressed, and continued to work for British recognition of the open door in Russia—and for all economic development, not just for oil development.

The British played their trump card at Genoa on May 5, 1922, in an attempt to force American agreement to the British consortium approach for the revival of Russia. Lloyd George told Child that if the overall approach at Genoa failed there would be a rush by private interests, including the British groups, to make separate private or "national" agreements with the Russians for the development of Russian resources.[47] On the same day Child sent a second confidential message to Hughes in which he indicated the more general scope of British aims at Genoa, of which the oil consortium was only a small, symbolic part:[48]

46. A. R. Ledoux to Dearing, April 13, 1921, 800.6363/255.
47. Child to Hughes, May 5, 1922, 550.E1/250.
48. Child to Hughes (confidential), May 5, 1922, 800.51/325; Grant Smith, Budapest, Hungary, to Dearing, April 18, 1922, 800.51/324.

I desire to emphasize that all information gleaned here over conference pending treaty discloses interesting secret British delegation viewpoint and purpose. It is to manage so far as possible the process and capture the profits and trade on products and influence investments or credits we may make in Europe leaving us the bare interest rates. Nations such as Germany and Italy desire to act as commercial agents or in joint enterprises, as for instance in future development of Russia, in distinction from the British who unquestionably regard us as gullible enough to be anxious to put our gold surplus out through British controlled pipe lines as are owned or may be procurred by treaties concessions or international conferences such as this.

By May 5, therefore, Hughes was confronted with a serious dilemma. The United States had been partly successful in foiling a settlement with the Russians which recognized the right of the Soviets to nationalize, a feat accomplished by adroit use of the French and Belgian delegations at Genoa. If the principle of restitution (rather than compensation) was the basis of reopening economic relations with Russia, then the large French-Belgian investments in Russia would rise in value, and the deals to get concessions out of the property nationalized by the Soviets would be denied to British interests. In reply to the invitation to attend the conference the Soviets had promised to restore private property to former owners or, "in the event of that being impossible," to negotiate on compensation for nationalized foreign investments. Except for the French and Belgian delegations, which demanded restoration of private property to foreign investors, the Allies were willing to accept long-term leases in place of the restoration of prewar investments. The French and Belgians were able to force modifications in the language of the Allied counter-proposal to the Russians. When the memorandum was submitted to the Russians on May 11, it provided that "in cases where it is impossible for the Russians to return property to the former owners," the

Soviets would agree not to "dispose of it to third parties." This change provided that if in the future nationalized property was to be disposed of, "preference [would] be given to former owners."[49] The most significant change was that which left the question of restitution versus compensation to be decided by a mixed tribunal of four westerners and one Russian.[50] These changes provided for recognition of prewar property rights consistent with the American position, and at the same time conceded to the Soviets a limited right to nationalize some foreign property.

The Soviets rejected the changes as both an impairment of their sovereignty and as a threat to a system of socialist ownership in Russia.[51] Thus the consortium was defeated and the Anglo-Soviet Trade Agreement of 1921 was virtually nullified. The day before the Soviets rejected the revisions, Child told the British and French that these revisions still did not adequately protect private property rights.[52] His aim was to provide additional insurance in the event the Russians accepted the revisions.

After he had defeated the overt attempt at the "consortium development" of Russia, Hughes next had to fend off Lloyd George's threat of private concessions. He instructed

49. "The Genoa Conference," Federal Reserve *Bulletin*, May 1922, 550.

50. Command Documents 1667 and 1724 of 1922, the texts of the respective Allied and Russian proposals, are printed in an appendix to Paslovsky and Moulton, *Russian Debts and Reconstruction*. See also Bedford to Hughes, May 5, 1922, in *Foreign Relations*, 1922, II, 787. Bedford suggests to Hughes that the United States join the French and Belgians in protesting the British effort to compromise with the Russians on the key issue of the Soviet right to nationalize. It is highly likely that Hughes had some informal arrangement with the French along lines suggested by Bedford.

51. Child to Hughes, May 12, 1922, 550.e1/316. See also Command Document 1667 of 1922 in Paslovsky and Moulton, *Russian Debts and Reconstruction*, Appendix.

52. Child to Hughes, May 10, 1922, 550.E1/260.

Child to intimate to the British that if the conference proved
to be a failure, the United States might be willing to negotiate, if necessary, in order to forestall private deals with the
Soviets by private interests at the conference.[53] This had the
desired effect. The British asked Hughes whether the
United States would attend a new conference if the Allies
promised to call upon the Russians only for information, and
if no separate agreements were signed during the interlude
between the two conferences.[54] Once Lloyd George was
hooked, Hughes began to hedge. We would consider attend-
ing, he said, if the projected meeting was made up of economic experts only, if these experts would deal with the
economic situation and nothing else, if its decisions were
taken as merely advisory, and if the pledge of no separate
agreements with the Russians was kept.[55] The next day
Child was instructed to issue an American declaration
against separate agreements already made public by the
Allied Powers.[56] This last was a direct blow at the British
position embodied in the Anglo-Soviet Trade Agreement
of 1921, which accepted the principle of state trading; it also
struck at the specific Royal Dutch Shell-Russian agreement
to market oil from the nationalized wells in Russia.[57]

After frustrating the consortium and calling into question
private concessions, Hughes moved to obliterate the British
position by refusing to participate in the Hague meeting on
the grounds that the Allied response to Russian objections
to Allied demands on nationalization meant that the proposed
conference would end in failure.[58] Later that day Hughes

53. Hughes to Child, May 11, 1922, 550.E1/250.
54. Child to Hughes, May 14, 1922, 550.E1/Russia—: Telegram.
55. Hughes to Child, May 14, 1922, 550.E1/—: Telegram.
56. Hughes to Child, May 14, 1922, 550.E1/Russia/4: Telegram.
57. U.S. Senate, *Oil Concessions in Foreign Countries*, 17.
58. Hughes to Child, May 15, 1922, 550.E1/Russia; Hughes to Child
(telegram), May 17, 1922, 550.E1/9b.

amplified his reasons for refusing to attend the Hague Conference. He argued that the Hague, like Genoa, would become a political meeting, since the Russians were planning to propagandize for a large loan. An economic study was needed, he said, and political questions should be subordinated to it. But even before anything practical could be done about the study, Hughes maintained, the Russians would have to withdraw their objection to Allied demands on nationalization.[59]

Hughes won a signal victory. The British-favored consortium was defeated and Lloyd George was forced to join in a statement with the other Allies maintaining that private agreements with the Soviet government involving nationalized property of foreigners should be banned. All this was accomplished by the Secretary's first hinting that the United States would attend the Hague, and then refusing to do so. The United States now struck out on a policy of its own, a policy largely at variance with England's.

The United States, Britain, and the other European Allies agreed that European economic life should be reactivated, and that effective reconstruction of Western Europe was dependent on the reactivation of the German economy. German industry was in turn dependent on the reopening of Russian trade with Central Europe. Yet before Russia could export it had to produce, and as a result of the war and the revolution it needed an influx of foreign capital before production could be resumed.[60] The conditions under which this capital should be invested were the fundamental issues discussed at Genoa, and later at the Hague. Child's insistent pressure at Genoa for the open door (American observers at Genoa were fond of saying, "Child could not vote but he

59. Hughes to Child, May 17, 1922, 550.E1/Russia/9b.
60. Paslovsky and Moulton, *Russian Debts and Reconstruction*, 5–6.

could veto") destroyed any chance for the success of the British scheme.[61]

American policy on Russian reconstruction was based on the premises that any effort to bring Russia into the economic life of Europe should be based on equal opportunity, and that the open door could function only under conditions of economic security for investors. The net effect of Hughes' position was that Russian reconstruction had either to await the fall of the Soviet government, or proceed under the Soviet government under very different circumstances. Hughes, Hoover, and Harding were firmly convinced that the Soviet system could not last. They felt that when the proper time for reconstruction of Russia came it should be based on American-managed penetration. Hoover developed the policy based on the concept that "permanent American foreign commerce can never be based upon the reshipment of goods at the hands of other nationalities. The hope of our commerce lies in the establishment of American firms abroad, distributing American goods under American direction: in the building of direct American financing abroad and, above all, in the installation of American technology in Russian industries. . . ."[62] With only minor differences, such as his abortive attempt to work out a joint system with German business for the penetration of Russia in 1921, Hughes adhered to the policy worked out by Hoover.[63]

After the failure of Genoa, but before the Hague meeting, the French ambassador to the United States proposed that

61. E. H. Davenport and Sidney Russell Cooke, *The Oil Trusts and Anglo-American Relations* (New York, 1924), 148. While true that the authors overstate their case, it is nonetheless apparent that the United States unofficial representative was in a position to veto, for the simple reason that any decision at Genoa was dependent on American credit; at the very least, United States credit to Germany.

62. Hoover to Hughes, December 1, 1921, 661.6215/1a.

63. *Ibid.*

France and the United States join in suggesting a meeting of an economic committee of experts to develop a program for the reconstruction of Russia.[64] Hughes replied the following day with a polite but firm refusal. Such a proposal, said Hughes, might be construed as an attempt to thwart the forthcoming Hague Conference. If the European powers wished to adopt new proposals which fell into line with the American position they could do so; "the American government stood upon the suggestions which it had made." On the other hand, Hughes said, it was "quite competent for France, in the light of the American suggestion, and the inability of [the United States] government to be represented at the Hague to take the matter up with the British Government, the Italian Government, or other Governments to see what, if any, change in the proposed plan was desired. . . ."[65]

When the Hague meeting took place in July 1922, the Belgian and French delegations were able to force on the British a declaration that none of the governments at the Hague would render assistance to any private interests trying to obtain concessions which involved nationalized or confiscated foreign property in Russia. This pressure was applied with the encouragement of the United States after the Soviets and the European powers were unable to reach agreement on the question of restitution versus compensation.[66] While this declaration was agreed to at the government level, "big private interests," especially British, Dutch, and Scandinavian, were nevertheless negotiating for concessions.[67] All but the British delegate, who hesitated to sub-

64. Jusserand to Hughes, May 26, 1922, 550.E1/Russia/22½.
65. Memorandum of conversation of Hughes with Jusserand, May 27, 1922, 550.E1/Russia/24½.
66. U.S. Chargé in Hague Louis Sussdorff to Hughes (telegram), July 13, 1922, 550.E1/Russia/58.
67. *Ibid.;* Sussdorff to Hughes, July 14, 1922, 550.E1/Russia/59.

scribe, agreed to the declaration.[68] He finally agreed after forcing the use of very specific language in order not to affect adversely the oil marketing agreement that was concluded.[69] The American Ambassador to the Netherlands, Louis Sussdorff, maintained that although the statement would not prevent special deals with the Soviet government, it would act as a deterrent to such deals.[70] The United States was still unwilling to associate itself in any way with the decisions of the Hague Conference. Hughes maintained in August 1922 that the United States stood on its open door statement of March 25, 1921.[71]

After the halfhearted British attempt at the Hague was defeated, Hoover asked Hughes if he was "inclined to favor sending a strong technical mission to Russia to study the economic situation." The primary purpose of such a mission, he said, would be to determine what purpose America could serve in the regeneration of the Russian economy.[72] Hughes immediately agreed:

In view of the failure of the powers to accomplish anything of great importance at Genoa and The Hague, and on the assumption that an international expert commission would not be permitted to conduct such an investigation in Russia, the opportunity seems to be ours and we should take such action as would dispel the notion that we are indifferent, and, on the other hand, should encourage the view that we are proceeding carefully to find out the facts and shape our policy in accordance with them. . . .[73]

68. Fletcher, ambassador to Belgium, to Hughes, July 15, 1922, 550.E1/Russia/60.
69. Sussdorff to Hughes, July 27, 1922, 550.E1/Russia/69.
70. *Ibid.*
71. Hughes to H. L. Fletcher (telegram), August 17, 1922, 550.E1/Russia/68.
72. Hoover to Hughes, July 14, 1922, *Foreign Relations*, 1922, II, 825–26.
73. Hughes to Hoover, July 15, 1922, *Foreign Relations*, 1922, II, 826.

Hughes promptly began to make arrangements to exploit the opportunity offered the United States.

Hughes asked Alanson Houghton, United States Ambassador in Germany, to make certain that an international commission of experts was *not* welcome, "in view of the practical failure of the negotiations at Genoa and The Hague." If such a commission was not welcome, then the United States had the opportunity to determine what can be done in a business way to improve economic conditions in Russia." Houghton was first to "try to make sure that the Soviet authorities will not admit an international commission and then suggest that possibly the American government might consider sending such a commission . . . if the necessary facilities were offered." The commission was to "consist of real experts representing agricultural, industrial, transportation and other activities."[74]

The Soviets began to see the growing American interest as a way to bring about a change in the American open door position outlined in the note of March 25, 1921. Houghton warned the State Department that such might be the result of the United States request to send in a committee of economic experts. The Russians tried to convert the proposal for a unilateral visit to Russia into a bilateral exchange of trade delegations. To help their cause, the Soviets began to issue statements to the press indicating a hinted change in the United States position on recognition of Soviet Russia. The State Department ended the discussion by a public announcement that the Soviet refusal terminated the discussion.[75]

74. Hughes to Houghton, July 24, 1922, *Foreign Relations*, 1922, II, 826–27.
75. Houghton to Acting Secretary William Phillips, September 16, 1922, *Foreign Relations*, 1922, II, 832–34; Houghton to Hughes, July 28, 1922, *ibid.*, 827–29.

By September 16, 1922, the three positions, American, British, and Soviet, were in mutual deadlock. This situation had been brought about by the United States. The Soviets were in no position to force any nation to do anything. They played from weakness. The British position was not so obviously weak. But Lloyd George could not go ahead with his program for the rehabilitation of Russia without a general settlement of war debts. The loan control machinery of the Commerce and State Departments prevented foreign countries which had not settled their war debts from borrowing capital in New York. Without access to American capital the British attempt to develop Imperial economic resources and to take the lead in the reconstruction of Russia was doomed to failure. But indebtedness was a chain stretching along many lines: one led from Moscow to Berlin, Paris, and Brussels; another from Berlin to London and Paris; a third from Rome, Brussels, and Paris to London; and the main line from London to New York. On the other hand, from the British point of view, reconstruction had to begin before they could settle their war debts.

Russia was thought in 1922 to lay at the heart of reconstruction. The American condition for the reconstruction of Russia was that it be based on the open door. America wielded the war debts as a club to insure that the reconstruction of Russia, when it came, would proceed on the open door principle. By the end of 1922 the British had not only surrendered on the projected "Chinese," or sphere-of-influence solution for Russia, they had also agreed to compromise with United States' demands in the Middle East. Paraphrasing the report by Child and Joseph G. Grew on the Lausanne Conference, Hughes told Harding on November 25, 1922 that "the British began to abandon any moves toward zones, concessions and special privileges and were now prepared to support at the conference [the] open door policy in the Near East."[76] Using an intricately complicated procedure, the State and Commerce Departments combined had opened the door to the possibility of commerce in Russia and the Near East on American terms. The essential tool they used was the unofficial but real control of American private capital issues for foreign investment.

76. Hughes to Harding, November 25, 1922, Charles Evans Hughes Manuscripts, Manuscript Division, Library of Congress, Washington, D.C., Letters, 1921–1925.

CHAPTER VII

Loan Control: Hoover's Program to Stabilize the World for Investment

THE ORIGIN of the government's policy of controlling foreign investment was imbedded in the attempt by the United States to win general recognition of the open door in China. When Woodrow Wilson withdrew government support from the bankers' participation in the first China Consortium in 1913, he was attempting to use the flow of American capital to prevent the European and Japanese spheres of influence from evolving into colonial possessions. Wilson and Bryan were simply continuing by other means the attempt by Taft and Knox to shore up Chinese nationalism. When Wilson withdrew backing from the prewar consortium he was not withdrawing from China; rather, he was trying to gain a better position for American interests by obtaining recognition of the open door.[1]

1. Herbert Feis, *Europe the World's Banker, 1870–1914* (New Haven, 1930), 441–56. According to Feis, "The preceeding haggling created in the mind of the American State Department mistrust of the situation created by the Consortium loan. See *Foreign Relations of the United States*, 1913, pp. 164 *et seq*." (Quoted from p. 449, footnote 37.) Feis shows that Wilson's break with the past American position on the Consortium was not an abrupt departure, but in accord with the later trend under Taft.

Because of British and French capital shortages, the Wilson Administration found an opportunity to push for the open door when, in January 1917, Japanese, British, and French bankers invited (with the approval of their governments) "the American Group to resume its participation or to designate other American financial organization to succeed to its rights" in the old consortium.[2] In addition, the Administration was considering a recommendation by American Minister to China Paul Reinsch that the United States extend a government loan to the government of China.[3] Reinsch's suggestion was discarded because, in Treasury Secretary McAdoo's view, "commitments to European countries and . . . [financial] needs in America were such as to make a loan to China then [in the fall of 1917] impracticable."[4]

Reinsch then proposed in November 1917 that the United States accept the offer to resume participation in the consortium. Such an arrangement, Reinsch argued, "would obviate [the] difficulties inseparable from direct participation by our Government."[5] Lansing agreed with Reinsch and began arrangements to organize a new American consortium group.[6] Although no formal record appears in the State Department files, as soon as the Administration began to organize a new group, it began to control capital issues. For example, G. M. Gest, Vice-president of Lee, Higginson and Company, an

2. Paul Reinsch to Robert Lansing, November 2, 1917, U.S. Department of State, *Papers Relating to the Foreign Relations of the United States*, 1917, 29 vols. (Washington, 1925–1944), 152–53. (Hereafter cited as *Foreign Relations*.)

3. Reinsch to Lansing, August 31, 1917, Lansing to Reinsch, September 7, 1917, *ibid.*, 194–95.

4. Lansing to Wilson, June 20, 1918, *Foreign Relations*, 1918, 169–70.

5. Reinsch to Lansing, November 2, 1917, *Foreign Relations*, 1917, 152–53.

6. *Ibid.*, 153.

investment banking firm, inquired of Lansing on December 17, 1917, whether or not the Administration objected to a projected loan by that firm to the Chinese government. Lansing replied on the same day that "in so far as the State Department was concerned the loan seemed to be desirable," and that the Treasury Department also "had no objection."[7]

In seeking approval from Wilson for the reentry of American bankers into the consortium, Lansing, on June 20, 1918, outlined three projects in which he thought it was "very advisable to have American financiers interested." Japanese interests, he reported, were negotiating a loan with the Chinese wine and tobacco tax as security. The Japanese were using the loan to secure "control of the whole tobacco and wine industry of China—its manufacture, production and sale." American participation in the consortium, he inferred, could block this move. Second, Lansing pointed out that American participation would enable the bankers to obtain control of the British-contracted railroad from Canton to Hankow. The British and French interests involved in the road were in desperate need of finance to complete the line. If assistance were rendered, Lansing thought, the British and French interests would be willing to turn control of the road over to the Americans. But more important, the British and French governments "would because of such aid, be likely to withdraw their claims to the spheres of influence in the regions affected." Third, and finally, the Chinese government was seeking a loan for currency reform. This loan had to "be made with the old consortium from which the American group withdrew." Since the British and French did not have the capital, this left Japanese capital "in control." The results would be that "unless we are able to participate Japan can and probably will proceed alone with this large

7. Lansing to Gest, Gest to Lansing, December 17, 1917, *ibid.*, 157–58.

and important loan."[8] Lansing's brief won Wilson's approval with the reservation that "everything necessary would be done to protect the Chinese Government against such unconscionable arrangements as were contemplated by the former consortium."[9]

More important in determining Wilson's adherence to the new consortium than the immediate advantages Lansing cited was the fact that the capital shortage the British and the French were suffering would make them subject to additional United States pressures to support a wider open door approach to China. Under the prewar consortium the Russians and Japanese had sphere arrangements with respect to Manchuria, and could use their votes within the consortium to protect positions won by means of such agreements. Both Russia and Germany were out of the new consortium, and France and Britain were reduced to a level of financial dependency on the United States. On most questions within the four-power group the United States would now have a three-to-one vote controlling Japan. Because the new consortium would be supplying loans to China, with the United States effectively setting the conditions upon which the loans would be made, Japan would be denied any economic leverage to press for exclusive concessions from China. The United States would in practice be the major foreign political influence on the Chinese government.

When in July 1918 the bankers accepted the Administration's proposal that they participate in the new consortium they suggested that "one of the conditions of membership in such a four-power group should be . . . a relinquishment by the members of the group either to China or to the group of any options to make loans which they now hold, and all

8. Lansing to Wilson, June 20, 1918, *Foreign Relations*, 1918, 169–71.
9. *Ibid.*, 171.

loans to China by any of them should be considered as four-power business. Through cooperation of England, France, Japan and the United States," the bankers pointed out, "much can be accomplished for the maintenance of Chinese sovereignty and the preservation of the open door."[10] The next day Lansing accepted the bankers' further condition that the Administration agree to issue a public statement that it had suggested a loan to China on the specific understanding that "the terms and conditions of each loan are submitted to and approved by this Government, and the other cooperating Governments and by the Government of China."[11] In other words, the Administration pledged public support for loans to China if the bankers would make only those loans which the Administration approved. In exchange for the bankers' agreement to accept loan control, Lansing expressed "willingness to take all possible steps to insure the execution of equitable contracts made by its citizens in foreign lands."[12] Though the only foreign country discussed was China, the implication of Lansing's pledge seemed far wider.

For example, on July 1, 1918, Franklin Sands, a vice-president of American International Corporation, proposed to Treasury Secretary McAdoo in regard to Russia that "it might be possible to work out a plan for an Allied non-governmental financial group something on the order of the Six Power or the Four Power Group of China, which under the circumstances would probably be composed of American, British, Japanese and possibly French capital. In order to

10. The American Banking Group to Lansing, July 8, 1918, *ibid.*, 172–73.
11. Lansing to the American Banking Group, July 9, 1918, *ibid.*, 174–75.
12. Lansing to Walter Hines Page, American ambassador to Great Britain, July 11, 1918, *ibid.*, 176–77.

overcome the risk attaching to such an investment even under the direction of governments, it might be advisable to consider the possibility of insuring actual investments in the same manner as war risk insurance is granted now by governments to shippers. I think that it may be necessary to consider some such action in order to overcome the legitimate objections of corporations to the risk attaching to such operations of capital belonging to their stockholders." Acting Secretary of State Frank L. Polk wrote McAdoo July 16, 1918, that "the suggestions of Mr. Sands have been carefully noted and will be given consideration whenever an opportunity occurs to take advantage of them." In August 1919, when the State Department approved a Kidder-Peabody loan to the Kolchak government of Russia, it demonstrated clearly that United States government direction and control of capital investments had indeed been extended to Russia.[13]

The British were the first to recognize that the proposal to pool all rights to lend in China was a powerful offensive weapon to obtain international recognition of the open door. Arthur Balfour, British Secretary of State for Foreign Affairs, in a memorandum of August 14, 1918, informed the American Ambassador to Britain, Walter Hines Page, of the unwillingness of his government to agree to the pooling of industrial as well as administrative loans in the new

13. Sands to McAdoo, July 1, 1918, Assistant Secretary of the Treasury Russell Leffingwell to Lansing, July 5, 1918, Acting Secretary Polk to McAdoo, July 16, 1918, in State Department Files, National Archives, Record Group 59, 861.51/335. (Unless otherwise labeled, decimal number will indicate Record Group 59 in State Department files in National Archives.) The State Department's approval of the Kidder-Peabody Loan to Kolchak is in Lansing to Kidder-Peabody, August 18, 1919, U.S. Senate, *Special Committee on Investigation of the Munitions Industry*, 74th Cong., 2d sess. (Washington, 1936), 9707, 9712. (Hereafter cited as *Munitions Industry Hearings*.)

four-power consortium.[14] Within a month of this communication both Japan and France protested the pooling proposal. All three powers felt the Americans were attempting
to deprive them of the special concessions which they had
secured up to that time. The Japanese Foreign Office
pointed out that pooling of industrial and administrative
loans would "put an end to any financial operations in China
which may be planned by independent [of the consortium]
commercial concerns."[15]

In a memorandum of October 8, 1918, to the British
Chargé, and to the French and Japanese ambassadors, Lansing defended the American position. Each "interested government must necessarily make its own arrangements with
its own national group." The new consortium could not
function properly unless banks in the other national groups
relinquished all options on loans to China "without distinction as to the nature of the options held." The American
government suggested, Lansing said, that "the interested
Governments should by common consent, endeavor to
broaden the membership in the newly formed national
groups that all financial firms in good standing . . . might
be included in the respective groups."[16] British and French
objections were resolved in early 1919 by an agreement that
only those firms participating in the new consortium would
pool their options. To the extent that French and British
bankers refused to join the consortium they formally
blocked the application of the open door to China. Nevertheless, since in practice those two nations had no capital to
lend, only Japanese resistance stood in the way. The State

14. Balfour to Page, August 14, 1918, *Foreign Relations*, 1918,
189–90.
15. Roland Morris, American ambassador to Japan, to Lansing, August 26, 1918, *ibid.*, 191–92.
16. Lansing to the French ambassador and the British chargé, October 8, 1918, *ibid.*, 193–96.

Department therefore concentrated its diplomatic efforts on convincing the Japanese to join the new consortium on the American basis.

To assure the Japanese that the United States was seeking no special position in China, Wilson and Lansing controlled capital exports. This was expressed in the form of exclusive diplomatic support for American banks which were members of the American group. For example, on March 20, 1919, Paul Reinsch telegraphed Acting Secretary of State William Phillips that important Chinese interests proposed the formation of a Chinese-American deposit and industrial bank in cooperation with the International Banking Corporation (a National City Bank affiliate).[17] Phillips reproved Reinsch for allowing the Legation in China to become intimately involved in a private commercial venture which might threaten the proposed consortium and thereby lend credence to the belief that the United States was promoting American enterprise in China "to the exclusion of other nationals."[18] This projected industrial bank was the tag end of a proposal formulated during the period January to November 1917, when the State Department and certain American bankers had considered pursuing an independent American policy in China in open competition with Japan.[19] By discussing this bank with the Chinese two years later, Reinsch was in effect pressing for an independent policy in the face of Japanese stalling. While reproving Reinsch, Phillips did not (as he could have) kill the whole proposal. Instead, he held it in reserve as a means of pressuring Japan to adhere to the new consortium.

Lansing used another projected American investment in

17. Paul Reinsch to William Phillips, March 20, 1919, 893.516/62.
18. Phillips to Reinsch, March 31, 1918, 893.516/62.
19. Reinsch to Lansing, January 10, 1917 and January 13, 1917, Lansing to Reinsch, September 20, 1917, *Foreign Relations*, 1917, 114–15, 142.

China in much the same manner. During the summer of 1919 the Continental and Commercial National Bank of Chicago (known as the Chicago Bank, and a Morgan associate bank) negotiated a $30 million loan to the Chinese government. Japan immediately protested the agreement as a violation of the spirit of the proposed consortium.[20] Lansing responded with a thinly-veiled accusation that Japanese stalling was holding up the consortium, and promised that when and if the consortium was established the loan rights of the Chicago Bank could be taken up by the four powers.[21] The Board of Directors of the Chicago Bank refused to approve the loan, ostensibly because the Chinese government changed the conditions of security. John Jay Abbott, President of the Chicago Bank, notified the Pacific Development Corporation of the demise of the loan; and that group, led by Albert H. Wiggin, Chairman of the Chase National Bank, Galen L. Stone of Hayden Stone and Company, and Edward B. Bruce, immediately tried to save the operation.[22]

Upon receiving news that Pacific was replacing the Chicago Bank, the Japanese government protested again. Lansing responded with a combination of reassurance and pressure on the Japanese to allow implementation of the consortium. The United States had disapproved the loan, he said, but was "loath to interfere with the activities of its citizens abroad unless the consortium should be organized." When the four-power plan went into effect the State Department would give exclusive diplomatic support to the formal American Group and all activity would be channeled through the consortium.[23]

20. Morris to Lansing, October 27, 1919, 893.51/2503.

21. Lansing to Morris, November 11, 1919, 893.51/2503.

22. Chargé in China Charles D. Tenney to Lansing, November 10, 1919, 893.51/2550.

23. Lansing to Morris, December 23, 1919, 893.51/2587.

It was not until December that Lansing became strongly suspicious that Japan was secretly opposed to the implementation of the consortium. Ambassador Reinsch had become convinced the Japanese were trying to undermine the plan shortly after the Paris Peace Conference awarded Japan the former German rights in Shantung. Reinsch reported that Japanese residents in China thought Wilson had been defeated at Paris on Shantung.[24] For a month Reinsch deluged the State Department with protests on the Shantung decision framed by American business groups in China. The American Chamber of Commerce in China, for instance, protested the decision; they declared that Japanese pledges to maintain the open door were meaningless without guarantees.[25]

The most important issue holding up the organization of the consortium was the Japanese demand for recognition of a sphere of influence in South Manchuria and Eastern Inner Mongolia. Involved was an interpretation of the Lansing-Ishii Agreement of 1917. The Wilson Administration was willing to exclude from consortium operations vested rights which Japan had acquired before the war. But they refused to exclude the area as a whole, which would have meant recognition of a Japanese sphere. The Japanese claimed that the Lansing-Ishii Agreement in effect gave them this right.[26] This Japanese-American dispute held up implementation of the consortium until mid-1921. In lieu of agreement on outstanding issues, the State Department ceased to discourage competing American interests in China. It announced in

24. Reinsch to Lansing, April 25, 1919. 793.94/819.
25. Reinsch to Phillips, acting secretary of state, May 22, 1919, 793.94/821.
26. Japanese Embassy to State Department, April 3, 1920, *Foreign Relations*, 1920, I, 523–26; see also Polk, acting secretary of state, to Morris, ambassador to Japan, February 28, 1920, *ibid.*, 497–99.

1919 that the Pacific Development Corporation, the Chase National Bank, and Hayden Stone and Company were participating in a Sino-American bank.[27]

In addition to its action on Chinese loans, the State Department also sought to control projected loans to Russia, at least after the Bolshevik Revolution. Through the Russian Corporation of the War Trade Board, established on November 5, 1918, the Department was in a position to deny licenses to export to certain areas, in this way controlling the flow of capital to Russia and other areas of the old Russian Empire.[28]

The State Department meanwhile became interested in the increasing evidence that some of the Allies were controlling their capital exports. Arthur C. Millspaugh, Foreign Trade Adviser in the State Department, suggested to his superiors Wilbur J. Carr and D. H. Hart on October 24, 1919, that all American consuls report on the extent to which other nations relied on exclusive contracts to promote

27. *Foreign Relations*, 1919, I, 640. This was simply an editorial note explaining the ultimate fate of the Sino-American Bank.

28. *Munitions Industry Hearings*, 9707, 9712. On August 18, 1919, Secretary of State Lansing notified the investment house of Kidder-Peabody & Co. that the Department did not disapprove of the projected loan to the Kolchak (Omsk) government by the American (Kidder-Peabody, Guaranty Trust Co. and National City Bank), British syndicate. At the same time, Lansing refused to encourage the loan. Because the Administration had set up the Russian Corporation of the War Trade Board on November 5, 1918, it was still in a position to control the proceeds of the loan by refusing to allow export or import licenses. On at least one occasion Lansing used the Russian Corporation and licensing provisions under its regulations to frustrate British attempts to use American capital to channelize Russian foreign trade into British managed "pipe lines." On this see U.S. Department of State, *Papers Relating to the Foreign Relations of the United States*, 1918, *Russia*, 3 vols. (Washington, 1931–1932), III, 155–59, 149. Against this background, control of capital export seemed to be exercised with respect to Russia as well as China.

foreign trade. In his projected instruction, Millspaugh pointed out that during the war "Committees set up by the British Board of Trade . . . expressed the opinion that British interests in foreign countries would be furthered if British Banks in making loans would stipulate that the proceeds of the loans should be expended partly for the purchase of British goods. It is believed," Millspaugh wrote further, "that the exclusive loan contract is already in use to a considerable extent by British banks, as well as other foreign banks."[29]

After reading Millspaugh's memorandum, Wesley K. Frost of the Economic Intelligence Section of the Foreign Trade Advisers Office of the State Department requested the Bureau of Foreign and Domestic Commerce (BFDC) of the Commerce Department to send Millspaugh's instruction to all commercial consuls abroad. J. K. Towles, director of the Division of Research of the BFDC agreed to Frost's request on November 6, 1919. But he expressed opposition to adopting the British practice "if we find that they have been insisting on exclusive contracts."[30]

Carr and Hart reworked the Millspaugh instruction. They deleted specific references to Britain and shifted to the more general statement that "a number of committees which were set up in foreign countries to investigate and report on the possibilities of extending commerce after the war expressed the opinion that the banking institutions of their respective nationalities in making external loans should stipulate that the proceeds of each loan be expended for goods of their own nationals."[31] Even though British practices were

29. October 24, 1919, 800.51/182a.

30. November 6, 1919, in Commerce Department files, National Archives, Record Group 151, Bureau of Foreign and Domestic Commerce, indexed 640, File No. General. (Hereafter cited as R.G. 151, BFDC, indexed 640, File No. General.)

31. February 7, 1920, 2w800.51/182a.

not specifically named in the final draft, the State Department's interest was still concentrated on Britain because the British were the only other significant foreign lender besides the United States.

The United States government was regulating the flow of private capital to China and Russia by 1920. The purpose of regulation was to make certain that the open door would govern economic development of both China and Russia. The consortium approach was thought by the Wilson Administration to assure that loans would be used to increase the productive capacity of the Chinese economy.[32] Similarly, control of loans to Russia was designed to preserve the territorial integrity of Russia and to make certain that when American investment took place it would contribute to the expansion of the Russian economy.[33] Indeed, it is evident that Hoover, his predecessor Redfield, and Hughes wanted to see Russian economic development handled as a unit, just as they wished to see future Chinese development take place without distinct spheres of influence. They conceived of Russia and China as "new frontiers" open under equal conditions to the capital of all the industrial nations, and believed that American policy toward Russia and China would contribute to the future peace of the world by blunting economic rivalries.

An expansion of loan control to include American foreign investment in general was eventually proposed by Hoover. In the winter of 1920 he took the lead in calling for an organized effort to "prevent fraud, waste and loss" in foreign investment.[34] Partly through his impetus and partly due to a

32. Lansing to Wilson, June 20, 1918, Wilson to Lansing, June 21, 1918, *Foreign Relations,* 1918, 169–71.

33. See Chapter VI, this volume; also note 28 above.

34. Herbert Hoover, *The Memoirs of Herbert Hoover, The Cabinet and The Presidency,* 1920–1933, 3 vols. (New York, 1952), II, 36.

general concern for the creation of some system of regulating the flow of badly needed capital to Europe, the American Bankers Association called a Foreign Trade Financing Conference in Chicago on December 10, 1920. The purpose of the meeting, according to Hoover, "was to organize a corporation [under the Edge Act] through which these credits could flow, with proper checks against speculative, wasteful, and bad loans."[35] The Edge movement to release a flow of foreign investment fell apart and Hoover, when he became Secretary of Commerce, was forced to consider other means of achieving his goals.

As Secretary, Hoover enjoyed a special position with respect to both foreign and domestic economic policy. He accepted the post only after Harding acceded to his request that he have a "voice on all important economic policies of the administration." This amounted to the right to veto foreign policy decisions in economic areas. Successful treatment of economic and reconstruction problems, Hoover told Harding, would involve a grant of special authority to him in the areas of "business, agriculture, labor, finance, and foreign affairs so far as they related to these problems."[36]

Installed as Secretary, Hoover took the lead in seeking a long-range foreign loan policy. Although discussions on this problem began as a strictly governmental affair between the Commerce, State, and Treasury Departments, by May 1921 the New York banking community was astir with rumors that the Administration was in the process of framing an expanded foreign loan policy. The New York investment banking house of Harris Forbes & Company wrote Hughes inquiring whether the Administration was discouraging the flotation of loans in the United States unless the proceeds of

35. *Ibid.*, 13–14.
36. *Ibid.*, 36.

such loans were spent in this country.[37] This letter may have
stimulated the Hoover-instigated meeting held two weeks
later. Secretary of State Charles Evans Hughes, Secretary of
the Treasury Andrew Mellon, and President Harding were
the government men present at this meeting. The banking
representatives were Thomas Lamont of the House of Morgan and Milton E. Ailes of the Riggs National Bank.[38] This
meeting appears to have been the first step in a general
program of extending the principle of loan control beyond
the long-standing practice with respect to China and Russia.
As a result of this discussion, the bankers formally agreed to
loan consultation. In a letter to President Harding on June
6, 1921, J. P. Morgan agreed to keep the State Department
"fully informed of any and all negotiations for loans to
foreign governments." Further, the House of Morgan had
communicated with "all the people who have anything to do
with issuing foreign loans, including . . . National City
Bank, Guaranty Trust Company, Bankers Trust Company,
Kuhn, Loeb & Company, Brown Brothers & Company, and
Equitable Trust Company."[39]

On December 7, 1921, six months after the liaison between the Administration and the bankers was set up, the
State Department sent a proposal for clarification of the
goals and procedure of the loan control arrangement to
the Commerce and Treasury Departments. The Administration found it necessary to undertake "careful scrutiny of
proposed loan transactions" in view of the mounting indebtedness of Europe and the need to see to it that loans to

37. Harris-Forbes & Company to Secretary Hughes, May 23, 1921,
800.51/244.

38. Memorandum of State Department Foreign Trade Advisor Arthur
N. Young, April 3, 1925, 800.51/510½.

39. J. P. Morgan to President Harding, June 6, 1921, 800.51/503.

foreign governments were used for productive ends "and not for military expenditures or to make up budgetary deficits." A public statement by the government was promised soon, but did not appear in 1921.[40]

The *New York Evening Sun*, however, printed a story on January 6, 1922, to the effect that the government and the bankers were cooperating to "promote American banking and industry in Europe and in South American countries. . . . Under the plan," the news story said, "agents of the Department of Commerce will investigate conditions in countries asking for loans to carry on public or private projects. . . . Before the loan is made . . . the applicant will be obliged to promise to purchase materials in this country, thus benefiting both bankers and manufacturers. A commercial attaché [of the Commerce Department] will be on the ground to observe fulfillment of the contract." When confronted with this story by Professor Frank Mussey of Wellesley College on March 29, Assistant Secretary of State Leland Harrison refused to affirm or deny the arrangement.[41] Later developments seem to indicate that there was such an agreement, or at any rate one very similar to it.[42]

Difficulties began to plague the arrangement almost at once. On January 7, 1922, Harold Stanley, President of Guaranty Trust, requested clarification on what the State Department wanted from the bankers. He asked that the Department voice its objections before bids were out on loans. Undersecretary Henry P. Fletcher replied evasively,

40. A. N. Young to Assistant Secretary of State Fred M. Dearing, February 1, 1922, 800.51/3108.

41. Frank Mussey of Wellesley College to Assistant Secretary of State Leland Harrison, March 29, 1922, 800.51/301.

42. Hoover, *Memoirs*, II, 89–90. Hoover indicates that Harding retreated from full dress control when the New York bankers objected.

asking that the Department be kept informed during the course of negotiations.[43] On February 8, Assistant Secretary Fred M. Dearing sent a letter to Lee Higginson & Company, calling attention to their failure to consult with the Administration in connection with a recent foreign loan.[44] The first public hint of trouble between the Administration and the bankers came in the surprising form of a State Department press release issued March 23. The release claimed that the desire of the Administration to be informed "regarding such transactions" did not seem "sufficiently well understood in banking and investment circles."[45]

Spokesman for the banking opposition was Benjamin Strong, Governor of the Federal Reserve Bank of New York. In a memorandum to Secretary of State Hughes on April 14, he discussed restrictions or partial restrictions designed to influence foreign borrowers in balancing their budgets and reducing unproductive expenditures. Borrowers buy where goods are cheapest, Strong maintained. "It is my belief," he said, "that restriction of the character now being discussed will result in a reduction of our export trade just to the extent that the restriction attempts to require borrowers to buy goods in this market at higher prices than they can be obtained elsewhere. . . ."[46] The expansion of American export trade, he claimed, was entirely dependent on the ability of foreign corporations and governments to borrow in the American money market without regard to whether or not they bought American goods, for the money ultimately

43. Harold Stanley, President, Guaranty Trust Company to Undersecretary of State, Henry P. Fletcher, January 7, 1922, Fletcher to Stanley, January 13, 1922, 800.51/265.

44. Dearing to Lee Higginson & Company, February 8, 1922, 800.51/282a.

45. State Department Press Release, March 3, 1922, 800.51/287½.

46. Memorandum from Benjamin Strong, governor of the New York Federal Reserve Bank, to Secretary Hughes, April 14, 1922, 800.51/316.

would be spent in the United States—if not by the borrower, then by someone else.

He denied that the British government required foreign persons, governments, and corporations borrowing in London money markets to spend loan proceeds in England.[47] Strong readily admitted that it was "not uncommon that the London banker endeavors to secure some sort of understanding that the proceeds will be spent" in England. But this practice was "simply the result of better cooperation after many years of experience between that department of British business . . . which supplies credit and another . . . which manufactures and exports goods."[48]

Hughes sent a copy of Strong's memorandum to Hoover with a request for written comments. Hoover began with his several points of agreement with Strong: Strong was right when he said loans made in the American market would result in the export of either goods or gold by the United States without regard to where initial buying took place, and the banker was equally correct when he maintained that these loans were "vital" for the world and for American commerce. But Hoover disagreed sharply with Strong's conclusion that standards were not needed "in the placing of foreign loans in the American market." The bankers should have set these standards, Hoover said. If they did not, Congress would do so because there were "other and larger considerations than those enumerated by Governor Strong." The bankers, Hoover claimed, had "certain internal responsibilities to our commerce."[49]

Unproductive loans failed to provide the wherewithal for repayment. As Chinese and Central American experience

47. *Ibid.*
48. *Ibid.*
49. Hoover to Hughes, April 14, 1922, 800.51/316. Hoover's comments on Strong's memorandum of the same day.

demonstrated, default on loans led investors to pressure the government to intervene and collect debts forcefully. This in turn helped to create political tensions, such as the Chinese Revolution, which to all intents and purposes withdrew that area from world markets. If bankers used productive criteria for foreign investment then the danger of default, diplomatic intervention, revolution, and the consequent narrowing of world markets could be minimized. In this way bankers would be meeting their internal responsibilities to American commerce. Since American bankers were not setting such standards, Hoover believed it was the duty of the Administration to act in advance in order to prevent these conditions from erupting. Reproductive loans would not only increase the standard of living in the borrowing country, but increase its assets in such a way as to "strengthen its ability to meet its obligations to the United States Treasury."[50]

Hoover agreed with Strong "that it was undoubtedly bad economic theory to attach compulsory purchases of American goods as a condition of loans in our market." But it was "a fact" that such conditions were applied in foreign countries, both by British bankers and others. These foreign bankers set "conditions that specifications for public works expenditure from money borrowed" at least give "their contractors and builders of equipment an equal chance to compete on equal terms with other foreigners." A second usual condition, according to Hoover, was that in construction of a public project which necessitated "continuous subsequent purchase" of spare parts and supplies, the bankers strongly insisted on selling the "initial plant to the borrowing country." As an example he cited the history of the China railway loans floated in the London market, almost all of which embraced "one or more of these considerations." Where it

50. *Ibid.;* Hoover, *Memoirs,* II, 85–89, 34–36, 13–14.

proved feasible, American bankers could and should make the same reservations.[51]

No decision was reached in the government on the Hoover-Strong debate. Inside the Administration Hoover raised the issues, and in June of 1921 the bankers had apparently agreed to his proposals. But Strong's memorandum demonstrates that in less than a year the bankers were fighting back hard against Hoover's system. Apparently the Hoover-Strong debate was an outgrowth of unsuccessful efforts by the bankers and Commerce Department to maintain a consensus which would have enabled both sides to cooperate in implementing a foreign loan policy. The American Bankers Association announced in January 1922 that the Commerce and Marine Division and the Department of Commerce had established a liaison committee "to establish a closer working relationship for the purpose of enabling greater cooperation between the government and the bankers of the United States."[52] Had it functioned smoothly, then certainly no Hoover-Strong debate would have taken place.

In addition to this debate, a bitter argument was developing inside the business community between the bankers and the manufacturers. A propaganda program for restrictive clauses in loan agreements was launched by the manufacturers on March 10, 1922. Oscar K. Davis, Secretary of the National Foreign Trade Council (NFTC) wrote to Charles T. Gwynne, Secretary of the Chamber of Commerce of New York, requesting the cooperation of that body "in an effort to secure the adoption by American underwriters of foreign loans of a definite policy" to the end that "all or a part of the loan proceeds shall be expended for the purchase of American products." Davis pointed out that the prosperity of the

51. *Ibid.*
52. American Bankers Association, *Journal of the American Bankers Association*, XV, January 1922, 569. (Hereafter cited as ABA *Journal.*)

United States would increase through the additional employment. The NFTC spokesman denied the bankers' claim that foreign loan competition prevented restrictive loan agreements by remarking that the United States was "practically the only country in the world with the capacity to make foreign loans in any considerable amount. . . ."[53] Davis approached Hoover with a similar argument, although the solution he proposed in his letter to the Secretary was more closely tied to the specific interests of United States manufacturers. Then, on March 29, 1922, Maurice A. Oudin, Vice-president of General Electric International and an architect of the policy decisions of the NFTC, met with State Department Foreign Trade Advisor Arthur N. Young and urged that bankers be forced to require the purchase of American goods as a part of their loan contracts.[54]

On the same day the American Asiatic Association expressed support for State Department pressure to obtain such restrictive clauses. The President of the Association, John Foord, also sent along a clipping from the March 13, 1922 *New York Journal of Commerce*, which provided an analysis of wide support for the NFTC position from firms such as U.S. Steel, Standard Oil, Westinghouse, U.S. Rubber, International Harvester, and the American Radiator Company.[55]

By May 16, the NFTC had completed its preparatory work in urging business groups to take public positions for restrictive clauses in loan contracts. On that day Davis met with Young, and informed him that manufacturers and bankers had been meeting continuously and discussing their respective points of view. "Apparently there had been vigor-

53. March 10, 1922, 800.51/319.
54. Memorandum of Arthur N. Young, March 29, 1922, 800.51/481.
55. John Foord, president of the American Asiatic Association to A. N. Young, March 29, 1922, 800.51/482.

ous discussions on the subject," Young reported later, but "neither group had been able to reach a point of common understanding." The NFTC and the American Bankers Association could not agree. Davis acknowledged to Young that sound economics dictated a policy of "free trade" in loans. But this in no way helped "a manufacturer with a village of idle people on his hands." Davis also used Hoover's argument that the purchase of manufactured articles from the United States would mean a "continuous demand over a indefinite period for spare parts and replacements. He believes," Young went on, "that this latter point is very important."[56]

Young forwarded the substance of his conversation with Davis to Secretary Hughes and recommended that Hughes examine the *Acceptance Bulletin* for April 1922, in which the bankers had presented their position. An editorial item in that journal expressed the view that there was a "quite common misunderstanding" of "the relation of loans to exports." On restrictive clauses, the Acceptance Council "believes that the imposition of such conditions would be a serious error, wrong in principle and disappointing in prac-

56. Young memorandum, 800.51/481. In his conversations with Young, Davis does not explicitly indicate which NFTC leaders are arguing with which bankers. I have not been able to find in the business papers for February through April any indication of who is actually discussing the problem. There are many indications that discussions were taking place—for example, in the Federal Reserve Board's *Federal Reserve Bulletin* for February, March, and April (hereafter cited as Federal Reserve *Bulletin*), and in the American Acceptance Council's *Acceptance Bulletin* for March and April—but no direct attribution is given. It is a strong possibility that Davis conferred directly with the leading investment bankers on the Board of the American Acceptance Council on this problem. Davis was the only non-banking member of the Council and the *Acceptance Bulletin*, the Council's organ, was spokesman for the banking point of view in the public propaganda campaign. Banking spokesmen could have been any member of the Executive of the American Acceptance Council.

tice." The editorial went on to illustrate in simple economic terms that position which Strong had stated in the intergovernment debate with Hoover. In response to the NFTC's argument that machinery exports were not generally determined by free trade criteria, the bankers maintained that it "stands to reason that if purchases requiring large capital expenditure . . . are contemplated, as for instance, the purchase of ships, heavy machinery units or equipment, that other things being fairly equal, the work will go to the country that will finance the operation. . . ." The editorial concluded with a disquisition on the history of French loans to Russia and how they had worked in a triangular fashion, stimulating French "luxury manufactures" exported to Argentina. In conclusion the bankers' organ maintained that "operations against these natural laws" would defeat their own purpose and harm the American export trade.[57]

The Administration was thus confronted with a complex and difficult situation by the middle of April 1922. The investment banking houses objected to Hoover's attempts to limit foreign loans to reproductive purposes. On the other hand the manufacturers, through the National Foreign Trade Council, generated substantial pressure (which they dramatized by referring to the relatively heavy unemployment) for stipulations in loan contracts forcing foreign borrowers to purchase American capital goods. At least until the fall of 1922, Harding, Hughes, and Mellon acquiesced in Hoover's program[58] that the bankers should limit somewhat their appetite for commissions on bond issues and agree to make only reproductive loans. Hoover refused, however, to follow the manufacturers' suggestion for restrictive purchase clauses in loan contracts. He believed that if they were combined with substantial equality of opportunity in bids,

57. *Acceptance Bulletin*, April 1922, 3–4.
58. Hoover, *Memoirs*, II, 88.

reproductive loans would generate an expanding volume of business for American manufacturers sufficient for them to operate their plants at a high level of capacity.[59]

Hoover's loan control machinery was designed to (1) channelize capital into reproductive projects; (2) allow Secretary of the Treasury Mellon to close the capital market to governments which had not funded their war debts to the United States; and (3) allow Secretary of State Hughes to veto loans that threatened diplomatic objectives, primarily in regard to Soviet Russia and China.[60] Upon receipt of a request for a loan, the bankers were expected to forward the pertinent information to the State Department, which in turn sent copies to the Treasury and Commerce Departments. State and Treasury usually responded in a perfunctory manner.[61] Hoover, however, was more active.

Hoover and his advisers in the Commerce Department took a direct interest in these loans on several grounds. First, they were concerned about the overall effect which a particular loan might have on American foreign commerce; and second, they manifested a more specific interest whether equality of opportunity existed in connection with the expenditure of the loan. While internally the government debated the nature of American foreign loan policy, Hoover was testing the feasibility of informal procedures. In January 1922 industrial machinery manufacturers complained to W. R. Rastall, chief of the Industrial and Machinery Division of the BFDC, that the hundreds of millions of dollars of

59. Hoover to Hughes, April 14, 1922, 800.51/316; Hoover, *Memoirs*, II, 89–90.

60. Grosvenor M. Jones to Secretary of Commerce Thomas Lamont, July 13, 1929, R.G. 151, BFDC, indexed 640, File No. General; Arthur N. Young memorandum for Secretary Kellogg, April 2, 1925, 800.51/509½; also, Young to Kellogg, March 21, 1927, 800.51/560.

61. Grosvenor M. Jones to Secretary of Commerce Whiting, February 8, 1929, R.G. 151, BFDC, indexed 640, File No. General.

foreign bonds floated by New York bankers in 1921 had been of no assistance in increasing their export trade. Rastall also received complaints that building contractors in New York lost some foreign markets because the New York banks refused to finance certain projects.[62] By January 24, 1922, Hoover was trying by informal coersion to win the bankers to a loan policy based on equality of opportunity for American manufacturers.

Hoover's work in directing the Queensland Railroad loan was typical of the manner in which he wanted loan control to function. The State of Queensland in Australia, where previously British banks enjoyed a near monopoly of loans, asked the National City Bank for a $20 million loan to build a railroad. Hoover was first informed of the project on February 8, 1922. Early in the morning of that day, Assistant Secretary of State Fred M. Dearing read a letter over the phone to Julius Klein, BFDC director, from Milton E. Ailes (of the Riggs National Bank) who was serving as the bankers' liaison man with the State Department.[63] The purpose of the loan was to open up an area containing 3,500 farms unable to move agricultural commodities to market. Ailes requested quick approval by Dearing. On the same day Hoover approved the loan as "reproductive," and at the same time asked that the loan arrangements assure American manufacturers equality of opportunity in bidding for equipment and supplies for the project. This could be done, Hoover maintained, if particular attention was paid in the loan contract to engineering specifications for the road.[64] Richard

---

62. W. H. Rastall to Commercial Attaché in London Walter S. Towers, January 24, 1922, R.G. 151, BFDC indexed 640, File No. General.

63. Dearing to Julius Klein, Director, BFDC, February 8, 1922, R.G. 151, BFDC, indexed 640, File No. General.

64. *Ibid.*

Emmett, Hoover's secretary, telephoned the text of Hoover's letter to Dearing that day.

Dearing then phoned Ailes, and repeated the substance of Hoover's request. By phone Ailes relayed Hoover's suggestions to R. W. Byrne, Vice-president of the National City Bank of New York. Byrne in turn assured Ailes that "the National City Company will be willing to do everything possible to bring about the expenditure of the loan proceeds in the United States, and in such ways as to benefit Americans." After he had received this assurance Dearing formally approved the loan on behalf of the Administration.[65]

By late in the afternoon Hoover and Klein had drawn up a set of instructions which they wished to have Dearing include in any written communication to National City formally approving the loan. Klein told Dearing he approved the loan with the reservation that "the interests of American manufacturers . . . be adequately protected in the event of any purchases . . . with the proceeds of the loan. . . ." Klein suggested "such protection should properly include the drafting of any specifications for bids so as to secure a reasonable equality of opportunity for Americans," and "the elimination of any discriminatory tariff obstacles," as well as provision for "the publication of specifications simultaneously in London and New York."[66]

These instructions were included in the State Department's letter to National City approving the loan. Hoover and Klein found that in order to assure equality of opportunity for United States manufacturers in the Queensland Railroad loan, it was necessary for them to attack the appli-

65. Hoover to Dearing (with enclosure of Milton E. Ailes to Dearing), February 8, 1922, R.G. 151, BFDC, indexed 640, File No. General.

66. Klein to Dearing, February 8, 1922, R.G. 151, BFDC, indexed 640, File No. General.

cation of the Imperial Preference agreements between England and Australia. Under that system, British machinery
exporters received a 5 percent tariff preference on manufactures exported to Australia. The only way such discrimination could be removed was by the United States receiving
the same preference. The National City Bank began to feel
tremors of doubt as their representative took up the equality-of-opportunity request with Sir Dennison Miller, Governor of the Commonwealth Bank of Australia. "It is," Byrne
maintained, "naturally a delicate matter and it may take
some little time before we can have any definite assurances
on the matter."[67] He then hinted that it did not make much
difference anyway, because the loan would "eventually be
spent by some one in the United States, either to liquidate
existing debt or to buy products or services here. . . ." But
Byrne continued, "It is . . . a more difficult matter to say
that any portion of the proceeds be spent directly by Queensland in this market."[68]

When faced with the possibility of losing the loan if they
insisted on equality of opportunity, even the cooperative
National City bankers were ready to desert Hoover. But
Hoover and Klein were interested in using the Queensland
loan as a means of installing United States technology in a
railroad which American bankers were financing. American
bankers had "internal responsibilities to our commerce,"
Hoover believed, and under his leadership the Commerce
Department tried to influence the bankers to meet those
responsibilities. They thus refused to let the National City
Bank off the hook. On February 14, Klein wrote to Roger L.
Farnham, a National City vice-president, requesting details

67. R. W. Byrne to Dearing, February 14, 1922, R.G. 151, BFDC,
indexed 640, File No. General.
68. Dearing to Hoover, February 14, 1922, R.G. 151, BFDC, indexed
640, File No. General.

on what was to happen to the proceeds of the loan and what the details of the technical specifications were. He wanted the specifications, Klein said, so that he could protect American interests against discrimination. To this end he proposed sending the specifications to a Commerce Department Trade Commissioner in China (probably Frank R. Eldridge), who had made a "special study of the Railroad situation in Australia," to obtain his "opinion regarding the possibility of American competition."[69]

Little more was heard from the bankers on Australian railroads, although they continued to try to obtain equality of opportunity. The most effective work along these lines, however, was done by the Commerce Department (BFDC) Trade Commissioner in Sydney, J. W. Sanger. Sanger met with Commonwealth Bank Governor Miller and discussed all the issues connected with the railroad project. Miller expressed unalterable opposition to the establishment of American branch banks in Australia. On this issue, considered important by Hoover and Klein, Sanger was unable to move Miller. With respect to the railroad loan proper, Sanger won the concession of an equal 5 percent preference, the same advantage British competitors had over all others. However, no concession was obtained on the request to bid from New York and to quote in dollars, rather than from London and in sterling, as was the custom. Sanger may have been allowed the temporary preference equality with the British as a blind, for there was a strong movement in Australia to force purchase of steel rails from the high-cost but native Australian Broken Hill Steel Mill in Queensland. On non-steel rail equipment for the railroad, British testing standards for quality were used and favored over American

69. Klein to Roger L. Farnam, Vice-president, National City Bank, February 14, 1922, R.G. 151, BFDC, indexed 640, File No. General.

testing standards.[70] The Queensland Railroad loan saga ended with American firms unable to obtain any equipment orders.[71] Australian policy was Australia first; and then "Mother" England.

By the summer of 1922 the debate over the extent of government control of foreign issues was resumed. The leading figure in the banking community, Thomas Lamont, who was the operating head of the House of Morgan, expressed firm opposition to restrictive clauses on American foreign loans. The results of existing methods of lending, Lamont claimed, disproved "the theory that American trade is not getting the benefit of these foreign loans." After noting that Lamont spoke for American bankers, the *Federal Reserve Bulletin* explained that such restrictions would limit, at least temporarily, the extent of American foreign trade.[72]

Inside the Cabinet, Hoover was the only member of the Administration who continued to push for a program of informal but widely-based control over foreign capital issues. Both President Harding and Secretary Mellon "insisted upon a retreat" from the "original standards."[73] Harding's decision made it necessary for Hoover to seek equality of opportunity without the weapon of formal loan direction, control, and consultation. Throughout July 1922, while Hoover watched the possible positive results of the Queensland loan vanish, reports poured into the State and Commerce Departments demonstrating consistent policies of discrimination against American producers. On July 19, for

70. Sanger to Klein, June 9, 1922, R.G. 151, BFDC, indexed 640, File No. General.
71. W. H. Rastall to Klein, July 28, 1922, R.G. 151, BFDC, indexed 640, File No. General.
72. Federal Reserve *Bulletin*, June 1922, 644, editorial comment.
73. Hoover, *Memoirs*, II, 88.

example, the Western European Affairs Division of the State Department reported that the 1922 loan to the Netherlands seemed to have been used "to carry the accounts of the Java rubber planters," thus "aiding them to restrict the production and export of rubber in order to keep the price up."[74] On the same day, Stanley K. Hornbeck of the same Division reported that a number of recent loans by United States bankers to the Belgian government had released Belgian capital for work on the Lunghai Railway in China. In turn, orders for equipment to supply the line were placed in such a way as to discriminate against United States producers and favor Belgian and Dutch manufacturers.[75]

Aside from Russia, the one area where the American government continued complete control of capital issues in close cooperation with the bankers was in China. Moreover, in 1920 the bankers had been instrumental in the success of the one last attempt made to win Japanese acceptance of the China consortium. Thomas Lamont, a representative of the American group, negotiated with Japanese bankers in an attempt to resolve the dispute directly.[76] After prolonged negotiations agreement was reached on conditions for Japanese participation in the new consortium with the approval of both governments. The agreement involved Lamont's commitment, on behalf of the American group and the State Department, that certain Manchurian railways, mainly the South Manchurian Railway, and including a number of

74. Stanley K. Hornbeck to Arthur C. Millspaugh and William Phillips, July 18, 1922, 611.003/1380.
75. Hornbeck to Millspaugh and Phillips, July 19, 1922, 611.003/1380.
76. Polk, acting secretary of state, to Roland Morris, American ambassador to Japan, February 28, 1920, *Foreign Relations*, 1920, I, 497–99.

202 Heir to Empire

others, were "outside the scope of the joint activities of the consortium."[77]

The negotiations, concluded on May 11, 1920, paved the way for the Washington Conference of 1922. The Lamont-Kajiwara agreements also spelled out the meaning of the Lansing-Ishii Agreement of 1917. Hughes, like Lansing, accepted Japanese vested rights in the Manchurian railroads. Therefore, when negotiations began in Washington in December 1921, some of the underlying principles for economic competition in China had already been agreed upon. The Nine-Power Treaty, especially Article I, merely reflected the Lamont-Kajiwara Agreement.

While Article I of the Nine-Power Treaty was only a paper guarantee by Japan and the other major powers that they would respect the open door and Chinese territorial integrity, Hughes had no intention of relying upon good faith alone. He fully intended to use control of capital issues as a means of pressuring Japan to abide by the open door pledge. For example, when the Japanese Oriental Development Corporation requested a loan from American banking houses in December 1922, the State Department withheld approval until they determined that the loan would not be used in a manner that threatened the open door.[78] In similar fashion, when the Japanese-controlled South Manchurian Railway requested a $25 million loan in New York, the bankers submitted the request to the State Department, which then approved it.[79] Had the loan been judged a threat

77. The representative of the American group, Thomas Lamont, to the representative of the Japanese group, Nakaji Kajiwara, president of the Yokohama Specie Bank, May 11, 1920, *Foreign Relations*, 1920, I, 556–57. For the story of the Lamont-Kajiwara negotiations, see *ibid.*, 536–59.

78. Hornbeck to Millspaugh and Phillips, July 19, 1922, 611.003/1380.

79. *Ibid.*

to the open door agreement, Hughes would have been in a position to deny Japan the capital necessary to develop its interests in China.

But the situation in regard to China loans was unusual. As late as July 1929 the State Department maintained control of capital issues for China without objection on the part of the bankers. Control of investment in China was viewed as the key to maintaining Chinese sovereignty and thereby protecting it as an area for future expansion of American investment. As Hughes explained to Lamont, the "organization of the new consortium . . . was largely in the nature of a public service. . . . The reason for these policies is to be found in the conviction that, in the interests of the future economic development of our country, it is essential that our interests should preserve the opportunity for practical participation in the financial and industrial development of China." America wished to preserve the open door in China not as a "matter of mere academic concern but [as] a provision for a future stage" in which American bankers, manufacturers and merchants "will feel a need for expansion into the potentially rich markets of China."[80]

Hughes, having secured Japanese agreement to the open door in China, and confident that loan control would enable him to pressure the Japanese to abide by their pledge, could confidently seek general disarmament in the Far East. Loan control in China functioned then as both a way to preserve future commercial opportunities for Americans and as the principle means of bringing about a concert of power in the Far East. Loan control and disarmament were the Republican substitutes for Wilson's program of naval expansion.

Except for special areas such as those in China, Soviet

<hr />

80. Hughes to Lamont, April 13, 1922, *Foreign Relations*, 1922, I, 764–65.

Russia, and Mexico,[81] the State Department seemed to agree with President Harding and Secretary Mellon that rigid control of foreign loans in general could not be maintained. It was also true, however, that a block of civil servants in the Department argued for a general policy of investment control as a means of forcing equal treatment for American commerce. William Phillips, Ambassador to the Netherlands, urged in February 1922 that "it is not reasonable that [Dutch] colonial authorities should receive the benefit of American financial assistance without giving in return some encouragement to American business desiring to expand within the colonies." He pointed out that Dutch colonial officials were refusing to grant American petroleum and other firms the right to develop the raw material resources of the East Indies.[82] Stanley K. Hornbeck went further than Phillips. "Is there not," he told Millspaugh on July 17, 1922, "too great a disposition on the part of the American Government to accept references to agreements and the giving of general assurances as conclusive in relation to questions of treatment accorded to American and other interests? Should we not insist on the enjoyment of the equality of treatment which we insistently claim but seldom demand? Should we not use the superior economic and political weapons which we now possess to compel respect for the principles which we advocate and for certain rights which are clearly ours?" Other governments went much further than the United States in paving the "way for their financiers and construction companies abroad."[83]

81. Young memorandum, May 2, 1925, 800.51/509½; Jones to Commerce Secretary Lamont, July 13, 1929, R.G. 151, BFDC, indexed 640, File No. General.
82. Quoted in Hornbeck to Millspaugh and Phillips, July 17, 1922, 611.003/1380.
83. *Ibid.*

In a second memorandum to Millspaugh two days later, Hornbeck admitted that it was unfortunately true that "American capitalists, industrial producers, and commercial or trading groups and individuals have not worked out . . . the methods of common and united effort . . . which are so great a factor in the success of overseas activities of several other countries. . . ." Until private methods of cooperation were worked out, Hornbeck argued, the government "should assume a more definite and positive leadership toward creating and maintaining the desired degree of cooperation." The Hornbeck-Phillips group, however, was in a distinct minority, and in no way reflected the position of the State Department as a whole.[84]

Although Hoover made a strong case for loan control as a lever to be used in obtaining equality of opportunity, he apparently agreed to the rejection of this approach on the dual premises that it conflicted with an overall open door solution to the economic problems which arose out of World War I, and that control of loans was a dangerous substitute for a policy of voluntary cooperation between bankers and manufacturers. After the campaign to secure extensive loan control was lost, Hoover and Klein immediately launched a campaign to pressure bankers by means of an aroused public opinion to concert their loan activity with the needs of manufacturers. At the same time they took steps to create a division within the Commerce Department to facilitate such cooperation.

The BFDC of the Commerce Department established in July 1922 a Finance and Investment Division under Grosvenor M. Jones to deal with financial and economic questions which were "international in scope and not limited to a

84. Hornbeck to Millspaugh and Phillips, July 19, 1922, 611.003/1380.

specific country, and to matters concerned with the flotation
of foreign securities, . . . with the investment of American
capital abroad and with the general aspect of foreign trade
financing." In addition it was to act as the principal connecting link between the banks and the Commerce
Department.[85]

This new Division began an immediate campaign to edu-
cate the business community on the mechanics and principles of British foreign investment policy. Among the studies
prepared were *British Investment Trusts, Foreign Credit
Facilities of the United Kingdom, Financial Review of Great
Britain and British Banking* and *Foreign Policies of the Big
Five Banks.*[86] These studies tended to show that British
manufacturers and investment bankers worked closely to
regulate foreign investment in order that British industry
and commerce might obtain the maximum possible benefits
in terms of export markets. Following closely on this series
was a report on how the Swiss government developed informal consultation with Swiss bankers so that foreign investments contributed to the exports of Swiss manufacturers.
Despite objections to control of foreign loans, Swiss bankers
accepted the consultation system rather than face legislative
control.[87] This was an implied but firm threat to American
bankers that legislation might force cooperation.

The most powerful salvo fired in the public campaign to
force bankers to join manufacturers in a joint policy was a
speech entitled "The Need of a Sound Foreign Loan Policy,"

85. Julius Klein, "Report of the Chief of the Bureau of Foreign and
Domestic Commerce," *Eleventh Annual Report of the Secretary of Commerce* (Washington, 1923), 140–41.

86. *Ibid.*

87. Bureau of Foreign and Domestic Commerce, *Commerce Reports*,
September 18, 1922, 803. Editorial comment by Grosvenor M. Jones on
a report from the American Embassy in Bern, Switzerland, on Swiss
control of foreign loans.

delivered by Grosvenor M. Jones before the National Foreign Trade Convention on December 5, 1922. Jones began
by saying it was necessary to sell American surplus production abroad if American industries were to be "fully and
efficiently employed and if the cost of production . . . [was]
to be kept down to proper levels." America had no adequate
policy with respect to "loans to foreign governments" and
"investment of American capital in foreign enterprises," and
no effort was being made to develop such a policy.[88]

"To play the part England has so long filled as the
great international loan market," Jones explained, "we need
more preparation than we have as yet been able to get."
Britain had a relatively long chronological period in which
to develop her international commercial system. Yet, "despite her experience in world affairs, the ability and conserv-
atism of her bankers, and the cautiousness of her investors,
she sometimes made costly mistakes." If a loan policy could
be formulated which would guide and protect the American
investor it would almost automatically place the capital
"where it will do the most good." Public opinion should
come to a consensus in answering eight questions which lay
at the heart of a "sound foreign loan policy."[89] These were:

88. Grosvenor M. Jones, "The Need of a Sound Foreign Loan Policy,"
Commerce Reports, December 18, 1922, 708–09. Reprint of a speech
given by Jones at the NFTC convention on December 5, 1922.

89. It is interesting to note that the disciples of Keynes, in following
through the implications of the master's argument, tend to claim that
foreign investments are broadly beneficial even if in the narrow sense
they are wasted, so long as the investments are continuously made—as in
the current American foreign aid program. In this respect, Hoover and
the statesmen of the 1920's are regarded as hopelessly old-fashioned.
Though Congress may be coerced into accepting that argument, the
international financiers associated with the International Bank for Reconstruction and Development (the World Bank) and the International
Monetary Fund reject the economics of that argument. But even if these
bankers may be regarded as anachronistic holdovers from an unfortunate
bygone era, the ethical poverty of such an argument is glaring. The

"(1) Whether foreign loans should be restricted to constructive purposes. . . . (2) Whether loans to foreign governments should be scrutinized so as to preclude the offering to the American investing public of the securities of any National, State, or municipal governments having a poor debt record. (3) Whether certain restrictions should be made on foreign loans, such as a requirement that no loans be made to a government the service of whose debt, including the loan under consideration, exceeds a certain percentage of its average annual revenue over a period of years. (4) Whether loans should be granted to nations whose political stature is uncertain or involved. (5) Whether loans should be issued in foreign currencies; and if so, under what restrictions or safeguards. (6) Whether any restrictions should be imposed with a view to providing that all or a part of the proceeds of foreign loans shall be spent in the United States. (7) Whether the Federal Government should actively support the efforts of American bond-holders to collect in cases of default. (8) Whether any attempt should be

---

American people accept foreign aid by and large because they believe such aid (1) helps stabilize foreign countries politically, and hence contributes to the security of the United States, and (2) because it supposedly helps to develop the economy of the aided country, in this way satisfying a beneficent strain in the American character. If this aid is wasted, the taxpayer is cheated on both counts and cannot, as the investors of the 1920's did, stop investing his savings when he concludes they are being wasted. He must continue to pay his taxes; he has no other option. Therefore, the foreign aid managers bear even greater responsibility to the public than did the bankers managing American foreign investment in the 1920's. There is also a moral obligation to the American taxpayer and to the foreign peoples being aided; the managers of the aid program violate this moral obligation if they accept waste in foreign aid, since such waste creates expectations among foreign peoples which cannot be realized. This in turn leads to political insecurity which in turn results in probable consequent economic underdevelopment. Hence, accepting waste practices trickery on donor and recipient alike.

made to allocate the loans so as to secure wide distribution of risk to place them where they can be used most effectively."[90]

The investment bankers as a group refused to consider limitations on their lending power except in those areas in which the government had a legitimate political interest. The bankers agreed that the Administration had a right to control loans to China in order to safeguard the new consortium, to bar loans to states (such as Russia and Mexico) which confiscated American property without adequate compensation, and to prevent loans to Germany until the indemnity was fixed in a way agreeable to the United States. But from the summer of 1922 to the middle of the decade they resisted Hoover's attempts to pressure them into financing only reproductive ventures. They also largely refused to enter into any voluntary system of cooperation with the manufacturers.

An economic expansion began again in 1922 when the capital-short nations of the world turned to American banks to raise capital through the flotation of bonds. These bonds were attractive to investment banks, both because the commissions were high and because they frequently carried foreign government guarantees. Of a total of $763 million for all foreign capital issues for 1922, some $625 million was in government-guaranteed or government-controlled issues. That is to say, no more than one-fifth of total foreign investment was in equity financing.[91] In substance then, the investment bankers refused to undertake what Hoover called their

90. Grosvenor M. Jones, "The Need of a Sound Foreign Loan Policy," *Commerce Reports*, December 18, 1922, 708–09. Reprint of a speech given by Jones at the NFTC convention on December 5, 1922.

91. Ralph A. Young, *Handbook of American Underwriting of Foreign Securities*, Trade Promotion Series No. 104, Bureau of Foreign and Domestic Commerce, Department of Commerce (Washington, 1930), 14–15.

domestic responsibilities to American commerce.[92] The
major portion of foreign investment in 1922, 1923, and
1924 was made without any substantial attempt to consider
the interests of the major industrial corporations. With the
exception of the Dawes loans, in which the whole economy
was interested, and the Japanese earthquake loan of 1924,[93]
for which Hughes and Lamont worked out a system to
channel portions of the orders to American machinery manufacturers, the bankers paid little attention to the interests of
the economy as a whole.

Having lost their program for a government-sponsored
foreign loan policy, the manufacturers, through the National
Foreign Trade Council, joined the Commerce Department
in a campaign for voluntary cooperation. The Secretary of
the NFTC, Oscar K. Davis, wrote to Julius Klein in December 1923 requesting data which might show that European
banks restricted the expenditure of loan proceeds. Klein
promised in January 1924 to send Davis "from time to time
such data as can be had" on European practices. He emphasized, however, that specific information was often hard to
obtain, since loan restrictions were often in the form of
"gentlemen's agreements."[94]

Some of the information Klein supplied began immediately to appear in attacks on the bankers. Franklin Remington, President of the Foundation Company of New York (an
international harbor construction company) attacked them
at the 1924 National Foreign Trade Convention. The "only
advantages to a foreign loan do not lie merely in the under-

92. Rastall to Walter H. Tower, January 24, 1922, R.G. 151, BFDC,
indexed 640, File No. General.

93. Lamont to Hughes, February 4, 1924, in Charles Evan Hughes
Manuscripts, Manuscript Division, Library of Congress, Washington,
D.C., Letters 1921–1925.

94. Klein to Davis, January 10, 1924, R.G. 151, BFDC, indexed 640,
File No. General.

writing fees and commissions," Remington argued. He criticized the bankers for the fact that "our foreign investments are almost entirely in non-productive issues such as government and municipal loans," while "British loans are . . . largely reproductive ones."[95] Despite this concerted campaign by the Commerce Department and the NFTC the bankers did not respond. Indeed, by 1925 some investment houses were threatening to make loans to foreign raw material monopolies in defiance of Cabinet policy.[96]

The bankers thought the 1920–1921 depression was caused by a surplus of productive power in the domestic economy, which in turn made for a shortage of domestic investment opportunities. Since they could not put their capital to work at home they had to do so abroad. But purchase of foreign equities was, from their point of view, a risky business. The instability of conditions in Europe, and the consequent general instability of world markets, increased the risks in equity ventures (direct investment in common stock) abroad. Bonds guaranteed by foreign governments therefore appeared the safest investment. In addition, it was this type of investment rather than equity investment which was in demand from abroad. Finally, fees and commissions from such issues were generally quite high. With their eyes focused on immediate safety in the form of guarantees they were blind to Hoover's point that the long-term safety of loans lay in their reproductive character. Hoover understood what the bankers failed to see—that government guarantees meant little if loans were frittered away on many unreproductive ventures which would (and did in 1929) someday make debt service impossible.

95. Remington's address, "Foreign Loans as a Trade Builder," National Foreign Trade Council, *Proceedings of the Twelfth Annual Convention* (New York, 1924), 171–73.

96. James Speyer to Leland Harrison, November 10, 1925, Harrison to Speyer, November 25, 1925, 832.51 Sa6/47 and 832.51 Sa6/48.

CHAPTER VIII

❧ *The Open Door Tariff*

THE TREND toward a new, more effective American tariff system flowed from two concurrent phenomena: the expansion of American foreign commerce (and its acceleration during the war), and the desire of the business community and the government to keep the Allies and Central Powers from regaining the commerce they had lost to the United States. The American business community and the Wilson Administration believed that the maintenance and expansion of foreign commerce was extremely important for the viable operation of the American economy.

Both official administrators and private economic managers thought of the tariff as an instrument to stabilize and expand the productiveness of the economy. In an address to the National Foreign Trade Council in January 1916, Frank A. Vanderlip pointed out that tariff policy had widespread implications for the proper functioning of the credit structure and the general prosperity of American society. Under the Federal Reserve Act, the amount of bank credit available at any given time was dependent, in a ratio of eight to ten times the level of the reserves, on the amount of gold which banks normally held as reserves.

This provided some elasticity for domestic currency credit relationships. Seasonal movements of gold from one section of the country to another, for example, ceased to wreak havoc and cause panics. But the Act offered little direct help in warding off anarchic contractions in the credit system "through the operation of trade balances." The "enormous influx of gold" occasioned by expanded export sales during the war produced an overall expansion of loans and discounts by American banks to a total of some $2 billion by January 1916.[1] According to Vanderlip, the "interior farmer, merchant or manufacturer, wholly local in his interests, may think he has but the remotest interest in foreign trade," but "he is interested in bank reserves, and the course of foreign trade as it reacts on those reserves will effect his business future to an extent that may some day amaze him." A key way to defend the gold reserve and America's commerce, Vanderlip thought, was to make the tariff "an instrument for national service, rather than a field for the display of individual and political selfishness." He believed a tariff commission "wisely selected and properly empowered may mean the beginning of a movement of vast significance in taking the tariff out of politics."[2]

A new tariff program was necessary, Vanderlip maintained, because "the nations now at war will use every method of legislation to benefit their position." He saw the threat in terms of a "tariff union not only between Britain and her colonies, but between Great Britain and her allies, and probably another tariff union of the central European powers."[3] In January 1916, Alba B. Johnson, President of the Baldwin Locomotive Works, also criticized the "old methods of tariff revision" as "incapable of providing a tariff

1. National Foreign Trade Council, *Proceedings of the Fourth Annual Convention* (New York, 1916), 431. (Hereafter cited as NFTC Convention *Proceedings*.) The pages in the text on the effects of the Federal Reserve Act on foreign trade, domestic credit, economic expansion and contraction are based on Frank A. Vanderlip's analysis at the 1916 NFTC convention.
2. *Ibid.*, 436.
3. *Ibid.*, 437.

adaptable to the changing conditions of business." A flexible and scientific tariff could be obtained by means of a "permanent non-partisan tariff commission."[4] The consensus of the NFTC meeting of January 1916 held that such a flexible bargaining tariff was the way in which American foreign trade "may be encouraged by commercial agreements and protected from undue discrimination."[5] The single-level tariff was seen as useless in the event of European preferential tariff agreements. Such a tariff policy would fail to provide any trading margin in a postwar world where the danger of economic alliances running parallel to wartime military alliances was regarded as likely.[6]

In 1912, before his election as president, Woodrow Wilson had committed himself to the idea of a "flexible" or bargaining tariff, as it came to be called. As President, he recommitted himself to the idea in a letter of July 25, 1916, to the President of the Illinois Manufacturers Association. Wilson's concept of the tariff was one which routinely and almost automatically adjusted itself to "employing to the utmost the resources of the country in a vast development of our business enterprise." Such a tariff had to be based on the findings of a nonpartial commission. It could not be developed as a patchwork of government revenue problems and interest-group desires for protection.[7] Quoting Wilson's words approvingly, Benjamin F. Harris, an Illinois banker, suggested in January 1917 dropping the "old tariff bugbear of 'high' or 'low,' " protection or revenue; instead, it should be thought of as "a great business getting and nation developing organization."[8]

4. *Ibid.,* 12–13.
5. *Ibid.,* vii–viii, ix.
6. *Ibid.,* vii–viii, ix.
7. NFTC Convention *Proceedings,* 1917, 104–05. Harris read the text of Wilson's letter on the tariff to the convention.
8. *Ibid.,* 107.

Both corporate business and government spokesmen were more specific in 1917 about the need for a flexible bargaining tariff. According to Willard Straight, Vice-president of the American International Corporation, postwar conditions were in February already "uppermost in the minds of our commercial and financial leaders." Straight predicted that world tariff systems would "be revised." The prewar unconditional most-favored-nation structure would "be at an end." All debtor nations would develop export drives to rid themselves of accumulated debt. It was highly likely, Straight reasoned, that the American market would be a key export goal for Europeans trying to regain from the United States their war-lost gold. The tariff would be of significance not only in protecting the vast American market against such organized incursions, but it "should be," and could be made, an instrument to protect American industry and the home market. Further, it could be "utilized for the maintenance and development of our export trade." The new trading relationships the Europeans would set up would discriminate against the United States; the American tariff would have to be used to win concessions or enforce retaliation.[9]

A question which agitated Straight and C. H. Bentley, Chairman of the Foreign Trade Commission of the National Canners Association, almost as much as the threat of direct discrimination by the Allies was whether or not Allied nondiscriminatory treatment of American commerce was to be conditioned upon American discrimination against Germany.[10] A United States agreement to discriminate against Germany would place indirect burdens on American foreign commerce, because an anti-German policy would tend to

9. *Ibid.*, 62–74. This address by Willard Straight seemed to inspire the remarks of the other speakers, who return again and again to Straight's analysis to make their own points on the tariff.
10. Bentley's address, *ibid.*, 82; Straight, *ibid.*, 65.

narrow world markets at a time when both official and private leaders were convinced that American industry needed the widest possible nondiscriminatory world market system. William B. Fleming, State Department advisor on Commercial Treaties, spoke out at the 1917 NFTC convention on the problem of the individual manufacturer. The economy as a whole had reached the point where foreign markets had to be found for the surplus products of American industry, since "a number of our big manufacturers" confronted the problem that "in normal times [they] can produce enough to supply the home market in seven months." Foreign markets were necessary to keep labor and capital busy for the other five months. The end of the war would simply intensify this existing situation.[11]

Fleming urged business and government leaders, and the public, to be prepared for "the war after the war." He explained how the existing Underwood Tariff was "weak because it permits only the reduction of duties," and "no power to raise them." A strong tariff for the "war after the war" was dependent on retaliatory provisions. The most significant modification of the Underwood system, Fleming held, would be one which would "enable the executive, under limitation imposed by Congress, to make treaties conclusive," without the need to refer them "back to Congress." In the past, sectional and interest-group fights in Congress had doomed such treaties. The responsibility for success, Fleming said, rested on both business and government. He commended to his audience the recommendations made by Straight, particularly the proposal that the tariff be modified to give the executive the necessary freedom of maneuver.[12]

Many delegates placed strong emphasis on the assumed discriminatory effect of the predicted European protection

11. *Ibid.*, 84–86.
12. *Ibid.*, 84–86.

and trade preference systems on the American exports of agricultural commodities, which amounted to 50 percent of the total. Benjamin F. Harris, a banker operating in the agricultural districts of Illinois (he was actually listed as "farmer" on the roster of delegates), expressed such fears. European discriminations ought to be fought with the weapon of the large American market. In the long run the American market would absorb such surpluses, Harris predicted, but agricultural exports had to be protected by the tariff in the interim.[13]

In keeping with these arguments and recommendations, the 1917 NFTC convention reiterated its 1916 call for a flexible bargaining tariff to protect United States exports against discrimination and to "guarantee" continuance of the favorable treatment enjoyed by that commerce before World War I.[14] Similar demands for a bargaining tariff were repeated at the 1918 convention.[15] Then, at its 1919 convention, the Council heard a long analytical address by William S. Culbertson, Vice-chairman of the United States Tariff Commission, on the advantages of the flexible bargaining tariff.[16]

Culbertson's plea demonstrated how, in the course of development, the initiative in policymaking often shifts from its point of origin, be it business or government, to the other party and back again until a consensus is reached. The first

13. *Ibid.*, 102.
14. *Ibid.*, viii.
15. "Final Declaration," NFTC Convention *Proceedings*, 1918.
16. NFTC Convention *Proceedings*, 1919, 71–81. Culbertson's emphasis was on the broad interests of the American economy. By the time he spoke on the need for a bargaining tariff, there was very nearly a community of thought among government officials and export trade leaders. Then as now this "consensus" did not appear to include typical members of Congress who were more concerned with the fate of specific interests in their districts than the broad interests of the whole economy.

sustained push for a bargaining tariff appeared in a referendum conducted by the United States Chamber of Commerce in late 1915.[17] Early in the next year the NFTC took up the issue and helped advance the cause. At the same time, and immediately thereafter, government bureaucrats took up the idea of a nonrevenue, nonprotective flexible tariff. This was remarkably close to the scientific tariff Wilson had first advocated in 1912.[18] In 1919 then, Culbertson spoke with as much urgency as did the foremost export traders in the country, if not more.

Concern for revising tariff policy grew sharply throughout 1919. The war was over, and although the exigencies of the present situation and those which were expected were not known precisely, the basic outlines of the alternatives could be seen. In a letter to Oscar T. Crosby, Assistant Secretary of the Treasury, Frederick Strauss of the Federal Reserve Bank of New York highlighted the probable dangers. Two possiblities were yet open, said Strauss: a peaceful, disarmed, low-tariff world without struggles for "paramount spheres of influence"; or the reverse—a world of high tariffs, heavy arms burdens, and general commercial war. A general move toward self-sufficiency and commercial warfare might confront the United States with "the risk of large importations at low prices. To meet such competition would not be easy, for it would require as a fundamental condition absolute readjustment of the money wage scale in this country. . . ."[19]

17. NFTC Convention *Proceedings*, 1916, 123–24, 128.

18. William Diamond, *The Economic Thought of Woodrow Wilson* (Baltimore, 1943), 97–99. Diamond's footnotes 25 to 30 give a short clear summary of Wilson's tariff ideas from 1912 to 1916. Of course, the idea of a bargaining tariff was not new in 1916. It had already been the subject for discussion for some years before 1916.

19. U.S. Senate, *Special Committee on Investigation of the Munitions Industry*, 74th Cong., 2d sess. (Washington, 1936), 10429–30. (Hereafter cited as *Munitions Industry Hearings*.)

Business and government policymakers therefore had to frame a tariff which could be used as a means of protecting the American economy in the event of widespread commercial war. If the United States framed a tariff which gave cheap European exports easy access to American markets, it would find itself inundated with highly competitive imports. If the United States lost control of the flow of gold and the international exchange situation, it could meet the exigency only by massive deflation, which would bring about price and wage cuts and unemployment. Though Crosby did not say so, the most powerful American weapon against worldwide discriminatory tariffs and consequent deflation was protection of the domestic American market for home producers. American political and economic leaders involved in framing a postwar tariff policy understood the threat of deflation inherent in a situation in which competing European industries could use their depreciated currencies as a means of flooding the United States with cheap goods.

Historians and economists who subsequently criticized protection as a shortsighted measure failed to note the very real deflationary danger to the American economy inherent in the disintegration of the gold standard.[20] This was precisely what Vanderlip, Straight, and other leading foreign traders had been talking about so worriedly in and out of NFTC meetings since 1916. They were not simpleminded, inflexible, extreme high-tariff protectionists. They wanted a

20. Culbertson to Hughes, July 14, 1922, in State Department files, National Archives, Record Group 59, 611.003/1092. (Unless otherwise labeled, decimal number will indicate Record Group 59 in State Department files, National Archives.) While Culbertson admitted that the duties were too high he argued that since Congress had plumped for protection, all doubts had to be resolved in favor of domestic producers, at least until British prices were stabilized. Culbertson revealed the same fear, as Vanderlip had in 1916, of an America inundated with cheap British goods passing under U.S. tariff walls by means of the weapon of unstable British currency.

bargaining tariff in order to trade access to the largest market in the world, the United States, in exchange for the acceptance of open door commercial policies by the European powers.

The nature of European commercial relations had not been settled by 1919, but the trend was unmistakably toward Imperial Preference within the British Empire, and with such protectionism extended to Britain's European allies. France and Japan were moving consciously and openly toward a policy of tariff assimilation, converting imperial possessions into overseas segments of metropolitan markets. For example, at the Conference of Algeciras in April 1906, France had pledged agreement to "economic liberty without any discriminations" in the administration of Morocco. Although France had reaffirmed its recognition of the open door in 1912 when it converted Morocco into a protectorate, the introduction of the franc as the official currency tended to make Morocco an economic colony. The French continued to close the door when they secured Anglo-American agreement to Articles 141, 142, 143, and 144 of the Versailles Treaty, which deprived Germany of open door privileges in Morocco. Subsequent to Versailles, the French Chamber of Deputies expressed the view that the "act of Algeciras is still an international reality," but that the French government "should by a diplomatic convention break the last bonds already well loosened, of the accord imposed by Germany now conquered." By 1919 France had virtually assimilated Morocco into the French tariff system.[21] Japan had begun its policy of tariff assimilation in 1909 with Formosa. Then in August of 1920, after the expiration of a ten-year treaty obligating Japan to administer Korea on open door principles, she also assimilated Korea into her tariff system.[22]

21. U.S. Tariff Commission, *Colonial Tariff Policies* (Washington, 1922), 206–07, text and footnotes; also 78–79, including footnotes.
22. *Ibid.*, 438–41.

Tariff policies pursued by the Europeans in their metropolitan areas were of little concern to American interests as long as they treated the United States as well as they treated one another. Equality of treatment within all metropolitan countries was the objective of both business and government under the Wilson Administration. Wilson had intimated as much in his 1912 call for a scientific tariff fashioned to facilitate the largest possible development of American resources.[23] Wilson believed any expansion of the domestic economy was dependent on the growth and development of foreign markets; therefore, the tariff should reflect the need of expanded export markets. He argued that if the industrial nations accepted equality of treatment, then American productive efficiency would naturally convert the whole world into the American market. Culbertson repeated Wilson's broad sentiments at the 1919 NFTC convention when he enlarged on the government's conception of tariff policy. With the exception of those in the minority,[24] who viewed

23. NFTC Convention *Proceedings*, 1917, 104–05, 106–07.
24. George M. Gillette, president of Minnesota Steel & Machinery Co., in remarks before the 1916 NFTC convention, NFTC Convention *Proceedings*, 1916, 122–25, argued for a

> return to the principle of a tariff which will reasonably protect American industries, and after that I favor the creation of a tariff commission to administer such a law. . . . [Later Gillette explained,] I fully realize that the Chamber of Commerce of the United States . . . is advocating the creation of a tariff commission as a cure all, and I appreciate that body now more nearly than any other body, has the ear of Congress and the President, and still I beg to state my own peculiar and individual belief that the Tariff question will not be settled by a tariff commission. . . . I believe the element of protection is one of the most essential elements in a tariff law. . . .

But Gillette was the only speaker in this vein. All others either stressed foreign markets as primary or interpreted domestic and foreign markets as equally necessary. There was a group of medium- and smaller-sized corporations, not represented at the NFTC, called the American Tariff League, with the journal, *American Economist*, as their organ, which propagandized almost exclusively for protection, irrespective of conse-

the tariff principally or even exclusively as a way to protect parts or all of the domestic market, most business spokesmen respected the right of the metropolitan countries (industrial producers) to maintain protective schedules. In the words of William H. Douglas, such tariffs, once established, were part of the system so long as "no favoritism or inequality" was allowed.[25] Some businessmen analyzed very carefully the consequences of free trade between the United States and the European metropolitan states. Maurice Coster, Vice-president of Westinghouse Electric International, did not see how any "intelligent" American businessman could desire free trade with Europe. "I am firmly of the opinion that nothing could be worse for the future of America's foreign trade than the permission to enter into unrestricted competition with the manufacturers of England, France and Italy in their home markets. . . . If we were permitted to go freely into these markets and compete without restriction, it would mean the temporary, if not the permanent destruction of Europe's industries. . . ."[26]

Like Wilson, Coster thought of postwar trade relations as resting on a community of interest among the industrial powers which would have allowed the protection of domestic markets and competition in the underdeveloped areas. Again like Wilson, Coster conceived of the open door for all industralized nations in nonindustralized markets as the economic equivalent of Wilson's League in the political sphere. Coster was arguing that eliminating industrial competitors was not the way in which to expand world markets.

---

quences on foreign markets. But Gillette was correct when he stated that this group did not have the President's (Wilson then, but Harding later) ear. The NFTC and the Chamber of Commerce operating on the basis of a consensus for the Wilson Tariff Commission view, were the principal business influences on tariff planning.

25. NFTC Convention *Proceedings*, 1919, 141.
26. *Ibid.*, 389–90.

The broad objectives American business and government leaders wished to attain through the weapon of tariff policy were thus clear by 1919. But decisions about specific features were, in large measure, dependent on whether or not the Allies would permit Germany to enter the world market under conditions of equality, and whether or not the Allies would administer the mandates and other territories that had changed hands as a result of the war in a manner consistent with the open door. During the course of 1920 it became clear that the Allies were restricting the opportunity for Germany's economic recovery. Particularly important in this context was the clause in the Versailles Treaty which denied Germany most-favored-nation treatment for the first five years of the Treaty while at the same time forcing it to grant such treatment to the Allies. This meant not just ruin for the most significant industrial complex in Europe, but put great obstacles in the way of the American policy of encouraging the widest possible markets for American production by developing world markets generally. The systems of tariff preference and tariff assimilation evident in the Versailles clauses, when added to the clear tendency of England, France, and the other Allies to monopolize the world's oil resources, convinced American business leaders of the need to "fortify" equality of treatment against the assaults "to which it apparently is soon to be subjected."[27]

27. NFTC Convention *Proceedings*, 1920, 303. Robert R. Patchin, president of W. R. Grace and Co. did not refer specifically to the treaty, but the average American export businessman was aware of the anti-open-door implications of Articles 264 to 270 of the Versailles Treaty. For an opposing view see Bernard Baruch, *The Making of Reparations and Economic Sections of the Treaty* (New York, 1920), 90–95. In 1920 Baruch tended to see the economic clauses as fair. He even "found it difficult to perceive any harshness" in the clause which forced Germany to grant unconditional most-favored-nation treatment to the Allies without reciprocal treatment for German goods (see pages 92–93).

By the spring of 1920, the danger of a sharp tariff war seemed clear. Robert R. Patchin of W. R. Grace and Co. called for speedy development of American tariff policy. Patchin doubted "whether American foreign commerce can be greatly advanced in the long run by the negotiation of a series of reciprocity treaties. . . ." The reduction of tariff duties for the sake of reciprocal relations would evoke active opposition in Congress from representatives of the domestic interests affected, "rendering ratification difficult if not doubtful. . . ." Patchin therefore dismissed reciprocity as an effective approach. Instead, he advocated using access to the large American domestic market "in return for which every country would accord American commerce equality of treatment in its own markets."[28] In its Final Declaration on May 1920, the National Foreign Trade Council (NFTC) Convention declared in favor of a bargaining tariff, with provisions to fight discrimination, "by tariffs or administrative practices, against the trade of the United States."[29]

Decisions on the formulation of an effective tariff treaty policy were suspended during 1920 because two broader questions had to be decided. First, would the United States accept the special-privilege commercial relations flowing from the political-economic decisions of the Versailles Peace Treaty? Second, would the United States participate in the League of Nations, implicitly accepting the Versailles Treaty sections on the disposal of the German and Turkish colonies and those concerning commercial relations in those areas? In the broadest sense, the 1920 election was seen by top American leaders as a time of deciding whether or not to accept the postwar political and economic structure worked out by the Netherlands, Belgium, France, and Great Britain.

28. NFTC Convention *Proceedings*, 1920, 300–01.
29. NFTC Convention *Proceedings*, 1921, xi.

The opposition of some Wilsonions, some Progressive Republicans like Hoover, Stimson, and Root, and certain Democrats like Robert Lansing, foreshadowed rejection of a treaty and League which seemed to institutionalize a closed door world instead of establishing an open door system.[30] While the election sealed the doom of Wilson's conception of the League, it did not basically alter tariff planning. William S. Culbertson, Vice-chairman of the Tariff Commission under Wilson, continued to develop the principle themes of tariff policy under the Republicans.

The depression of 1921, which sharply reduced the level of agricultural prices throughout the world, interrupted temporarily the process of fashioning a tariff which would facilitate the long-range development of American resources. As a result of the decline in world prices during the depression, a danger developed that the American market would be inundated with low-priced commodities already in surplus in

30. Robert Lansing, *The Peace Negotiations: A Personal Narrative* (Cambridge, 1921), 151, 156–57, 159–60. According to Lansing, he early recognized the role of the mandatory system as a means of transferring effective sovereignty to the major European Allies in former German and Turkish possessions. He noted that while the Europeans were to exercise mandatory responsibilities over commercially valuable areas, the United States was offered mandatory power over commercially useless territory. Wilson's annoyance with Lansing's advice led Lansing to confine his objections "to those based on legal difficulties." See also Margaret L. Coit, *Mr. Baruch* (Cambridge, 1957), 234–35, 269, 289–90. According to Coit, Herbert Hoover was the sole member of the American delegation at Paris to criticize the treaty before Wilson openly. But Baruch himself had doubts, though he testified loyally for the treaty before the Senate Foreign Relations Committee in 1919. Lansing did not testify against the treaty, though, according to William Bullitt, he was opposed to it. Baruch, as Wilson, apparently believed that American control of all the available capital could be used as a club to force "equal trade," and cancellation of preferential treaties or other closed door devices. See also Richard N. Current, *Secretary Stimson* (New Brunswick, 1954), 25–28, 29. Here Current describes the positions of Stimson and Root on Article 10.

the United States, such as hard wheat and wool. According to the Tariff Commission, "the demoralization of world markets" led American agricultural interests to demand immediate "emergency duties."[31] The result of these demands was the Emergency Tariff Act of May 27, 1921, which placed heavy (almost prohibitive) duties on agricultural imports. Because the Emergency Act contained no bargaining features and no new rates on manufactures, it bore no relationship to the broad tariff policy which had been under discussion during and immediately after the war.[32]

A week before President Harding signed the Emergency Tariff Act, the Administration picked up the problem of a long-range tariff where it had been left by the outgoing Administration. On May 20, 1921, Wallace McClure, head of the State Department Commercial Treaty Division, sent a memorandum to W. W. Cumberland, Acting Foreign Trade Advisor of the Department, stating the need for the immediate formulation of "a consistent and effective" policy to meet open and hidden discriminations in foreign tariffs. Within the week, State Department Solicitor Dearing asked Cumberland to call a meeting of the various government departments concerned with the problem. The meeting was held on May 26, 1921.[33] Present were Cumberland (presiding), John H. Murray, Joseph S. Gittings, Frederick Simpich, Ray O. Hall, and Wallace McClure from the State Department; Charles E. Herring, the Acting Head of the BFDC and Louis Domeratzky of the BFDC Tariff Division; and Dr. William S. Culbertson of the Tariff Commission.

Cumberland outlined the purposes of the meeting as being (1) to assist the State Department in the formulation

31. U.S. Tariff Commission, *Report on the Emergency Tariff Act of May 27, 1921* (Washington, 1922), 1–4, 99.

32. *Ibid.*, 1–4.

33. May 27, 1921, 611.003/841.

of a policy against discrimination by foreign tariffs, and (2) to cooperate (if requested) on possible recommendations to Congress. Domeratzky observed that Congress might not want advice. Cumberland responded that the Secretary of State might present the Department's views even if they were not directly requested, and that joint recommendations by several departments "might prove very effective."[34] To marshall support for preparing a recommendation to Congress, Culbertson pointed out that Oscar K. Davis, Secretary of the NFTC, and the NFTC as an organization, had endorsed the Tariff Commission's draft of a proposed clause in the projected tariff. Culbertson's views won and a consensus developed favoring a formal recommendation.[35]

Culbertson then proceeded to explain the specific problem confronting the Administration. There were two points of view on the clauses framed by the Tariff Commission. One was represented historically by the bargaining tariff clauses in the tariff acts of 1890 and 1897. These tended to encourage special bargaining for tariff favors. The Tariff Commission condemned such clauses as contrary to the open door commercial policy espoused by Secretary of State Charles Evans Hughes. The difficulty was that special bargaining seemed to be the tariff principle most favorably discussed in Congress.

The other view had its origins in the 1909 tariff which abandoned special privilege in favor of a maximum-minimum principle. The maximum rates were enforced except against countries not discriminating against the United States, which enjoyed the minimum tariff rates. To further perfect the equality-of-opportunity tariff, Secretary of State Knox had proposed in 1911 that the President

34. Minutes of a meeting in W. R. Cumberland's office, May 26, 1921, Exhibit 2, 611.003/841.
35. *Ibid.*

be given the power to raise rates when discrimination was found in foreign tariffs. Culbertson thought that the Knox Draft (with some minor changes) was the best means of obtaining the principle of equality of opportunity. Domeratzky and Herring of the BFDC expressed only mild dissent on the singularly pragmatic ground that retaliation against discrimination would not work well.[36]

Once agreement was reached on a tool of the kind Knox had designed, Culbertson raised the issue of how extensively the equality-of-treatment provisions should be applied. Until then (1921) the United States had regarded the British Imperial Preference system as a domestic British phenomenon. The State Department was confronted with a need to review this position, since it affected the equality-of-opportunity principle. Culbertson thought self-governing dominions should be considered independent nations with respect to tariff policies. If the United States changed its position on foreign preference, however, it would be confronted with its own preference arrangements with Cuba, the Philippines, and Brazil.[37] No case could be made for continuation of Philippine preference, Culbertson maintained. Despite Domeratzky's mild dissent, Culbertson came to the same conclusion on the United States' special tariff relation with Brazil.

All agreed that it was another matter to eliminate preference for Cuba. Such a course would be unjust because Cuba was economically dependent on the United States. "Taking geographical matters into consideration," Culbertson argued, "we should recognize the necessity of customs unions embracing nations and adjacent dependencies or other inter-dependent sovereign nations." France and Algeria and Austria and her neighbors were in much the same category

36. May 27, 1921, 611.003/841.
37. May 26, 1921, 611.003/841.

as Cuba and the United States. In these areas, tariff preference was justified on both geographical and economic grounds.[38]

Domeratzky and Herring proposed that the executive recommend to Congress the inclusion of both equality-of-treatment and concession-negotiation (reciprocity) provisions. Herring argued that the threat to retaliate against discrimination by increasing the American tariff on imports would not work. He suggested that "missionary work" be "done [in Congress] for the concession method." Domeratzky defended the results of some reciprocity agreements between the United States and other nations. He thought Brazilian preference for American exports "more justifiable than other" preference systems because it had been granted to the United States voluntarily.[39] Both Domeratzky and Herring argued that the special-concession method was most likely to obtain for the United States the wider markets it was seeking. Despite the opposition of the two BFDC officials, Culbertson convinced the meeting that the executive departments should recommend to Congress only clauses to secure equality of treatment.[40]

Concurrent with the meeting of representatives from the Tariff Commission and the State and Commerce Departments, the House Ways and Means Committee was framing a permanent tariff bill. The first firm results of the Congressional discussion appeared on June 21, 1921, when Representative Fordney introduced tariff bill H.R. 7465. The same day Assistant Secretary of State J. Reuben Clark sent a memorandum to Undersecretary Fletcher and Secretary Hughes explaining the objectives behind a list of clauses the Tariff Commission and the State and Commerce Depart-

38. *Ibid.*
39. *Ibid.*
40. *Ibid.;* May 27, 1921, 611.003/841.

ments wanted inserted in the Fordney Bill. "We believe," Clark said, "in the open door and desire equality of treatment, and equality of commercial opportunity. We have no means of securing this equality if it is not freely granted. These clauses are expected to provide these means. They are primarily defensive and not offensive. . . . They are necessary to our well being and development. . . ."[41]

The Fordney Bill confronted the State Department with the first threat to its own program. Section 301 of the bill called for special concessions. Section 302 authorized the President "to impose penalty duties on specified products of any country which imposes duties or similar exactions . . . upon like or similar products" of the United States. This provision was designed to force foreign nations to lower tariff rates on any commodities on which the President might wish to negotiate. Section 303 reiterated the demand for general reciprocity treaties contained in section 301, but required that such agreements be concluded within three years of the date of the passage of the bill, and that such agreements remain operational for a maximum of five years. These parts of the Fordney Bill were aimed at reducing the tariffs of foreign nations, rather than at securing equality of treatment for American exporters competing with the exporters of third nations. Congressman Dingley told McClure that the reciprocity sections of the bill had probably been added at the suggestion of the White House. Two days later, on July 14, Clark asked Fletcher if the State Department had discussed with the White House the problem of equality of treatment as opposed to a concessionary tariff.[42] No reply appears in the State Department files, but since Hughes and the State Department continued to work for

41. June 21, 1921, 611.003/844.
42. July 14, 1921, 611.003/845; Wallace McClure, *A New American Commercial Policy* (New York, 1924), 97–99.

equality of treatment as the underlying principle of the tariff, without objection by Harding, the President must either not have been responsible for the offending provisions, or have reversed himself orally to Hughes.

Dearing and McClure were apparently reassured. They discussed the problem of whether or not the State Department should formally oppose sections 301, 302, and 303 of the Fordney Bill. McClure advised Dearing to meet informally with the members of the House Ways and Means Committee and first make all criticisms orally.[43] Apparently McClure thought this an effective means of expressing the Department's views to Congress. Oral criticism would deny to the supporters of reciprocity the opportunity to make the State Department a specific target. He justified such informal advice by arguing that from the point of view of efficient conduct of diplomacy, it was proper for the State Department to criticize and otherwise discuss legislation initiated by Congress. McClure cited the practical economic fact that a majority of business leaders and economists opposed concession tariff bargaining and favored the equality-of-treatment principle. Special concessions were also objectionable on political grounds, because they would leave the Administration open to the charge of favoritism toward special domestic interests.[44]

On July 16, 1921, Culbertson entered the fray against the Fordney Bill with a long memorandum to Dearing. Section 301 would institutionalize a system of tariff discrimination, he maintained. "The policy of special agreements . . . was attempted under the reciprocity provisions of the Dingley Act," but unsuccessfully. "The experience of nations indicates that the benefits from such agreements are not compa-

43. July 14, 1921, 611.003/843.
44. *Ibid.*

rable with the loss which comes from retaliation and international ill-will." It would "result in uncertainty and instability in our tariff policies." Section 302 also violated United States equality-of-opportunity positions; it was designed to force foreign countries to lower specific tariff rates even though they applied equally to all countries. This proviso, said Culbertson, flatly contradicted the American interpretation of the most-favored-nation clause in treaties.

Section 302 violated the "fundamental doctrine" that a nation may impose tariff rates it believes necessary to secure revenue and to encourage the development of domestic industry. This clause in the Fordney Bill also accepted implicitly the French tariff view that high tariff rates in a foreign country are an "offense to a country with low duties." Culbertson reasoned that section 302 would "condemn in foreign countries a practice which we at the same time are asserting our right to pursue at home." It was unlikely, he added, that the section would actually work to reduce rates, for an industry which needed high protection in its home market would hardly be tempted by low tariff rates in foreign markets; "it would not be able to compete in the American market and therefore, would not be concerned with the height of the tariff penalties imposed by the United States."[45]

Culbertson condemned paragraph 369 as a specific application of section 302 to support a drive by the American Automobile Association to promote its export trade by forcing tariff reductions on American automobiles in Great Britain, France, and Canada. He applied similar objections to paragraph 371 on bicycles, and to paragraph 1,545 on coal. They were violations of the American interpretation of the most-favored-nation clause which the government wished to see applied throughout the world. All these provisos violated

45. July 16, 1921, 611.003/835.

the equal treatment policy. Foreign nations could hardly fail, said Culbertson, to respond with retaliation against American commerce. He concluded by urging Dearing to replace sections 301 to 303 with a substitute draft, prepared by the Tariff Commission from the equality-of-treatment approach proposal by Secretary of State Knox in 1911.[46]

At some point between July 1921 and April 1922, the State Department succeeded in convincing key Senate leaders of the necessity of following Culbertson's recommendations. Senator Reed Smoot, Chairman of the Senate Finance Committee, piloted the State Department-Tariff Commission versions of basic policy through the Finance Committee. In a committee report delivered on April 24, Smoot asked for equality of treatment and argued effectively against reciprocity on the same grounds that Culbertson had argued these points to Hughes in July 1921.[47] Smoot and other Senate leaders working with the Administration won a complete victory. The offending clauses of the Fordney Bill, sections 301, 302 and 303, were cut out. The result was the Fordney-McCumber Bill. The result of Senate-House differences was that the Conference Committee of the two houses accepted the Senate version.[48] Culbertson acknowledged that the rates in the conference bill were too high, but he reasoned that this was a minor fault—one which could be handled later. He regarded the bill on the whole as a great victory for the open door principle.[49]

Private business was not so uniformly pleased as Culbertson. Thomas Lamont, whose view was typical of the bankers involved in foreign trade and investment, criticized the tariff

46. *Ibid.*

47. Undated, unsigned memorandum in State Department file which appeared to be an intra-department communication, 611.003/162.

48. *Ibid.*

49. Culbertson to Hughes, July 14, 1922, 611.003/1092.

because it protected "a lot of industries which do not need protection, and cuts off from our farmers and manufacturers a lot of foreign markets that are ready to buy our commodities." The policy outlined in the Fordney-McCumber Act, Lamont argued "will, if pursued, surely wreck a big part of our foreign trade."[50] Paul Warburg, President of the American Acceptance Council, took the same position and reasoned further that the high tariff would make it impossible for Europe to pay its war debt to the United States.[51] The bankers generally favored much lower tariff rates than those written into the Fordney-McCumber Act.

The manufacturers were divided into two groups. One group favored a tariff policy which protected the domestic market against foreign competition; the second believed their industries needed foreign markets to enable them to develop domestic markets most fully. The smaller and medium-sized manufacturers who made up the bulk of the first group argued their views through such journals as the *American Economist*, published by the American Protective Tariff League, and *The Protectionist*, published by the (New England) Home Market Club. They demanded total protection against foreign competitors, argued against "taking the tariff out of politics," and voiced deep suspicion of the Tariff Commission and its efforts to use the flexible provisions of the Fordney-McCumber Act to obtain wider access for American goods in foreign markets.[52]

Those corporations which desired the widest possible markets for American goods acted through the National

50. American Bankers Association, *Journal of the American Bankers Association*, XV, May 1922, 259.

51. American Acceptance Council, *Acceptance Bulletin*, May 1922, 7.

52. See Home Market Club of Boston, *The Protectionist*, XXXVI, May 1925–April 1925, 170–72, 296–97, 402–03, 484–85; *American Economist*, LXXI–LXXII (1923), 1, 19, 74, 95.

Foreign Trade Council. Paralleling Culbertson's analysis, James A. Farrell, Chairman of the NFTC, argued in May 1922 that the American "industrial establishment has reached such a stage that it can produce much more than the domestic market can consume, and that the domestic market can be most highly developed only when substantially all that our industry can produce under normal conditions can be sold."[53] James S. Alexander, President of the National Bank of Commerce, told the 1922 NFTC that "it is idle to think of continuing our course of domestic development without a corresponding development of foreign trade."[54]

Consistent with sentiments expressed in its debates, the Final Declaration of the National Foreign Trade Council (NFTC) Convention, on May 12, 1922, came out in full support of the principle of equal treatment. At the same time, the NFTC called for penalty provisions to retaliate against nations with "tariffs or administrative practices" which discriminated "against the trade or shipping of the United States."[55] Implicitly, the Council endorsed the Culbertson-framed penalty section 317 of the Fordney-McCumber Act.

Culbertson sent a long memorandum to Secretary Hughes on May 31, 1922, suggesting that the United States adopt a whole series of policies to implement its broad commercial policy of the open door. Since 1919, said Culbertson, the Tariff Commission had studied "the tariff relations between the United States and foreign countries, commercial treaties, preferential provisions, economic alliances, [and] the effect of preferential transportation rates." The Commission made three reports, *Reciprocity and Commercial Treaties* (1919),

53. NFTC Convention *Proceedings*, 1922, 573.
54. *Ibid.*, 51–52.
55. *Ibid.*, xiv.

Colonial Tariff Policies (1922), and *Handbook of Commercial Treaties* (1922, in page proof).

Culbertson concluded from the reports of the Commission that equality of treatment in commercial relations between nations, the traditional American goal, could best be served through two policies:

I. The unconditional form and interpretation of the most favored nation clause in commercial treaties and a willingness to make a treaty with every country which will pledge such most favored nation treatment.

II. The open door in economically backward areas of the earth, including colonies.[56]

Culbertson believed these two policies, although connected with "different groups of commercial problems," were "closely related."

To secure the widest possible application of the unconditional most-favored-nation policy, which was made necessary by increased American interest in international trade and finance, Culbertson thought it would be necessary in the years immediately ahead to revise the entire American commercial treaty structure. By writing unconditional most-favored-nation clauses into new and revised treaties, the United States could lay a basis for insisting that foreign nations grant it equality in their markets. Culbertson saw the unconditional most-favored-nation clause as simply an application to commercial intercourse of the other equality-of-treatment principle "—the open door—adopted by western powers to regulate their competitive commercial activities in certain third countries."

But the most persistent and serious problems confronting any implementation of the equality-of-treatment principle went beyond tariff structures and commercial agreements. A

56. May 31, 1922, 611.003/155.

solution to these problems, Culbertson wrote, could be found in bringing to life the open door principle in economically backward areas. The Commission study, *Colonial Tariff Policies*, outlined broad practice for underdeveloped areas. But field studies of the actual commercial policy guiding "leading foreign powers, in particular, Great Britain, France, the Netherlands, and Japan in colonial administration," were needed. The investigation should "relate to two general fields": raw materials and markets.

Many raw materials . . . certain . . . fibers, various metals, numerous vegetable oils—which American industries are using in increased quantities are produced chiefly or solely in areas controlled by other powers. Any movement . . . restricting the use of these materials . . . should be investigated, together with the possibilities of offsetting these combinations by the action of our government or by the investment of American capital in mines and plantations. . . .[57]

The investigation of markets should not be confined to a study simply of explicit discrimination against American trade, but should include information on less obvious means of discrimination. It "should include a study of the possibility of enlarging American export trade by investment in banks, shipping, railroads, factories, and by obtaining contracts for public works and government supplies."[58]

Regardless of whether or not such investigations were made, Culbertson urged the United States to call an international conference on commercial policy to deal "with such questions as unfair methods of competition in international trade, including transportation and communication, [and] equal opportunity of access to the raw materials of the world." In connection with the latter problem, he stressed particularly the colonies and underdeveloped areas of the

57. *Ibid.*
58. *Ibid.*

Pacific and the Far East. Equal access to markets—often blocked by preference—was also stressed. Finally, such a conference should deal with "equal opportunity for the investment of capital in the development of China and other backward parts of the world." In brief, the conference would be called to apply equality of opportunity and the open door "first to nations and then to all colonial possessions and dominions." Culbertson urged such a commercial conference on the grounds that it would be a natural development of Hughes' recent labors at the Arms Limitations Conference.[59]

Culbertson's memorandum to Hughes evoked no direct written reply, but the broad, calculated approach he advocated became Administration policy. Hughes apparently gave verbal orders for various investigations of foreign violations of the equal treatment-open door policies. On July 19, at any rate, Foreign Trade Advisor Arthur C. Millspaugh, and Assistant Secretary William Phillips received reports from Stanley K. Hornbeck of the Trade Advisors Office and Frank Eldridge, the BFDC liaison man with the State Department.[60]

The reports indicted Britain, France, the Netherlands, Japan, and Belgium for a whole series of discriminations against American commerce. For example, the Dutch colonial office denied Americans equal opportunity to invest in railways and petroleum enterprise, and was applying pressure to stop Western Union from opening offices on Java, a move that discriminated against United States communications firms. The British, the Belgians, and the Dutch were reported to be following a similar pattern of discrimination against American interests.[61] Hornbeck advocated using sec-

59. *Ibid.*
60. July 19, 1922, 611.003/1380.
61. *Ibid.;* Hornbeck and Eldridge to Phillips and Millspaugh, July 18, 1922, 611.003/1382.

tion 317 of the projected tariff bill as a proper means for prompt handling of some of the discriminations; ultimately, he felt, cooperation between American banking, manufacturing, commercial interests, and governmental agencies was also needed.[62]

While Hornbeck and Millspaugh were detailing the extent of discriminations against American trade and investment, Congress passed (and, on September 21, 1922, the President signed) the Fordney-McCumber Act. Section 317 of the Act contained the equality-of-treatment provision Culbertson and the State Department had recommended. A week later, on September 28, Assistant Secretary Leland Harrison asked Arthur N. Young of the Trade Advisors Office to prepare a memorandum outlining the responsibilities of the State Department under the new Tariff Act.

Trade Advisor Millspaugh received a memorandum in reply on October 21. It was prepared by Wallace McClure and Hornbeck. They suggested that two areas of responsibility were implied by the language of section 317: the United States should convert its treaty structure from the conditional to the unconditional form of the most-favored-nation clause; concurrently, the term "discrimination," as it was used in foreign commercial policy discussion and legislation, should be defined broadly to include various systems of imperial preference.[63]

McClure argued that the growth of the American economy made a broad definition of discrimination necessary in order to undermine the British and French exclusive tariff systems. The war and prewar periods, McClure explained, had expanded American industry enormously to a point

62. Hornbeck and Eldridge to Phillips and Millspaugh, July 19, 1922, 611.003/1380.
63. McClure and Hornbeck to Leland Harrison, October 21, 1922, 611.0031/189.

where "exportation became essential to industrial prosperity." Under these circumstances, continued industrial expansion was dependent on the widest possible nondiscriminatory market system. American policymakers concluded that writing the unconditional most-favored-nation clause into treaties with a majority of the independent nations of the world would so widen the American market. But two foreign commercial systems succeeded in excepting a considerable portion of the world from such a nondiscriminatory system. The French two-column tariff discriminated against nations with high rates (the United States under the Fordney-McCumber Tariff) while giving minimum tariff provisions to other nations with low rates on French exports. The British imperial preference system also functioned to create exclusive markets and deny equal access to Americans. Under section 317 the State Department was obliged to press for elimination of imperial preference and the two-column tariff systems, and McClure argued that the penalty provision (317) of Fordney-McCumber "provides a supply of dry powder for use against . . . violators of the principle of equality."[64]

On the same day that McClure sent his memorandum to Millspaugh (October 21), Arthur N. Young suggested to Hughes that the Secretary organize a campaign to make the unconditional most-favored-nation principle the basis of commercial treaties. Young proposed that Hughes call a meeting at the White House to include the President, Hoover, and leading members of the Senate Foreign Relations and the House Foreign Affairs Committees. If a new treaty system were outlined by the Administration, Young thought that Congressional leaders would support it. Such a conference in any event was necessary, he argued, before Congress made a decision on treaty policy.[65]

64. *Ibid.*
65. Arthur N. Young to Hughes, October 21, 1922, 611.003/179.

Hughes followed Young's suggestion. An intra-adminis-
tration meeting was held, and the unconditional form of the
most-favored-nation clause was endorsed. On December 14,
1922, Culbertson, apparently at Hughes' request, sent the
Secretary a modified version of his memorandum of May 31,
1922. It repeated his arguments for the unconditional most-
favored-nation clause as the best means of extending the
open door to the whole world.[66] Hughes sent the Culbertson
memorandum to Senator Lodge of the Foreign Relations
Committee. On January 8, 1923, Lodge replied to Hughes
that he was impressed with Culbertson's recommendations
and that he wished to discuss the proposal again with
Hughes.[67] Apparently Lodge agreed orally to the changed
treaty policy. The new commercial treaty policy was formally endorsed by President Harding on February 27, 1923.
The unconditional most-favored-nation treaty structure,
Harding wrote, was "probably the surer way of effectively
extending our trade abroad." At the same time, Harding
expressed the hope that Cuba would be excepted from the
new policy. Here again Culbertson's recommendation was
followed.[68]

Once the State Department secured the President's approval of the new treaty policy, the Tariff Commission proceeded to investigate tariff discrimination by foreign nations.
In reviewing the report of the Commission, McClure reported that the French two-column tariff presented the most
immediate threat to the equality-of-treatment principle in
world tariff policies. To succeed, America's new policy had
to overcome the French policy of discrimination. He argued

66. U.S. Department of State, *Papers Relating to the Foreign Relations of the United States*, 1923, 29 vols. (Washington, 1925–1944), I,
123–24. (Hereafter cited as *Foreign Relations*.)
67. *Ibid.*, 126–27.
68. *Ibid.*, 128–29.

that France should be pushed hard at the final stage of ultimate negotiation, but that first the United States should lay the groundwork to show that its position was the wave of the future. This could be accomplished by the negotiation of a series of unconditional treatment agreements with those countries and regions clearly receptive because of their own immediate interests.[69] Once Central America, Central Europe, the Balkans, and perhaps Finland signed such treaties, he suggested, the United States could then move toward an equality-of-treatment treaty with Spain. If Spain signed such a treaty, then the United States should proceed to press France vigorously.[70] McClure's analysis was followed by a general instruction from Hughes to all United States diplomatic officers announcing the new American treaty policy.[71]

The State Department proceeded to open negotiation for the desired treaties. It generally succeeded in Central Europe, Latin America, and the Balkans. The first obstacle arose when the Senate was considering the treaty of Commerce Amity and Friendship with Germany in December 1923. The majority of the Senate Foreign Relations Committee approved the Commerce Treaty with Germany in February of 1924, but that same majority favored attaching reservations which would permit Congress to legislate in a manner so as to discriminate against German and in favor of American shipping.[72]

The Committee's action threatened the efforts of the State Department to obtain equality of treatment. On February 13 McClure explained that this action would block "the completion of unconditional most-favored-nation

69. July 17, 1923, 611.003/188.
70. *Ibid.*
71. Hughes instruction to American diplomatic officers of August 18, 1923, *Foreign Relations*, 1923, I, 131–32.
72. McClure to Young, February 13, 1924, 611.0031/240.

treaties" with nations having merchant marines. "More than anything else," he pointed out, "we want to obtain from the parts of the British Empire treatment not less advantageous than that which is accorded to foreign countries or to other countries of the Empire which maintain their . . . complete autonomy in regard to customs tariffs." To ask for such a high degree of equality in customs matters and at the same time reserve the right to discriminate on short notice in the matter of shipping would probably strike the British as humorous. "There seems to be little we can do [to attack the British preference system]," McClure lamented, "until we have succeeded definitely in making our commercial policy one of complete equality of treatment."[73]

Hughes attempted to convince the Chairman of the Foreign Relations Committee, Henry Cabot Lodge, to use his influence to have the Senate drop its shipping reservations. No doubt basing his remarks on McClure's analysis of the relationship between the German treaty and a campaign to crack the British imperial preference system, Hughes wrote to Lodge that "if the treaty with Germany is approved, we shall be in a position to conclude negotiations with other powers upon the same basis and in this way most effectively to remove whatever discriminations may now exist to the prejudice of the United States."[74] Lodge made no formal reply. Very probably he was unwilling to surrender the right of Congress to discriminate in favor of American shipping.

In any event, the German treaty remained stalled in the Senate throughout 1924. Arthur N. Young explained to Assistant Secretary of State Leland Harrison that until "the Senate acts on the German Treaty," the Department could not "advantageously proceed with further negotiations for

73. *Ibid.*
74. Hughes to Lodge, March 13, 1924, *Foreign Relations*, 1924, II, 183–92.

general commercial treaties, and therefore [it] is limited to making less formal arrangements to protect American interests."[75] Unfortunately the State Department was in no position to take advantage of the fact that in July 1924 a Labor government was elected in Britain, which, unlike the outgoing Conservatives, was not wedded to the imperial preference system.[76] American shipping preferences—provided for in the Senate's reservations about the German treaty— still blocked the antipreference program.

McClure, who became increasingly skeptical of favorable Senate action on the German treaty, suggested to Young on November 10, 1924, that the Department cut the "Gordion Knot" of shipping discrimination by submitting legislation to Congress to repeal the offending sections of the Merchant Marine Act (Jones Act) of 1920. Until the United States ended its own preferential rules, American criticism of British preference stood on weak ground.[77] Repeal of section 34 of the Jones Act would make Senate reservations about the German treaty academic and therefore clear the way for the conclusion of a large number of treaties. The Department did not act upon McClure's proposal, and its hope that the Senate would drop its reservations to the German treaty did not materialize. On February 9, 1925, the Senate ratified the treaty with the key reservations attached. In this manner the Senate frustrated the planned campaign against imperial preference.

The battle against the French two-column tariff which, "aside from imperial preference," was defined as the most difficult obstacle[78] to obtaining the widest possible markets for American goods, fared little better than the antipreference effort. Spain resisted American overtures. This in turn

75. Young to Harrison, July 3, 1924, 611.031/220.
76. McClure to Young, July 3, 1924, 611.0031/217.
77. McClure to Young, November 10, 1924, 611.0031/233.
78. McClure to Young, July 3, 1924, 611.0031/217.

relieved the French of any pressure which a Spanish treaty might have applied. By 1925, then, only vanquished Germany of the three major powers accepted the American treaty proposals. The two major discriminatory systems, British imperial preference and French two-column reciprocity, were undamaged.

In general, the European nations argued that their policy of discrimination was no more an impediment to trade than the high rates in the Fordney-McCumber Act. Culbertson and McClure agreed to the extent of admitting that the specific rates were excessively high. But Culbertson told Hughes in July 1922 that the high rates were probably necessary at least until British currency was stabilized.[79] When the European nations accepted the Dawes Plan in 1924, and Germany went on the gold standard and Britain was forced to follow suit, McClure proposed a lowering of American rates. In a note to Young on November 10, 1924, McClure suggested that section 317 of the Fordney-McCumber Act be amended to give the President power to lower tariff rates.[80]

Technically the President possessed such power under the

79. Culbertson to Hughes, July 14, 1922, 611.003/1092.

80. McClure to Young, November 10, 1924, 611.003/233. As the man directly involved in organizing the negotiation of commercial treaties with foreign nations, it was easy for McClure to note that the high level of the American tariff stood in the way of further extension of the American treaty system. He proposed to Young that Congress be asked to amend section 317 of the Tariff Act of 1922 to allow the President to proclaim limited reductions if this would enable the United States to obtain like reductions in the tariffs of other nations, arguing that "in this way our tariff could be gradually reduced, not as a free gift to other countries but in return for corresponding advantages." See also U.S. Tariff Commission, *The Tariff and Its History* (Washington, 1934), 83. Under the law, the President had the right to raise or lower duties, under section 315 of the Act, by as much as 50 percent, "after investigation by the Tariff Commission, in order to equalize foreign and domestic costs of production." But McClure's memorandum (above) seems to indicate that lowering rates was a dead letter under administrative procedures.

existing law, but the procedures under which he administered the law made that theoretical power a dead letter.
Throughout the 1920's the majority in Congress refused to
consider tariff cuts. The State Department was therefore
unable to use lower rates as an inducement to European
nations to accept the unconditional most-favored-nation
clause. By 1929 the United States had signed only eight of
the desired treaties. In addition, the Administration framed
a dozen executive agreements implementing the American
position in a less formal manner.[81]

The State Department failed, at least in a relative sense,
to establish the unconditional most-favored-nation clause as
the basis of world tariff relations. This failure sharply limited Hoover's efforts to implement the overseas investment of
American capital in the underdeveloped areas of the world.
In substance there were three possible areas (outside the
Western Hemisphere) in which Hoover could channel
American technology: Russia, China, or the British Empire.
Until the Bolsheviks fell, American capital would not go to
the Soviet Union. The Nationalist Revolution in China, combined with the off-again on-again effort by Japan to convert
much of that nation into a sphere of influence, temporarily
removed China from the world market for capital. The imperial preference system acted just as certainly, if more
subtly, to close Africa, India, and Southeast Asia to American capital.

The British imperial preference system did not in most
cases forbid American investment, but it gave to competing
British investors a significant advantage. American investors who might wish to enter the British Empire faced tariff
walls against their own capital goods which tended to wipe
out the lower costs of American production, except in Can-

81. McClure to Secretary Stimson, March 30, 1929, *Foreign Relations*, 1929, I, 988–93.

ada, where geographical proximity and currency convertibility tended to undermine the preference advantage which British investors possessed in relation to their American competitors. The foreign investment of capital—and the installation of national technology resulting from such investment—tended to create controlled export markets. The preference system limited the areas into which American capital could go, and therefore curtailed American export markets.

American leaders had hoped to use the Fordney-McCumber Act to help them undermine and finally eliminate preferences. Their failure contributed to the failure of Hoover's program. But their failure was in large part due to the adamant position maintained by Britain and France. New Deal leaders were to turn back to the tactical weapon of reciprocity treaties in their effort to break the preference system, yet Secretary of State Cordell Hull was still struggling with the same battle at the end of World War II.

CHAPTER IX

🐦 *Community and Its Disintegration: 1916–1929*

FROM 1916 to 1923 the Europeans threw up every conceivable roadblock to the seemingly new American plan to manage the world's economy. In reality the American plan was to displace the faltering leader of the previous century, Great Britain. One by one American leaders tore down the obstacles to United States commercial leadership and the Europeans—with Britain in the lead—fell back to new positions, until in 1924 they surrendered.

The Allies agreed with the American contention that the European economy had to be reconstructed if the great damage wrought to the European social system by the war was to be repaired and Bolshevism successfully repelled. They were unwilling, however, to pay the financial cost of eliminating the economic and political dangers. In all essentials they wanted Germany and the United States to bear the financial burden.[1] Indeed, on May 22, 1919, Lloyd George went so far as to suggest to Wilson that the Succession

---

1. Norman H. Davis to President Wilson, February 21, 1920, *Senate Document No. 86*, U.S. Senate, Committee on Judiciary, *Loans to Foreign Governments*, 67th Cong., 2d sess. (Washington, 1921), 77. Davis told the President that while "the allies have never bluntly so stated, their policy seems to be to make Germany indemnify them for having started the war and make us indemnify them for not having entered the war sooner."

States to the Austrian Empire be required to share in Austrian reparations obligations, explaining that they should not "get their freedom without paying for it."[2] If in the British view the Czechs and Hungarians were legitimately bound to pay for Austria's cocriminality with Germany in launching the war, so much more so were the Germans liable for the various costs of the war. Lord Cunliffe, former Governor of the Bank of England, a man educated to the facts of international economics and thus aware of the commercial disaster implied in his own proposal, argued that the Germans could sustain an overall reparations bill of $120 billion and an annual amortization of $5 billion. Lloyd George admitted that such a bill could never be paid, but insisted nevertheless that such an obligation should be written into the Treaty, with adjustment possible later.[3] By supporting Cunliffe in such an unworkable proposal Lloyd George undoubtedly hoped to score points for the British argument that reparations and inter-Allied war debts were intimately linked and to bring pressure to bear upon the United States for mutual cancellation of war debts. This would of course place the ultimate cost of financing the war upon American taxpayers. German reparations obligations were to be reduced in relation to the amount of Allied debts the American Treasury might cancel.

But despite the ex post facto popularity of the view among European and American academics that as chief commercial victor in the war the United States should have been willing to cancel Allied war debts as a condition of Allied agreement to a practical reparations bill for Germany, United States leaders could not reasonably have been expected to accept any such proposal. President Wilson and the succeeding

2. Seth P. Tillman, *Anglo-American Relations at the Paris Peace Conference of 1919* (Princeton, 1961), 258.
3. *Ibid.*, 238–40.

Harding Administration believed that German investments seized by the Allies in Southern, Eastern, and Central Europe and in the Turkish Empire, as well as the preferential trading agreements they had imposed on the weaker nations, were more than sufficient repayment for the costs of the war. Cancellation of war debts would simply provide additional spoils for the Allies, with American taxpayers footing the bill. American leaders were willing to cancel part of the war debts if the Allies would agree to a reasonable reparations bill for Germany, and if they would dismantle preferential trading agreements among themselves. But the British and the continental Allies were not ready to make concessions until their own preferential and closed door methods failed at the end of 1923.

It would have been impossible in 1918 and 1919 for British leaders to accept the relatively equitable American peace proposals. Public opinion in Britain during the war had been charged in the direction of a harsh peace, and so the British supported the successful French demand that Germany be denied her prewar commercial treaty rights for five years (as previously resolved at the Paris Economic Conference of 1916), while the Allies would continue to force Germany to give them unconditional most-favored-nation treatment. A Germany deprived of any sort of steady markets for five years would give to the Allies time in which to gain a lead on Germany in world markets. Even the threat of a Bolshevik Germany, which such commercial restrictions posed, failed to move British leaders to fix a definite payable reparations figure.[4]

The apparently more selfish view of Europe did not, as so many Americans assumed, reflect the innate superiority of the American plan. The differing British and American pro-

4. Tillman, *Anglo-American Relations at the Peace Conference,* 242.

grams reflected the disparate and conflicting national interests of each society. Leaders of the European nations, with
Britain in the vanguard, believed sincerely that they could
begin to view the world as a community only after they had
satisfied pressing demands of national interest which they
defined as keys to their continued existence as viable states.

The leaders of Europe had of necessity to define conditions of stability in terms of their own experience. The
Europeans lost material and human resources to such an
extent that in the case of Britain, for example, the population
was threatened with severely lowered living standards. Britain's means of creating national wealth, foreign investments,
export markets, and access to vital industrial raw materials
at low cost, and its ability to perform international services
in the fields of insurance, shipping, and finance were considerably diminished. At the same time the ability of the United
States to expand its wealth had grown immensely—to a
considerable extent at the expense of Great Britain. The
British believed fervently that before they could cooperate
with the United States in rebuilding a world market with a
system of trade, payments, and investment encouraging
growth and expansion—in other words, a world similar to
the one that had existed for most of the century prior to
1914—they had first to rebuild their own system of expanding national wealth. Together with France in Europe and
the self-governing dominions around the world, they hoped
to accomplish this by means of preferential trading agreements and tariff assimilation. Indeed, such policies reflected
a hard-headed assessment of national interest. But so too did
the more objectively generous American program reflect
national interest.

The difference among the great powers over priorities to
be observed in building a world community of interest were
compounded by the fact that for the first time in a century

the fundamental system of values shared by the nations of
Europe and North America were dangerously challenged by
the Bolshevik Revolution and, to an alarming extent, by the
Nationalist revolutionary movements of the Arab East,
North Africa, and China. Unlike the participants in the
liberal and democratic revolutions of the nineteenth century,
who wanted merely to extend to themselves full rights in a
system based on parliamentary democracy and free enterprise, and who believed the system itself to be equitable, the
leaders of the revolts growing out of World War I sought to
destroy the existing system.[5]

To a very large extent the outbreak of the Bolshevik
Revolution, causing the first breach in the international system evolved up to 1914, was the result of the interplay of
two factors to which World War I gave rise: (1) economically, the outbreak of war destroyed the delicate network of
commercial ties which constituted the world market, dimin-
ishing the amount of real wealth available to each contestant
for purposes of waging war and sustaining the civil population; (2) politically, the consequence of this economic
breakdown and the eroded living standards it implied resulted in a loss of faith in and respect for traditional hier-
archies of political authority. To a greater or lesser degree
all the European combatants suffered civil disaffection. But
in Russia the ideological impact was so great that it tended
to throw up political power to any element capable of seizing
it. Lenin recognized this reality and took advantage of it to
seize power in Russia. He also urged revolutionary leaders
in other countries, imperfectly enjoying the fruits of the
existing international division of labor, to follow Russia's
example.[6]

   5. Edward Hallett Carr, *Conditions of Peace* (New York, 1942),
11–12.
   6. *Ibid.*, 11–12.

But it was the war which gave the Bolsheviks an audience for their appeal; in the absence of the destruction of capital, natural resources, and human life flowing from the war, few people, even in the weakest national segments of the pre-1914 international economy, would have had probable cause for protesting the way in which the world market distributed income and concomitant privileges. President Wilson showed that he understood this when he argued at the Peace Conference that the "poison of Bolshevism" was a "protest against the way in which the world had worked," the antidote to which was in Wilson's view a "new world order."[7]

But while the world would benefit from the American version of a "new world order," the United States as the managing element in the recreated world market would benefit most. The United States was to be the "engine" of the world economy,[8] which would haul the world to prosperity.

7. Tillman, *Anglo-American Relations at the Peace Conference*, 61.

8. This phrase is Dean Acheson's. He was arguing his view of what America's role should be in the post World War II period. Acheson wrote: "the system has been destroyed which expanded the power of Western Europe and permitted industrial development in societies in which individual liberty survived. One to replace it will be devised, managed, and largely (but not wholly) financed by the United States; otherwise it is likely to be provided by the Soviet Union, under circumstances destructive of our own power and of an international environment in which independent and diverse nations may exist and flourish." *Power and Diplomacy* (New York, 1963), 19–20. America's leaders during the 1920's shared with Acheson the goal of constructing an American-led world community to replace the British-led community which World War I had destroyed. But Acheson and his successors are much more ready to use force than were Harding, Hoover, and Hughes to protect such an American-led community against challenge. Acheson argues that the measured use of force (which is a dangerous euphemism implying that any amount of force necessary to suppress a challenge is legitimate) is requisite to protecting the system. Acheson has of course deceived himself and the American public by arguing that the force is to be used against the Soviet Union. But in reality the Acheson view of the world (shared by Dean Rusk) sets the United States up in the business of

The United States was the only nation emerging from World War I with a surplus of capital available to develop at long term the world's resources and to finance the world's day-to-day merchandise trade. Before any new resources could be developed the products of previous investment had to be marketed. The links between Europe and Latin America, among other prewar commercial ties, had to be reopened. But in order for Europe to buy from and sell to Latin America on anything like its prewar scale, Europe had to be reconstructed—both vanquished and victor nations concurrently. Simple reconstruction of the victors would not suffice, because markets would continue to be too narrow.

During the period 1918 to 1922 American bankers made an effort to finance the orderly marketing of primary products in Latin America. The system of branch banks the Morgan and Rockefeller interests established in Latin America during these years were largely designed to funnel short-term capital on deposit in the United States banking system into financing Latin American merchandise trade. But by 1922 these efforts suffered dismal failure; many of the American branch banks sank into insolvency and suffered considerable losses. This proved to American bankers, and to some extent American manufacturers and political leaders, that without the reintegration of Germany into a world economy, markets would continue to be too narrow to absorb even existing production, much less encourage

---

revolution suppression. The ease with which revolutions of all kinds can be defined as Soviet (or Chinese) threats under this view of the world is well demonstrated in American policy toward the Dominican Republic and Vietnam. To suppress a revolution is *not* the first step toward building a community. On the contrary, it is the first step toward waste of resources which could be used to build a true community. In this connection American leaders of the 1920's had a healthy skepticism about the easy use of force, even for limited objectives. We could learn a good deal from them.

the investment of American capital in the development of additional resources.

Since American leaders thought of a recreated world market as the only long-run basis for social stability and economic expansion, they concentrated their efforts on forging weapons with which to force the Allies to dismantle preferential trading agreements affecting areas which had changed hands as a result of the war and the peace treaty and to allow Germany to reenter the world economy without excessive reparations obligations. The United States created tools to attain the former objective when it enacted into law the Webb-Pomerene Act in 1918, the Edge Act in 1919, and the Fordney-McCumber Tariff in 1922. The American weapon to obtain a workable place for Germany in the world economy consisted of its ability to refuse to lighten the burden of the war debts the Allies owed the United States, until they in turn eased Germany's burden.

The American effort was successful. By the fall of 1922 Britain found itself unable to sustain its own program without extensive United States investment in Europe and the underdeveloped countries. New negotiations began on the subject of German reparations, with Britain showing a strong willingness to compromise on the issue. The same was true on the issue of closed door administration of the mandates. By the time of the Lausanne Conference of 1922 the British acknowledged that the closed door had failed; and so they accepted the open door in the Near East.[9]

9. Hughes to Harding, November 25, 1922, Charles Evans Hughes Manuscripts, Manuscript Divison, Library of Congress, Letters 1921–1925. In reporting to Harding on the results of the Lausanne Conference and saying in effect that the British had come round to accept the American demand for the open door in the Middle East, Hughes told Harding: "Curzon stated, after some discussion, that as long ago as the Tripartite agreement, the British began to abandon any moves toward zones, concessions and special privileges and were now prepared

Shortly thereafter, during 1923, British and American banking officials began to cooperate closely in matters of international finance, a move symbolized on a grand scale by discussion of a joint loan by Anglo-American bankers to the German government to stabilize that country's currency. On the more mundane scale British banking leaders agreed that the pound and the dollar could both be used profitably in the day-to-day finance of world trade.

In 1922 and 1923 the United States leaders also made some concessions in order to obtain British and French adherence to the projected world community. For example, they expressed some willingness to discuss the extent to which British and other Allied war debts to the United States might be scaled down. Treasury Secretary Andrew Mellon agreed with his predecessor, David F. Houston, who argued that cancellation, "does not involve mutual sacrifices on the part of the nations concerned. It simply involves a contribution mainly by the United States." He agreed too that any adjustment of war debts would have to "take into account advantages obtained by such debtor countries under the treaty of peace." Such advantages of course included seized German investments, "discriminatory advantages and exclusive concessions."[10]

But under neither Harding nor Wilson was the United States unreasonable. With the active assistance of Mellon

---

to support at the conference open door policy in the Near East. He disclosed that the Italians and the French were not in accord as to this. Not withstanding press reports to the contrary, it is his belief that the French will abandon Cilicia, but that both the Italians and the French desire selected Prizes." The words are Hughes' paraphrase of Child.

10. U.S. World War Foreign Debts Commission, *Combined Annual Reports of the World War Foreign Debts Commission: With Additional Information Regarding Foreign Debts Due the United States* (Washington, 1927), 69–70, 74.

and over the confused opposition of such a future New Deal statesman as Congressman Cordell Hull (Dem., Tenn.), the Harding and Coolidge Administrations reduced the war debts on the basis of ability to pay. This kind of distinction meant, of course, that Britain as the great victor in terms of commercial spoils, and the wealthiest in terms of per capita income, would have to pay a much higher percentage of its original war debt than Italy with its much lower per capita income and its impoverished southern regions. Indeed, Mellon defended the extent to which the United States had reduced the debt against Congressional attacks urging a more intensive collection on two essential grounds: 1) the Allies should not have to pay that portion of their debts which they had actually spent in fighting World War I; 2) it was in the national interest of the United States to "think of the financial reorganization of Europe along the same general lines as the reorganization of some large industrial corporation heavily involved after some severe depression. We have become, whether we like it or not, the most important creditor of Europe. In this capacity we are like the general creditors of the embarrassed corporation. Our money is in and we want it out, but it is impossible to get more than the debtor can pay. If we insist on too difficult terms, we receive nothing. We must then settle upon such terms as will give our debtor reasonable opportunity to live and prosper."[11]

Rightly or wrongly, Mellon believed that the United States had fixed a level of payments that Europe could sustain and that would not interfere with the reintegration of the world economy and the development of world markets upon which the ultimate prosperity of the world depended.[12]

11. Speech to the Union League of Philadelphia, March 24, 1926 in *ibid.*, 299–300.
12. *Ibid.*, 301–02.

Once it was clear in 1923 that the European Allies were willing to allow Germany to reenter world markets on a relatively equal basis, American political leaders were willing to encourage American bankers to float, jointly with British bankers, a $200 million loan to a new German Central Bank. But American participation was conditioned on the agreement that these Dawes loans would take priority over reparations payments. Two problems remained. Some means had to be found to enable Germany to make fixed reparations payments, and some means had to be found or created to allow Germany to sell its exports in world markets. American leaders thought the Dawes Plan would create a mechanism to deal with reparations and, at the same time, create conditions for the long-run expansion of markets for German exports.

American leaders also regarded the Tariff Act of 1922 as a contribution to a reintegrated world economy and a world community of interest. During the debates and hearings in Congress on the Fordney-McCumber Bill the various special-interest groups had about arrived at a consensus that reciprocity, the exchange of mutual tariff-cutting concessions, was the best way for each interest and the collective majority to expand foreign markets for American goods. But such reciprocal negotiations led inevitably to special bargains and discrimination among nations. They encouraged preferential arrangements which would have tended to prevent the reformation of a true world market based on nondiscrimination. Without an integrated world market, world trade would expand at a relatively sluggish rate. The Administration had to muzzle the influence of special interests in the writing of the tariff. It did so; the Tariff Commission, together with the State and Commerce Departments, wrote the basic clauses of the Tariff Act of 1922 in such a way as to offer to foreign nations access to the huge American market on condition that they accept the unconditional most-favored-nation clause as the underlying basis of the network of world commercial agreements.

Once the United States and its former co-belligerents compromised on such basic issues as war debts, Germany's reparations bill, the open door, and an American tariff facilitating the unconditional most-favored-nation clause as the governing principle in the framing of commercial treaties, the United States was willing to open its formerly locked gates to American capital investment abroad. In that connection too, American leaders believed that they made a significant contribution to a world community of interest. Under Herbert Hoover's direction the United States attempted to frame a foreign investment policy which would (1) guide foreign investments into ventures expanding the production of real goods and services, therefore benefiting both the investors and the capital receiving nation and (2) prevent wasteful investment which might impoverish both foreign investors and the peoples of the investment-receiving countries.

Without a doubt American foreign economic policy from 1916 to 1929 was a continuum. Wilson and his Republican successors desired an economic community of interest which the United States would manage, with the Western Europeans and Japan acting as associates with full rights in the system. That was, in all essentials, what the United States in fact created from 1916 to 1929.

Epilogue I: Political, 1919–1921

But an economic foreign policy is carried out within a political framework. On the institutional structure of this political framework Wilson and his successors disagreed.

Wilson and the supporters of the League of Nations had about concluded that a concert of power should be created to enforce the peace and guarantee the territorial integrity of the members of the world organization. Yet Wilson did not believe Article 10, which gave this guarantee, would unalterably work against change, but merely proscribe violence as a means of obtaining change.

Harding, Hoover, and Hughes thought the framework provided by Article 10 unworkable. In an address before the Union League Club of Philadelphia on March 26, 1919, Hughes expressed the opposition's view that "the guaranty makes no allowance for changes which may be desirable. It ascribes a prescience and soundness of judgment to the present peace conference in erecting states and defining boundaries which nobody in the history of the world has ever possessed." Hughes argued that instead of encouraging desirable and even necessary change, Article 10 "attempts to make permanent existing conditions . . . in a world of dynamic forces to which no one can set bounds. It gives no fair opportunity for adjustments." Hughes asserted that the Wilsonions wrongly assumed "that helpful cooperation in the future will be assured by the attempted compulsion of an inflexible rule," and believed that a community of "ideals, interests and purposes," to which he was as committed as were the League advocates, was more likely to "be promoted by freedom of conference than by the effort to create [the] hard and fast engagements" implied by Article 10.[13]

Wilson was not so naive as to assume that voting majorities would appear automatically in the Assembly of the League sustaining in all, or even most, instances a course of action leading to equitable change. The Wilsonions were

13. Merlo J. Pusey, *Charles Evans Hughes* (New York, 1951), I, 396.

aware that power begets votes,[14] but in addition they believed the United States possessed an ideological weapon to create American-led majorities; the United States was the only power crusading for both rapid economic development *and* self-determination. With this policy Wilson thought the United States would become the natural advocate of the smaller powers, which would then vote for American interests because they would coincide with their own.

Wilson also had a powerful weapon in the nation's overwhelming commercial strength, which he was willing to use as a weapon for peaceful change.[15] Wilson's thinking on the

14. In a remarkable analysis of the relationship between power, justice, and votes at international conferences, Rear Admiral William S. Benson of the United States Naval Advisory staff explained to Wilson on April 9, 1919 how nations advocating justice could secure votes.

> Our own prospective world position needs special considerations. We are setting out to be the commercial rival of Great Britain on the seas. We know that increase of population, the development of our great national resources, and our lack of real dependence on the rest of the world, spread before us the promise of a greater future than any other power may expect. The gradual realization of this promise is bound to excite enmity and to cause unjust opposition to our expanding world interest. Heretofore we have lived apart, but now we are to live in constant and intimate relation with the rest of the world. We must be able to enter every world conference with the confidence of equality. We can have this confidence in but one way and that is by actually being equal to the greatest. The equality that counts in conferences as well as in conflicts is the equality of power, and especially for us the equality of sea power. Given that equality, our superiority of motive will attract to us a following that will mean better days in the world. But while we are weak we may expect the powers of the world to group themselves about strength rather than about the promise of a distant justice.

Cited in Ray Stannard Baker, *Woodrow Wilson and World Settlement* (New York, 1923), III, 213–14.

15. As early as July 21, 1917, Wilson wrote to House stressing the underlying assumption that controlling foreign access to America's surplus capital was the key method of constructing a proper postwar world. For example: "England and France have not the same view with regard

Japanese demand for a sphere of influence in the Shantung Peninsula illustrates how he hoped to implement his policies. When Japan threatened at the Paris Peace Conference that if the United States did not recognize the special economic privileges which it had seized from Germany in Shantung it would refuse to take part in the League, Wilson uncomfortably surrendered to Japanese demands.

He hoped, however, to use two means to press Japan to return sovereignty over Shantung to China. He thought he could marshall votes in the Assembly of the League for a proposal which would obligate Japan, in theory at least, to respect Chinese sovereignty. In addition, Japan was experiencing a desperate shortage of investment capital, and the United States could refuse access to private American capital for the development of Shantung unless Japan pledged that the investment would not undermine Chinese political sovereignty. Wilson planned to use control of private capital issues to sustain the open door in China just as he was using war debts to frustrate discriminatory agreements and special trading arrangements with respect to the other areas changing hands as a result of the War and the Peace Treaty.[16]

---

to peace that we have by any means. When the war is over we can force them to our way of thinking, because by that time they will, among other things, be financially in our hands." Cited in William Diamond, *The Economic Thought of Woodrow Wilson* (Baltimore, 1943), 190, footnote 75. As has been demonstrated, the Administration could deny to foreign nations access to American private capital investment by simply refusing to approve such loans. Without informal government approval, private bankers would not make the loans, fearful as they were that the United States government would insist that war debts repayment take precedence over subsequent private loans. Wilson did not overstate the degree to which the Europeans would be "financially in our hands."

16. Davis to Rathbone, May 12, 1920, *Special Committee on Investigation of the Munitions Industry*, 74th Cong., 2d sess. (Washington, 1936), 9490. Though usually ignored in this light, German rights in Shantung which Japan seized were indeed among "newly constituted states, mandatories and territories" which had "changed hands as a result

Critics of the League undoubtedly assumed that Wilson's political framework led away from world community of interest and toward the probability that the United States would be committed to fight on behalf of an unsustainable status quo. The United States might indeed end by policing the world against change which could not be prevented. As Hughes expressed it, Wilson's political framework tended to institutionalize a status quo which would impede the codification of real power relationships among nations. The only way to get reality expressed in a "world of dynamic forces," Hughes and his colleagues believed, was to hold periodic international conferences between the major powers, at which the world's political rules could be rewritten in accord with changed political and economic power relationships.

The Washington Conference of 1921–1922 and the treaty structure emerging from the conference were typical of what Wilson's critics believed were practical moves on the road to peace and community. Hughes, acting for the Harding Administration, was the chief architect of the decisions reached at the conference. He tried to mold these decisions to a shape which would give military security on the high seas to Great Britain and Japan as well as to the United States. This objective was codified in the Five-Power Treaty, which established a capital ship ratio of 5:5:3 among Great Britain, the United States, and Japan respectively. In accepting this arrangement the United States was voluntarily giving up its ability (which it possessed in abundance) to construct a fleet sufficient to threaten Japan with a potential American policing operation in the Western Pa-

---

of the war and the Treaty" of Versailles. Consequently, President Wilson continued to use American government control of foreign investment to obtain Japan's assent to the open door, defined as equality of commercial opportunity in China, as well as respect for the territorial integrity of China. Indeed, this is what I have shown in the first five pages of Chapter VII, this volume.

cific. The only condition Hughes required for this extraordinary self-limitation of power was that Japan accept the application of the open door principle to China as a whole. This in turn was codified in the Nine-Power Treaty, which emerged from the Washington Conference as a companion of the Five-Power Treaty. Subsequent scholars who have taxed Hughes with naïveté miss the point which Hughes well understood: the United States could not police Japanese actions in China *and* at the same time win Japanese adherence to the world-wide economic community of interest the United States was trying to construct. The only way Japan could be won to support the community concept was for Japan's long-run needs to be met. This is exactly what did not happen. In great measure the Japanese-American conflict over China took place finally because the world economy fell apart in 1929. In this sense militant Japanese expansion in China subsequent to 1929 was simply the Japanese expression of the general tendency of all the great powers, including the United States under Franklin Roosevelt, to resort to nationalist autarchy as a way to deal with the world economic crisis.

Epilogue II: Economic Community and Breakup, *1923–1929*

With the exception of a vocal minority of businessmen, most economic groups within the United States reached a consensus in support of community among the industrial powers. But there was a continuous guerrilla warfare over details of the program. Two important groups attacked, from opposite directions and with varying degrees of emphasis the community-of-interest policies of the government from 1916 to 1923. These were the manufacturers and bankers.

For example, the House of Morgan, leading the majority of the banking community, opposed the efforts of the Commerce and State Departments to control the flow of American capital in such a way as to prevent British economic leaders from using United States private capital to sustain a system of trade, payments, and investment under British majority control. These bankers were willing to make loans for British consortia as minority partners. Indeed, as early as 1919 banking interests had pressured the State Department in support of Lloyd George's request, which Wilson had rejected at Paris, to have the United States government guarantee private foreign loans to European governments at a time when the Europeans were most intensely pursuing a preferential program. In analogous fashion banking interests were for the most part favorable to proposals for cancellation of European war debts to the United States. The bankers assumed that repayment of war debts would make it very difficult for Europeans to sustain the volume of exports necessary for them to finance adverse international trade balances (on current account) and at the same time resume a volume of international investment large enough to assist in the development of resources needed to sustain an expanding world economy.

By refusing to establish a world-wide banking system in direct competion with the British, these bankers believed they were making a contribution to easing European entry into the general community of interest. And with remarkably accurate predictive ability, they argued that ultimately the vast productive power of the United States would convert the British-controlled international banking system into an instrument largely serving the needs of United States international commerce. Leaders of the House of Morgan argued that their more moderate approach made the development of American management of the world financial system more certain than the more aggressive approach American political leaders were advocating. They assumed correctly that European commercial leaders would be less prone to resist a partnership with American bankers which posed no immediate threat to vested British interests, and which made use of existing institutions.

Managers of American industrial corporations disagreed with the proposition implicit in the banking program, that the immediate foreign market interests of the manufacturers should be subordinated to the long-run interests of community, which seemed suspiciously similar to the immediate short-run interests of the bankers. Corporations which had expanded their production facilities during World War I needed immediate markets. The manufacturers also wished to see the Edge Act function according to its original Congressional intent, as a means of funneling American capital to foreign development projects managed and controlled by American interests. When the Edge investment banks failed to initiate operations the manufacturers pressured the government for a control of foreign banking investment that would directly sustain the volume of American manufactured exports, even to the extent of "tying" such loans to American technology.

The immediacy of their needs also colored the attitudes of the industrial executives toward war debts and the tariff. In 1922 James A. Farrell, President of the United States Steel Corporation, expressed a view widely held among industrialists that some "means might be devised whereby the enormous foreign indebtedness to us might be transformed to the status of investment—actual ownership—in foreign property of a more or less public service nature. . . . We would then be building for ourselves for the future and there need be no question then of wiping off these huge items of indebtedness." Such a happy conversion, Farrell argued, would

expand foreign markets by encouraging the "placing of orders with American manufacturers for the requirements of
these properties." In this way Farrell reasoned we could
export and, concurrently, maintain high protective tariff
rates. "By the means just suggested we would be purchasing
from them [foreign nations] but not in a flood of goods to be
imported here to the detriment of our own industries and
workers but by the purchase of properties abroad whether
located in the actual debtor country itself, in its colonial
possessions or in neutral markets."[17] Under Farrell's proposals the United States could be repaid for its war loans
and continue to impose high tariff rates on European exports
to the United States, in this way granting American tariff
concessions to Europe only in exchange for empires easing
their preferential tariff systems, thus allowing American exports easier entry into third markets.

All the major issues were resolved by compromise, with
Harding, Hoover, and Hughes acting as mediators among
the interest groups at home and rejecting any demands
which might interfere with the world-wide community. Yet
two serious economic flaws appeared in the overall program:
the difficulties Hoover encountered in his attempts to ration-
alize a productive foreign investment program and the long-
run inability to find a secure basis for the operation of the
German economy. Both of these factors, in combination with
the effects on Japan of the Chinese Revolution, led to the
breakup of the political community after 1929.

The Harding Administration itself was sharply divided
on the foreign investment policy of the United States. For
the most part President Harding and Secretaries Hughes
and Mellon accepted the contention of the bankers that the

17. National Foreign Trade Council, *Proceedings of the Tenth Annual
Convention* (New York, 1922), 576. (Hereafter cited as NFTC Convention *Proceedings*.)

government should not interfere in the foreign investment process except for clearly political purposes. On the other hand Hoover and the Commerce Department, while resisting pressure from the manufacturers to tie American foreign loans to the export of American technology and equipment, did contend that the bankers and the Administration should make some effort to obtain for American manufacturers the right to compete on a basis of equal opportunity on bids for supplies and equipment to be used on projects financed by American capital. Hoover also wanted the bankers to assume some responsibility in preventing the capital placed abroad from being squandered on unproductive schemes.

Hoover's approach was the most promising route to creating a world economic community because he advocated steady controlled expansion without any important waste of capital which might disrupt the desired production and trade expansion. But because the Harding and Coolidge Administrations refused to regulate capital exports to the extent that Hoover thought necessary, a certain weakness was built into the economic community; this weakness was a tendency toward partial waste of capital in the form of unproductive foreign investment. Such wasteful investment, if cumulative, promised balance-of-payments difficulties for borrowing countries.

But these difficulties became fatal only in a proper "mix" with other flaws. Ranking with wasteful investment was the inability of the community planners sufficiently to reintegrate Germany, the key industrial complex on the continent of Europe, into the general scheme for an expanding world economy. The scaled-down reparations payments the United States had won for Germany at the Dawes meetings in 1924 removed a basic impediment to German participation in a community, but this did not automatically find a practical place for Germany. Under the Dawes agreements the German annuity was to graduate to $625 million (2,500 million gold marks). German attempts to make what were for that day such huge payments posed the most difficult problems. In part Germany could make some payment through "exports to the general world market in an ordinary business way." A second means was by "special arrangements between the allied governments . . . and . . . Germany for deliveries in kind and performance of service." But deliveries and labor service were limited in potential scope because they would tend to interfere with employment and markets in the Allied countries. A third method was by "either or both the allies and the United States making permanent investments inside Germany . . . for adequate considerations." But this method too would be limited unless there was a complementary opening of new foreign markets to consume the production stimulated by foreign investment in the German economy. Another way for Germany to acquire new markets was by developing "colonial projects" or "assisted schemes," such as opening up the Belgian Congo and Morocco. But such ventures had "stopped almost entirely at the outbreak of the war."[18] For Germany to obtain a meaningful place in such newly opening markets the Allies had to allow to German industry equal access to their empires. Instead they were framing imperial preference and tariff assimilation policies within their respective imperial spheres.

Denied access to Allied-controlled underdeveloped markets, German industry turned toward Russia to develop ex-

18. Henry M. Robinson, "American Banking and World Rehabilitation," NFTC Convention *Proceedings*, 1925, 157–60. Robinson, a West Coast banker with steel interests, was, along with Owen D. Young, the most important American representative at the Dawes Plan meetings. Robinson certainly interpreted the decisions arrived at at the Dawes meetings as not simply a way to effect German reparations payments, but as also paving the way for the industrial nations to initiate the economic development of underdeveloped areas.

port markets. In 1925 a number of American bankers "expressed some willingness to advance funds to finance German activities in Russia."[19] The Germans extended a 100-million mark experimental credit to the Bolshevik regime. The loan worked so well that the same German interests sought to expand their venture after 1926. But to implement the loan the Germans needed American financial backing and asked a group of American banks, informally headed by W. A. Harriman and Company, to supply the investment capital. Acting for the American bankers Harriman submitted the proposed participation to the State Department for approval. The State Department rejected the proposal on the grounds that it would tend to sustain Bolshevik power in Russia.[20]

Failure of the Allies to open their imperial markets to Germany and the unwillingness of the United States to finance large-scale Russian development as a target for German exports left only one significant means of expanding world markets in a general way: an intense campaign to expand interindustrial nation trade in Europe and between Europe and North America. The American campaign to secure among the nations of the world general adherence to the unconditional most-favored-nation clause in commercial agreements represented the major effort to expand interindustrial nation trade. By 1928, subsequent to the International Economic Conference of 1927 in Geneva, almost all

19. S. H. Cross, Chief, European Division of the Bureau of Foreign and Domestic Commerce, to Hoover, November 18, 1925, in Commerce Department files, National Archives, Record Group 151, Bureau of Foreign and Domestic Commerce, indexed 640, File No. General.

20. See series of letters from W. A. Harriman & Co. to State Department, State Department to W. A. Harriman, March 17, 1926, to July 15, 1926, U.S. Department of State, *Papers Relating to the Foreign Relations of the United States*, 1926, 29 vols. (Washington, 1925–1944), II, 906–10. (Hereafter cited as *Foreign Relations*.)

important trading countries had accepted the unconditional most-favored-nation clause as the most desirable basis upon which to erect trade agreements. But despite the fact that such clauses were written into most trade agreements, nations tended to evade the nondiscriminatory obligations inherent in the clause.[21] Hence by 1928, a year before the gigantic break in the world economy, the organized effort to broaden and deepen interindustrial nation trade had faltered.

Only one other practical, but somewhat unsatisfactory, line of policy remained; that was for each industrial nation (but particularly the United States, chief trader, investor, and financier, and hence general manager, of the world economy) to expand its own domestic economy without dangerous inflation in order to expand the general world market for goods and service.[22] Roy Harrod had noted that beginning in 1923 it became Federal Reserve System credit policy "to secure a steady advance of the economy" by using appropriate monetary tools to check overexpansion and depression. In this connection the Federal Reserve authorities rejected the traditional criterion for credit policy "involving an

21. H. W. Arndt, *The Economic Lessons of the 1930's* (New York, 1944), 236–37, footnote 1.

22. An increase in the value of world trade, representing an inflation of existing values without an appreciable increase in the exchange of real goods and services, expressed solely or even mainly in increased prices, would, in my opinion, have been totally without value between 1927 and 1929. I argue this despite the fact that I am fully aware that at certain times and under certain circumstances price inflation can stimulate the development of resources (i.e., goods and services) which would otherwise go undeveloped at the given time. What was needed between 1927 and 1929 was not increased liquidity, but markets for existing goods and services which could be used to stimulate new production; in fact one could argue that there was a surplus of liquidity and that such inflation-created funds went into unproductive investment, compounding the initial problem by creating unmanageable balance-of-payment problems.

inflow or an outflow of gold." Instead Federal Reserve authorities tried to vary credit policy in relation to whether or not production and consumption were in even balance. "This policy was executed with seeming success for a period of some six years. Industry and trade grew and prospered in the United States. Only in 1928 did some unhealthy symptoms appear." But trade cycle experts *have not* produced any convincing evidence that the development of unhealthy symptoms, such as the slight decline in United States production indices and prices in the second half of 1927, were due to faulty credit policies initiated by the Federal Reserve System. On the contrary, rediscount rates were reduced in 1927 from 4 to 3½ percent. This was a perfectly proper response by credit authorities who wished to encourage the production of goods and services, halt the decline in prices, and sustain employment.[23] Despite these efforts the United States economy sank into depression in 1929. And because the United States, as the largest consumer of primary products and as the largest long-term international investor, was the most important segment of the world economy, it tended to pull Europe, which was on shaky economic legs anyway, down with it. But domestic American economic weakness was not in and of itself the cause of the general world depression.

Had the world economy as such entered a period of new resource development in Latin America, Africa, and Asia, or had interindustrial nation trade expanded on the basis of greater specialization—and hence more efficient resource allocation among advanced nations—the basic elements needed to sustain world commerce would have been present. But the basis for such developments had been undermined effectively when preferential empires "chopped up" the

23. Roy Harrod, *The Dollar* (New York, 1963), 53–57.

world market and when the unconditional most-favored-nation clause was imperfectly applied during the danger period after 1927, further splintering the world market into a series of partial markets.

Europe, including its main economic power plant, Germany, had concluded its essential reconstruction by 1927, and needed new markets. As early as May 2, 1927, Thomas W. Lamont, operating head of the House of Morgan, somewhat lefthandedly referred to the disappearance of legitimate investment outlets. In an address before the International Chamber of Commerce, meeting in Washington, D.C., Lamont urged his audience to help curtail " 'indiscriminate lending and indiscriminate borrowing.' " Five months later S. Parker Gilbert, the Director General of reparations, issued public warnings against further loans to Germany. The German Central Bank also tried to damp down foreign investment in Germany in 1927. These efforts were unsuccessful. During the years 1927 to 1929, American loans to Germany over repayments totalled $379.2 million. But with German foreign markets growing only slowly these loans intensified balance-of-payments problems.[24]

Instead of investing in the development of real resources, or in services encouraging resource development, which would have expanded world markets, some American bankers were pressing unneeded loans for worthless or at least questionable projects on Latin American nations. Despite the view of the President of the Reserve Bank of Peru that the loans American bankers were making to his government in 1927 were at least twice the amount which could be legitimately absorbed, American bankers made the loans, rejecting the advice of a Peruvian colleague. In 1928 and 1929 American bankers made new loans to Peru. Colombia's

24. Cleona Lewis, *America's Stake in International Investments* (Washington, 1938), 380.

experience was similar, prompting the U.S. Commerce Department's commercial attaché to warn the Department back home that "Colombia is going wild on borrowing. She has started too many railroads and too many highways. . . ." In the case of Colombia the Commerce Department propagandized successfully against new loans.[25] Lending practices such as those cited, which were typical of much United States foreign investment in Latin America in the period 1927 to 1930, instead of easing European (especially German) balance-of-payments problems, created identical problems for Latin American countries.

The debates and discussions at the International Economic Conference at Geneva in the summer of 1927 show that world political and economic leaders understood that the stability of the system depended on the development of the resources of underdeveloped areas. For instance on June 10, 1927, the Chairman of the American delegation at Geneva, Henry M. Robinson, reported to Secretary of State Frank M. Kellogg that it was the sense of the conference that " 'consumer's goods' were being used, even in Europe, at as high a rate per capita as prior to the war; but the production and consumption of 'capital goods' was considerably lower and that this, in the main, accounts for unemployment and, in turn had reduced wages and purchasing power to a lower level." Given the assumptions which the informed public, political leaders, businessmen, and economists made prior to the acceptance of the "new economics," the conference delegates concluded quite rightly that any significant increase in real wages and employment, and hence consumption of consumer goods, had to be preceded by an increased consumption of capital goods. "The discussion of the Conference," Robinson told Kellogg, "disclosed the fact that if

25. *Ibid.*, 380–81.

the development of unused or inadequately developed resources throughout the world could be initiated and financed, increased consumption of capital goods would follow, with the result of reduction or elimination of unemployment, and the probable increase in the wage level and consumption of consumable goods."[26]

Although the economic leaders recognized the problem at Geneva they did not work out the means to solve it, mainly because the continued infusion of American capital in largely wasteful projects obscured the seriousness of the crisis. Since, with the exception of a few individuals such as Hoover, Robinson, Owen D. Young, and their counterparts in other countries, the decision-making elite in the developed industrial countries did not follow the logical program inherent in their own assumptions, they failed to deal with the fundamental problem of the international economic system for whose management they bore major responsibility. The disintegration of that system by 1929 was the inexorable result of that failure to act between 1927 and 1929.

Again in 1929 when Owen D. Young advanced the proposals which Robinson had supported in 1924 upon completion of the Dawes negotiations and which the International Economic Conference of 1927 endorsed, the international decision-making elite showed itself again unable to act in the general interests of the system. Aside from its overt task—to facilitate reparations payments under growing depression conditions—the Young commission proposed the creation of a Bank for International Settlements (B.I.S.). The original version of the B.I.S. was vastly different from the emasculated institution which finally emerged out of international banking and political negotiation. The Young committee originally viewed the projected B.I.S. as a true international

26. Henry M. Robinson to Frank Kellogg, June 10, 1927, *Foreign Relations*, 1927, I, 240.

bank in the sense in which the International Bank for Reconstruction and Development functions today. Young and his fellow planners wanted to encourage and direct integrated investment "for opening up new fields of commerce, of supply and demand." But again opposition based on sectarian national economic interests in each nation doomed the proposal.[27]

No attempt at a "Keynesian" solution was really practicable between 1927 and 1929. Politically, no important interest was demanding it; theoretically, few if any economists were propounding it.

Since it is clear from the foregoing analysis that efforts made by American statesmen such as Hoover and Young bore some promise of success, even though they ultimately failed, one hopes that those currently directing America's second attempt at creating an economic community of interest through the foreign aid program are well versed in the causes of the first failure. It is also to be hoped that they are well read in Herbert Hoover, and that they do not conceive of a necessity for the United States to act as the world's policeman to create conditions for a true economic community of interest. In that event the community will never be built.

27. Arndt, *Economic Lessons of the 1930's*, 233, footnote 1.

Glossary

Administrative Loans. International loans to finance government administration, usually in underdeveloped countries.

Bargaining Tariff. Using the tariff law to trade equal access for American products in foreign markets for equal access of foreign products in the American market.

Branch Banks Abroad. Their purpose was to collect credit information on foreign customers, discount the "draft" of American sellers, and collect the proceeds when the draft came due.

Buying Pools. A combination of buyers of specific imports to decrease or prevent an increase in the price at which given goods or services are marketed.

Captive Markets. The ability to control markets in a foreign nation. Frequently the result of successfully installing national technology in the industries of another country.

Drafts (Bills of Exchange). Orders written by export sellers directing future payment. Once the buyer has accepted such a draft it becomes a negotiable instrument in a "discount market."

Free Trade. Literally the absence of tariffs. Generally modified to imply that tariffs should be relatively low. Not to be confused with the American-supported "open door."

Imperial Preference. Tariff argreements discriminating in some degree against the exports of nations not members of a particular imperial structure.

Inter-Imperial Preference. The practice of exchanging tariff and/or investment advantages among a number of empires.

Metropolitan Markets. The home markets of developed industrial nations.

277

Open Door. Buying, selling, and investing under conditions where the commerce of all nations is treated equally.

Preferential Tariffs. One or more nations granting "special" access to its or their markets.

Reciprocity. An exchange of tariff concessions.

Selling Pools. A combination of a number of sellers of a given good or service generally designed to sustain or increase prices by regulating supply.

Tied Loans. The result of a stipulation in loan contracts to the effect that imports financed by the loan be, in some degree, supplied by the industry of the lending country.

Tariff Assimilation. A powerful nation acting to include another nation within its domestic tariff structure.

Unconditional Most-Favored-Nation Clause. Two nations agreeing to extend to each other no less favorable tariff treatment than either accords to the products of third countries. The benefits under such treaties are automatically extended to third countries, "unconditionally."

Bibliography

UNPUBLISHED DOCUMENTS

Commerce, U.S. Department of. Record Group 151, Bureau of Foreign and Domestic Commerce, indexed 640, File No. General, for the years 1919–1929. National Archives. This source was important in illustrating the evolution of the Commerce Department's role in control of foreign capital issues.

Hughes, Charles Evans, Manuscripts. Manuscript Division, Library of Congress. Letters, 1921–1925.

State, U.S. Department of. Record Group 59, 1918–1927. National Archives.

Stimson, Henry L., Manuscripts, Diary, 1920–1930. Yale University Library, New Haven, Connecticut. Memoranda of Stimson's conversations with various Republican party leaders clarifies Republican opposition to American entry into a League of Nations based on Article 10.

Vanderlip, Frank A., Manuscripts. Butler Library, Columbia University, New York City (two boxes labeled "American International Corporation"). This source was helpful in showing the relationship of the Webb-Pomerene Act of 1918 to America's Russian policy.

PUBLISHED DOCUMENTS

Baker, Ray Stannard. *Woodrow Wilson and World Settlement*, III, New York, 1923. This volume contains letters to and from Wilson pertaining to the settlement of economic problems at the peace conference.

———, and William E. Dodd, editors. *The Public Papers of Woodrow Wilson*, 6 vols., New York, 1925–1927.

Commerce, U.S. Department of. *Ninth to Sixteen Annual Reports of the Secretary of Commerce, 1921–1928*, 8 vols., Washington, 1921–1928.

———, Bureau of Foreign and Domestic Commerce. *Commerce Reports*, September 18, 1922–November 27, 1927.

———, Bureau of Foreign and Domestic Commerce. *Special Agents Series*, Nos. 1–204, Washington, 1913–1922.

Congress, U.S., 65th., 3rd Sess. *Proceedings and Debates*, February 21–March 19, 1919, Washington, 1919.

Federal Reserve Board. *Federal Reserve Bulletin*, January 1919–December 1925.

———. *Third to Fourteenth Annual Reports Covering Operations for the Years 1916–1927*, 12 vols., Washington, 1917–1928.

Federal Trade Commission. *Cooperation in the Export Trade*, 2 vols., Washington, 1916. This source outlined problems that business and government leaders faced in their efforts to develop legislative proposals to expand American foreign commerce.

House of Representatives. U.S., 68th Cong., 1st Sess. Subcommittee of the House Committee on Appropriations, *Department of Commerce Appropriations Bill of 1925*, Washington, 1925.

Lary, Hal B., and others. *The United States in the World Economy*, Publication of the Bureau of Foreign and Domestic Commerce of the U.S. Department of Commerce, Economic Series No. 23, Washington, 1943.

League of Nations. *Proceedings of the International Conference on the Treatment of Foreigners*, 1st Sess., Paris, November 5th–December 5th 1929, League of Nations Document C.I.T.E. 62, II. B., Geneva, 1929.

———, Economic, Financial, and Transit Department. *Commercial Policy in the Interwar Period: International Proposals and National Policies*. League of Nations Publication II, A. 6., Geneva, 1942.

Lewery, Leonard J. *Foreign Capital Investment in Russian Industries and Commerce.* U.S. Department of Commerce Publication, Miscellaneous Series No. 124, Washington, 1923.

National Foreign Trade Council. *European Economic Alliances, A Compilation of Information on International Commercial Policies After the European War and Their Effect Upon the Foreign Trade of the United States. Also an Analysis of European and United States Commercial Inter-Dependence and Treaty Relations,* New York, 1916.

———. *Official Reports of the Second to Fifteenth National Foreign Trade Conventions,* 14 vols., New York, 1915–1928.

National Monetary Commission. *Publications of the National Monetary Commission,* vols. 1–20, Washington, 1909–1911.

Senate, U.S., 64th Cong., 1st Sess., Committee on Judiciary. *Trade Agreements Abroad,* Senate Document No. 491, Washington, 1916.

———, 64th Cong., 2d Sess., Committee on Interstate and Foreign Commerce. *Promotion of the Export Trade, Hearings on H.R. 17350,* Washington, 1917.

———, 67th Cong., 2d Sess., Committee on Judiciary. *Loans to Foreign Governments,* Senate Document No. 86, Washington, 1921.

———, 68th Cong., 1st Sess. *Oil Concessions in Foreign Countries,* Senate Document No. 97, Washington, 1923.

———, 68th Cong., 1st Sess., Committee on Foreign Relations. *Hearings on the Treaty of Commerce and Consular Rights With Germany,* Washington, 1924.

———, 68th Cong., 2d Sess., Subcommittee of the Committee on Foreign Relations. *Pursuant to Senate Congressional Resolution 22* (FOREIGN LOANS), Washington, 1925.

———, 72d Cong., 1st Sess., Committee on Finance. *Hearings Pursuant to Senate Resolution 19, A Resolution Authorizing the Finance Committee of the Senate to Investigate the Sale, Flotation, and Allocation by Banks, Banking Institutions, Corporations or Individuals of Foreign Bonds or Securities in the United States,* Part I, December 18, 19, 21, Washington, 1931.

———, 74th Cong., 2d Sess. *Special Committee on Investigation of the Munitions Industry*, LXXVIII, Washington, 1936.

State, U.S. Department of. *Papers Relating to the Foreign Relations of the United States*, 1916–1929, 29 vols., Washington, 1925–1944.

———. *Papers Relating to the Foreign Relations of the United States*, 1916, *The World War*, Supplement, Washington, 1929.

———. *Papers Relating to the Foreign Relations of the United States*, 1917, *The World War*, Supplement I, Washington, 1931.

———. *Papers Relating to the Foreign Relations of the United States*, 1917, *The World War*, Supplement II, 2 vols., Washington, 1932.

———. *Papers Relating to the Foreign Relations of the United States*, 1918, *The World War*, Supplement I, 2 vols., Washington, 1933.

———. *Papers Relating to the Foreign Relations of the United States*, 1918, *The World War*, Supplement II, Washington, 1932.

———. *Papers Relating to the Foreign Relations of the United States*, 1918, *Russia*, 3 vols., Washington, 1931–1932.

———. *Papers Relating to the Foreign Relations of the United States*, 1919, *Russia*, Continuation of 1918 Foreign Relations, Russia, Washington, 1937.

———. *Papers Relating to the Foreign Relations of the United States*, 1919, *The Paris Peace Conference 1919*, 13 vols., Washington, 1942–1947.

———. *Papers Relating to the Foreign Relations of the United States*, *The Lansing Papers 1914–1920*, 2 vols., Washington, 1939–1940.

Tariff Commission, U.S. *Colonial Tariff Policies*, Miscellaneous Series No. 9, Washington, 1922. This was a tariff commission study of various preferential arrangements in foreign tariff laws and their effects on the American goal of the commercial open door.

———. *Report on the Emergency Tariff Act of May 27, 1921,* Washington, 1922.

———. *The Tariff and Its History,* Washington, 1934.

Woodward, E. L. and Rohan Butler, editors. *Documents on British Foreign Policy 1919–1939,* 1st Ser., 13 vols., London, 1947–1963.

World War Foreign Debts Commission, U.S. *Combined Annual Reports: With Additional Information Regarding Foreign Debts Due the United States,* Washington, 1927.

Young, Ralph A. *Handbook of American Underwriting of Foreign Securities,* Trade Promotion Series No. 104, Bureau of Foreign and Domestic Commerce, Department of Commerce, Washington, 1930.

MEMOIRS AND PERSONAL PAPERS

Grew, Joseph C. *Turbulent Era, A Diplomatic Record of Forty Years, 1904–1945,* Walter Johnson, ed., 2 vols., Cambridge, 1952.

Hendrick, Burton J. *The Life and Letters of Walter H. Page,* III, New York, 1925.

Hoover, Herbert. *The Memoirs of Herbert Hoover, The Cabinet and the Presidency, 1920–1933,* II, New York, 1952.

Lansing, Robert. *The Peace Negotiations: A Personal Narrative,* Cambridge, 1921.

Seymour, Charles, ed. *Intimate Papers of Colonel House,* 2 vols., Boston and New York, 1926.

Wilbur, Ray Lyman, ed. *The New Day: Campaign Speeches of Herbert Hoover,* Stanford, 1928.

BOOKS

Acheson, Dean. *Power and Diplomacy,* New York, 1963.

Arndt, H. W. *The Economic Lessons of the 1930's,* New York, 1944.

Baruch, Bernard. *The Making of Reparations and Economic Sections of the Treaty,* New York, 1920.

Bidwell, Percy W. *Tariff Policy of the United States*, New York, 1933.

Brandes, Joseph. *Herbert Hoover as Secretary of Commerce: Economic Foreign Policy, 1921–1928.* (Unpublished Ph.D. thesis, New York University, 1958, announced for publication in the spring–summer of 1963.)

Brown, William Adams, Jr. *The International Gold Standard Reinterpreted, 1914–1934*, 2 vols., New York, 1940.

Buell, Raymond Leslie. *The Washington Conference*, New York and London, 1922.

Carr, Edward Hallett. *Conditions of Peace*, New York, 1942.

———. *German Soviet Relations Between the Two Wars, 1919–1939*, Baltimore, 1951.

———. *The Soviet Impact on the Western World*, New York, 1954.

Cochran, Thomas C. and William Miller. *The Age of Enterprise*, New York, 1951.

Coit, Margaret L. *Mr. Baruch*, Cambridge, 1957.

Corey, Lewis. *The House of Morgan*, New York, 1930.

Culbertson, William Smith. *International Economic Policies*, New York and London, 1925.

Current, Richard N. *Secretary Stimson*, New Brunswick, 1954.

Curry, Roy Watson. *Woodrow Wilson and Far Eastern Policy 1913–1921*, New York, 1957.

Davenport, E. H. and Sidney Russell Cooke. *The Oil Trusts and Anglo-American Relations*, New York, 1924.

Diamond, William. *The Economic Thought of Woodrow Wilson*, Baltimore, 1943.

Elliott, William Y., ed. *The Political Economy of American Foreign Policy*, New York, 1955.

Faulkner, Harold Underwood. *American Economic History*, New York, 1943.

Feis, Herbert. *The Diplomacy of the Dollar: First Era 1919–1932*, Baltimore, 1950. Feis gives a clear but somewhat misleadingly simple description of administration efforts to guide and control foreign capital issues.

———. *Europe The World's Banker, 1870–1914*, New Haven,

1930; paperback ed., W. W. Norton and Co., New York, 1965. This work is an excellent survey of the direction, course, and effect of the foreign investment movement until 1914.

———. *The Sinews of Peace*, 1st ed., New York and London, 1944.

Fleming, Denna Frank. *The United States and the League of Nations 1918–1920*, New York and London, 1932.

Grady, Henry F. *British War Finance, 1914–1919*, New York, 1927.

Graebner, Norman A. *Ideas and Diplomacy: Readings in the Intellectual Tradition of American Foreign Policy*, New York, 1964.

Griswold, A. Whitney. *The Far Eastern Policy of the United States*, New York, 1938.

Hancock, W. K. *Survey of British Commonwealth Affairs, Problems of Economic Policy, 1918–1939*, Part I, II, London, New York and Toronto, 1940. Hancock argues that the shift in British commercial policy toward preference was doomed from the beginning, and represented only half-hearted efforts on the part of British statesmen.

Harrod, Roy. *The Dollar*, New York, 1954.

Hicks, John D. *Republican Ascendancy, 1921–1933*, New York, 1960.

Hoover, Herbert. *American Individualism*, New York, 1923.

House, Edward Mandell and Charles Seymour, eds. *What Really Happened at Paris, The Story of the Peace Conference, 1918–1919*, New York, 1921.

Jolliffe, M. F. *The United States as a Financial Centre 1919–1933*, Swansea, Wales, 1935.

Lewis, Cleona. *America's Stake in International Investments*, Washington, 1938. An invaluable history of the American foreign investment movement.

Link, Arthur S. *Wilson the Diplomatist, A Look at His Major Foreign Policies*, Baltimore, 1957.

McClure, Wallace. *A New American Commercial Policy*, New York, 1924. This work contains a very useful explanation of

the shift in American commercial treaty policy after World
War I.

Morgan, E. Victor. *Studies in British Financial Policy, 1914–
1925*, London, 1952. This work contains the most recent
statistical data on the decline of British foreign investment
securities as a result of World War I.

Nicholson, Harold. *Dwight Morrow*, New York, 1935.

Nolde, Boris. *Russia in the Economic War*, New Haven, 1928.

Paslovsky, Leo and Harold G. Moulton. *Russian Debts and Russian Reconstruction*, 1st ed., New York and London, 1924.

Phelps, Clyde W. *The Foreign Expansion of American Banks,
American Branch Banking Abroad*, New York, 1927.

Pusey, Merlo J. *Charles Evans Hughes*, 2 vols., New York,
1951.

Reed, Harold L. *The Development of Federal Reserve Policy*,
Boston and New York, 1922.

Riesser, J. *The German Great Banks and Their Concentration*,
Washington, 1911.

Robinson, Leland Rex. *Investment Trust Organization and Management*, New York, 1924.

Smith, George O., ed. *The Strategy of Minerals*, New York,
1919.

Soule, George. *Prosperity Decade, From War to Depression:
1917–1929, The Economic History of the United States*,
VIII, New York, 1947.

Steiner, William Howard. *Investment Trusts and American
Experience*, New York, 1929.

Stuart, Graham H. *The Department of State*, New York, 1949.

Temperley, H. W. V., ed. *A History of the Peace Conference
of Paris*, V, London, 1921.

Tillman, Seth P. *Anglo-American Relations at the Paris Peace
Conference of 1919*, Princeton, 1961.

Vanderlip, Frank A. and Boyden Sparkes. *From Farm Boy to
Financier*, New York, 1935.

Vanderlip, Frank A. *What Next in Europe?*, New York, 1922.

Williams, Benjamin H. *Economic Foreign Policy of the United
States*, 1st ed., New York, 1929.

————. *The United States and Disarmament*, New York and London, 1931.

Wilson, Robert Renbert. *United States Commerical Treaties and International Law*, New Orleans, 1960.

JOURNALS

American Acceptance Council. *Acceptance Bulletin*, February, 1921–November 1925.

American Bankers Association. *Journal of the American Bankers Association*, V–XX, July 1912–June 1928.

American Economic Association. *American Economic Review*, XI, No. 1, Supplement, March 1921, *Papers and Proceedings of the 33rd Annual Meeting*, December, 1920, Princeton, 1921.

American Protective Tariff League. *American Economist*, LXV–LXXIV, January 1920–December 1924.

Home Market Club of Boston. *The Protectionist*, XXXVI, XXXVII, May 1924–April 1926.

ARTICLES

Abrams, Richard M. "Woodrow Wilson and Southern Congressmen, 1913–1916," *Journal of Southern History*, XXII, November 1956, 417–37.

"American Investment Abroad." Federal Reserve Board, *Federal Reserve Bulletin*, August 1920, 777–78.

"Foreign Trade Banking." Federal Reserve Board, *Federal Reserve Bulletin*, September 1920, 908.

"International Acceptance Bank, Inc." American Acceptance Council, *Acceptance Bulletin*, February 1921, 9.

"Report of the Commerce and Marine Division of the Executive Council of the American Bankers Association." American Bankers Association, *Journal of the American Bankers Association*, XIV, November 1921, 240.

Goodhue, F. Abbot. "Acceptance Syndicates to Finance Export Trade," American Acceptance Council, *Acceptance Bulletin*, August 1921, 3–4.

Hoover, Herbert. "Momentous Conference," American Bankers Association, *Journal of the American Bankers Association*, XIII, January 1921, 462–63.

Link, Arthur. "The South and the New Freedom: An Interpretation," *The American Scholar*, XX, Summer 1951, 314–24.

McHugh, John. "Report of the Commerce and Marine Division to the Executive Council of the American Bankers Association," American Bankers Association, *Journal of the American Bankers Association*, XIII, May 1921, 733.

Redfield, William C. "There Are Other Factors Yonder," American Bankers Association, *Journal of the American Bankers Association*, XIII, April 1921, 661–62.

Robinson, Leland R. "British Banking—The Foreign Policies of the London Big Five Banks," American Acceptance Council, *Acceptance Bulletin*, October 1923, 5–7.

———. "Foreign Credit Facilities of the United Kingdom," American Acceptance Council, *Acceptance Bulletin*, December 1923, 15–21.

Sherwell, G. Butler. "American Branch Banking in Latin America," American Bankers Association, *Journal of the American Bankers Association*, XVI, December 1923, 365–66.

Sonne, Hans C. "South American Trade Prospects," American Acceptance Council, *Acceptance Bulletin*, January 1922, 8–10.

Williams, John H. "Our Foreign Trade Balance Since the Armistice," American Bankers Association, *Journal of the American Bankers Association*, XIII, February 1921, 571–73.

Index

ABA *Journal*, 92
Abbott, John Jay, 180
Acceptance Bulletin, 125, 193
Africa, 246
Agricultural commodities, 74, 93, 97, 99, 102, 123, 125, 217, 226. *See also* Raw materials
Ailes, Milton E., 186, 196, 197
Alexander, James S., 235
Alien Property Custodian for Guatemala, 134
Allen and Harvey, London, 126
Allied Economic Alliance: and postwar commercial policy, 15–16, 20, 21, 22, 31, 35; and Germany, 31; views of U.S. leaders towards, 31, 32, 33, 215; considered by British, 32–33; failure to materialize, 40. *See also* Paris Economic Conference
Allied Powers Council of Ambassadors, 150
Allied Supreme Council, 151, 152
Allies: and open door, 13, 248; and U.S. commerce, 37, 73, 212; and postwar German trade, 46, 215, 223; and access to U.S. capital, 48, 67, 68, 138, 146, 147; Wilson Administration's view of, 147–48, 150; and reparations, 147–48, 250; and war debts, 148, 250; and Genoa Conference, 152, 154; and Soviet nationalization, 162, 165; and loan control, 182; and

reconstruction, 223, 248. *See also* individual nations
American Acceptance Council, 124, 193–94, 234
American and Foreign Banking Corporation, 57, 80, 95, 114, 115
American Asiatic Association, 192
American Automobile Association, 232
American Bankers' Association, 4, 78, 82, 83, 84, 91, 92, 95, 123, 185, 191
American Chamber of Commerce in China, 181
American Commission to Negotiate Peace at Paris, 68
American Economic Association, 123
American Economist, 234
American International Corporation, 8, 33, 61, 62, 63, 65, 75, 96, 110, 111, 130, 176, 215
American investors, 41
American Locomotive Corporation, 77
American Manufacturers Export Association, 81, 84, 86
American Mercantile Bank at Lima, 134
American national banks, 23
American Protective Tariff League, 234
American Radiator Company, 192
American Relief Commission in Paris, 66

Wilson, Thomas E., 91
Wilson, Woodrow: and foreign
trade, 8, 10, 90; and League of
Nations and Peace Treaty, 12,
13, 21, 139, 140, 141, 143,
147, 260, 261, 263; and the
open door, 12, 46, 138, 172,
175; and Germany, 12, 67, 69;
and Allies, 21, 65, 66–67, 143,
144; and China consortium,
172, 175; and loan control, 172,
179, 262; and Japan, 181, 262;
and tariffs, 21n15, 214, 218,
221, 222
—administration of: and foreign
trade policy, 3, 7, 22, 91, 108,
212; and the open door, 11,
150, 173; and Allies, 21, 68,
147–48, 150, 249–50; and tariffs, 21, 212, 221; and shipping,
33, 70; and Japan, 148, 149,
174, 181; and League of Nations, 149, 150, 225; and loan
control, 173, 174, 176, 180,
184; and China consortium, 173,
174, 176, 179, 181, 184; mentioned, 10, 69, 203
Wilson and Company, Chicago, 91

Withers, Hartley, 127
Woodruff, George, 107
Wool, 226
World community of interest, 10,
11, 12, 251–52, 253, 263–64,
268
World depression, 264
World markets: and proposals for
expansion of, 15, 16, 35, 44,
69, 160, 218, 274, 275–76; and
disintegration of, 78, 124–25,
211, 225, 226, 246, 264, 272–
73, 275; and U.S. views, 82,
102, 105, 123, 137, 160, 259,
270, 275; and U.S. need for
widest possible, 98, 215–16,
223, 240; and gold standard,
102, 118, 119, 219, 270, 271–
72. *See also* Reconstruction;
War debts; and Germany, views
on reparations
World War I, 19, 37, 73, 75, 76,
81, 109, 110, 127, 129, 252,
253

Young, Arthur N., 192, 193, 239,
240, 241, 243, 244, 245
Young, Owen D., 275–76